THE TRIUMPH
OF REALITY TV

THE TRIUMPH OF REALITY TV

The Revolution in American Television

Leigh H. Edwards

 PRAEGER

AN IMPRINT OF ABC-CLIO, LLC
Santa Barbara, California • Denver, Colorado • Oxford, England

Library of Congress Cataloging-in-Publication Data

Edwards, Leigh H., 1970–
    The triumph of reality tv : the revolution in American television / Leigh H. Edwards.
        p. cm.
    Includes bibliographical references and index.
    ISBN 978-0-313-39901-5 (hardcopy : alk. paper) — ISBN 978-0-313-39902-2
(ebook)   1. Reality television programs—United States—History and
criticism.   I. Title.
    PN1992.8.R43E49   2013
    791.45'655—dc23   2012031863

ISBN: 978-0-313-39901-5
EISBN: 978-0-313-39902-2

17   16   15   14   13   2   3   4   5

This book is also available on the World Wide Web as an eBook.
Visit www.abc-clio.com for details.

Praeger
An Imprint of ABC-CLIO, LLC

ABC-CLIO, LLC
130 Cremona Drive, P.O. Box 1911
Santa Barbara, California 93116-1911

This book is printed on acid-free paper ∞

Manufactured in the United States of America

Contents

Acknowledgments

In writing about the importance of popular culture and media studies, I am grateful to supportive colleagues who also believe deeply in this kind of work. Many thanks to the good folks at Praeger/ABC-CLIO, especially James Sherman, and Dan Harmon before him. A hearty thank you to colleagues for feedback and discussion over the years, especially Bob Batchelor, Cindy Fuchs, Jennifer Proffitt, Andrew Epstein, Meegan Kennedy, Nancy Warren, Darryl Dickson-Carr, Elaine Treharne, Kathi Yancey, David Kirby, Barbara Hamby, Jerrilyn McGregory, Ned Stuckey-French, Elizabeth Stuckey-French, Paul Outka, Michael Neal, Amit Rai, Chris Shinn, David Johnson, and David Vann. Thanks also to friends for their discussion and support, including Chris Goff, Brian Ammons, Patricia Thomas, Tatianna Flores, James Mitchell, Katie Conrad, Vall Richard, Bev Bower, Ann Duran, Cindy Michaelson, Vickie Lake, Maria Fernandez, Monica Hurdal, Jack Clifford, Fayanne Farabee, Pam Flynn, Feli Wilhelmy, Janet Dilling, Julie Relin, Michael Todd, Lori DiGuglielmo, Karen Barnett. A big thank you for support and good wishes from family, including my sister Ashley Carothers Edwards, Kim Hinckley, NancyAnne Carothers, Allison Carothers, Brittney Carothers Harvey, JuliaAnne Carothers Harvey, Melissa Anne Carothers Moon and family, Charles Graham Carothers, Jr., Sarah Jane Carothers, Milton Washington Carothers II, Theresa Loper and family, Karen Campbell Frank, Melanie Joyner and family. I dedicate this book to my parents, Steve Edwards, Jr. and Helen Carothers Edwards.

My thanks also to colleagues at conferences where I have presented this work (including FLOW, Console-ing Passions, American Studies Association, Modern Language Association, Popular Culture Association).

Portions of this work have appeared in different form in some of my published articles and reviews, including: Leigh H. Edwards, "Transmedia Storytelling, Corporate Synergy, and Audience Expression," *Global Media Journal* 12, no. 20 (Spring 2012); "Reality TV and the New American Family," *Cult Pop Culture: How the Fringe Became Mainstream,* ed. Bob

Batchelor (Praeger, 2012), 263–278; "Reality TV and the American Family," *The Tube Has Spoken: Reality TV and History,* eds. Julie Taddeo and Ken Dvorak (University Press of Kentucky, 2010), 123–145; "The Endless End of Frontier Mythology: PBS's *Frontier House*," *Film & History: An Interdisciplinary Journal of Film and Television Studies* 37, no. 1 (2007): 29–34; "Chasing the Real: Reality Television and Documentary Forms," *Docufictions: Essays on the Intersection of Documentary and Fictional Filmmaking,* eds. Gary D. Rhodes and John Parris Springer (McFarland Press, 2006), 253–269; "'What a Girl Wants': Gender Norming on Reality Game Shows," *Feminist Media Studies* 4, no. 2 (Summer 2004): 226–228; "British Nanny Invasion: Review of *Supernanny*," *PopMatters*, March 28, 2005, http://www.popmatters.com/pm/review/supernanny-2005/; "Good One: Review of *Meet Mr. Mom*," *PopMatters*, August 2, 2005, http://www.popmatters.com/pm/review/meet-mr-mom-050802; "Identity Props: Review of *Wife Swap*," *PopMatters*, October 11, 2004, http://www.popmatters.com/pm/review/wife-swap-2004.

Introduction:
Keeping It Real—
Reality TV's Evolution

Once considered a fad or copycat genre, reality TV now dominates American television programming and has become a lasting staple. Established franchises such as *American Idol* or *Dancing With the Stars* top the ratings. *American Idol* has been the highest-rated show on television each year since 2003, averaging over 20 million viewers, while *Dancing With the Stars* is among the top five shows in Nielsen ratings, averaging over 18 million viewers.[1] Meanwhile, newer shows of the moment, such as *Keeping Up with the Kardashians,* become buzzed-about phenomena and generate spin-offs. Why has reality TV continued to gain popularity? While the sensationalism and low production cost of these programs are obvious factors, there is nevertheless more to the story of the genre's continued success than just escapism or guilty pleasure cheap TV. Reality shows are also surviving because they are at the forefront of new and innovative media developments.

This book explains how reality TV has gained greater popularity by capitalizing on recent media trends, including new directions in storytelling, emotional appeals to audiences, and taking content from TV to other media platforms (with features such as smart phone applications and online videos). I argue that a second main factor in reality TV's success is how it powerfully portrays major anxieties of the era, be it fears of the rapidly evolving media landscape (such as how digital media is affecting American culture and society), or tensions about basic social units like the American family. Reality programs capture touchstone issues and emphasize their conflict and drama, grabbing viewer attention and fanning anxieties. Taken together, these two factors help account for the genre's surprising success and survival.

Many of the media trends reality TV exploits involve incorporating developments in new media. More than simply following the popularity of multiplatform storytelling, for example, the genre has consistently been a trailblazer in that area. It banks on what Henry Jenkins calls "transmedia storytelling," in which content is taken across multiple media platforms in a coordinated way that encourages viewers to seek out added features, such as webisodes, online games, music albums, books, films, and YouTube videos.[2]

A fan of *Keeping Up With the Kardashians* could, for example, experience multiplatform storytelling by watching several spin-off shows, read Kardashian books, watch webisodes, and listen to featured music. They could even play Kardashian-themed games on the E! website or join millions of Kardashian Twitter followers. Likewise, in addition to voting for the winner, a dedicated fan of *American Idol* could find webisodes and behind-the-scenes footage on the Fox website, buy related DVDs and albums, attend the *American Idol* concert tours, and sing along by downloading a karaoke *American Idol* smart phone application. For *Big Brother*, in addition to the usual range of DVDs and webisodes, viewers could pay to watch the live feed online, screening the raw footage before anyone else. For *Dancing With the Stars*, audiences can watch extra rehearsal footage online and attend the tour. They can even land themselves on the show, by competing in an online design a dance contest, in which the winners have their dance idea performed and also get interviewed on the live broadcast. On *The Voice*, fans can get on the show virtually by live tweeting the contestants and having their tweets included on-screen. They can vote by downloading the songs from iTunes, and can express their devotion by attending concert tours. Fan could interact with a similar range of media items from reality series such as *The Jersey Shore* (books, DVDs, reunion specials, online interviews, online deleted scenes, concert events, mobile phone apps), *The Real World* (a film, DVDs, books, cast blogs, online games), and *The Real Housewives* franchise (behind-the-scenes specials and reunions, Bravo talk show interviews, online games, mobile phone apps, promotional tours, and some atrocious music singles).

The goal of this multiplatform storytelling is to create an entire narrative universe that active fans are drawn to, with each additional element of the transmedia franchise able to exist on its own but also contribute to the larger whole. For a transmedia franchise to be successful, it has to have rich enough characters and stories to support such interest. The newest major development in television is for programs to generate a range of related media items envisioned at the same time, what Jennifer Gillan describes as a TV show becoming a "multiplatform series of networked texts." The aim is to have the broadcast series appear alongside a range of linked texts: DVDs with added features, video games, interactive websites, content and games for mobile phones, interactive DVD-ROMs, novelizations, tie-in books, companion volumes, fanzines, board games, trading cards, and even series-related sponsor content for advertisers, like *American Idol's* Ford commercials starring the contestants.[3] It is significant that reality TV can create strong enough characters and storylines to generate this kind of transmedia storytelling. Even for fictional shows expanding their transmedia repertoire, reality programs become important components. Witness *Glee* (2009–), which now has a companion reality game-doc, *The Glee Project* (2011–), in which fans compete to become an actor on the show.

This book examines such trends, assessing where the genre is headed today and how it is a bellwether for new developments in American media culture. I identify and explore five key media trends that reality TV exploits. In addition to transmedia storytelling, I examine: how reality TV mixes genres (documentary combined with fictional TV genres such as soap opera, sitcom, or game show); how it turns castmembers into characters (using familiar narrative codes to turn real people's lives into stories); how it sparks greater audience interaction and fan participation (what critics call participatory fan culture, often through new media features); and how it encourages viewers' emotional connections to castmembers (with techniques like confessionals, diary cams, and access to the cast on social networking websites).

In the second factor I identify in reality TV's success, how it banks on heated social topics of the moment, I explore the prevalence of family reality programs. Capitalizing on an underlying sense of worry about cultural change, these TV shows capture the changing demographics of the American family. Reality TV uses its quick production schedules to rush in and capture recent controversies. Like other television genres, reality TV does not simply reflect current beliefs and debates in a society but it also helps shape them. Because reality programs depict real people and their supposed real problems on-screen, this values-shaping dynamic is heightened for the reality genre. Many reality programs make themselves newsworthy, entering into public discussions of controversial issues important in American society at any given time. Reality shows have become lightning rods for press debates and public policy fights about the state of the American family, and some are even used as evidence in family court cases.

In scope, I focus on the period from 2000 to 2012 in order to account for the more recent developments in reality TV. This time segment is relevant because it begins with *Survivor*'s success in the summer of 2000 and the boom it sparked in reality programming. For my discussion here, I date the full advent of the current genre to when MTV's *The Real World* premiered (1992), although related forerunners like police and emergency nonfiction series emerged in the late 1980s. It is important to note that factual programming has, of course, been around since the medium's origins, particularly since television has always claimed the ability to convey liveness as a marketing tool.[4] While my focus is on the most recent decade, I also address relevant features since the beginning of reality TV's spread as a genre. While critics debate the looseness of the term reality TV, I use it to refer to factual programming with key recurring generic and marketing characteristics, such as unscripted, low-cost, edited formats featuring a documentary and fiction genre mix, often to great ratings success.

Using literary studies techniques of historicized textual analysis, I provide textual analysis of reality shows alongside discussions of relevant cultural and sociohistorical contexts. I examine recurring themes in a representative number of episodes of key U.S. programs during that time, with my logic of selection being programs that were controversial, enjoyed high ratings, spawned copycats, or are representative of a particular subgenre. The reality shows discussed include: *Keeping Up with the Kardashians* (2007–); *The Real Housewives* franchise (2006–); *American Idol* (2002–); *Survivor* (2000–); *Big Brother* (2000–); *The Real World* (1992–); *Jersey Shore* (2009–2013); *Wife Swap* and *Celebrity Wife Swap* (2004–); *Supernanny* (2005–2011); *Nanny 911* (2004–2009); *Extreme Makeover: Home Edition* (2003–2011); *Dancing with the Stars* (2005–); *The Osbournes* (2002–2005); *The Surreal Life* (2003–2006); *The Apprentice* and *Celebrity Apprentice* (2004–); *Dog the Bounty Hunter* (2004–); *Run's House* (2005–2009); the *Teen Mom* franchise (2009–); *Trading Spouses: Meet Your New Mommy* (2004–2007); *Meet Mister Mom* (2005); *Gene Simmons Family Jewels* (2006–); *Black.White.* (2006); *Renovate My Family* (2005); *Frontier House* (2002); *The Voice* (2011–); *Jon & Kate Plus 8* and *Kate Plus 8* (2007–2011); *Married by America* (2003); *Things I Hate About You* (2004); *Showbiz Moms and Dads* (2004); *The Bachelor* (2002–); and *The Amazing Race* (2001–).

Marketing Hot Topics: The Family

To elaborate on the family theme I will explore in greater detail in later chapters, my argument is that reality TV is a key cultural site at which contemporary politics of the family are being negotiated. Reality family shows depict conflict around the family in order to seize viewer interest and generate ratings, mining and stoking anxieties about social and cultural changes. More than that, however, they are also making their own arguments about family life, sometimes implicitly and sometimes explicitly, as they portray these real people going about their daily lives and dealing with stresses over current family life problems and issues. These issues range from changing gender role expectations to teen pregnancy, from economic struggles to divorce and blended family tensions. Reality programs proffer their own take on how best to approach family and the very viability of that social unit in America today. A critical discussion of the reality family shows is important, since TV has always played such a vital role in formulating fantasies of the American family; the suburban nuclear family unit has historically been television's favorite topic and target audience.[5] This book makes an extended argument about how reality TV depicts the family in order to give the fullest example of how reality TV banks on a volatile topic in society and turns it into a recurring theme, and I establish rich sociohistorical and cultural contexts for these depictions.

While obviously not the only recurring theme pictured, family is one of the genre's obsessions. The genre titillates by putting cultural anxieties about the family on display, hawking images of wife swapping, spouse shopping, and date hopping. Its TV landscape is dotted with programs about mating rituals, on-screen weddings, unions arranged by audiences, partners testing their bonds on fantasy dates with others, family switching, home and family improvement, peeks into celebrity households, parents and children marrying each other off on national television, and families pitching their lives as sitcom pilots.

I demonstrate specifically how the reality TV genre both reflects and helps shape changing American family ideals. In an era of rising cultural anxiety about alterations in family, gender, and work patterns (including dropping marriage rates, newer, more diverse household models, and greater numbers of women delaying marriage and childbirth for careers), reality shows express larger stress about the state of the family. A significant number of reality shows picture a seemingly newfound family diversity.

For every traditional modern nuclear family, with the wage-earning father, stay-at-home mother, and dependent children, we see a panoply of newer arrangements, such as postdivorce, single parent, blended, and gay and lesbian families. What is the significance of this family diversity as a recurring theme in factual programming? Concurrent with images of demographic change, we also see a familiar rhetoric of the family in crisis. Witness the emergency rhetoric of *Nanny 911* (where a British nanny must save inept American parents at their breaking point) or *Extreme Makeover: Home Edition* (a design team must renovate the home of a family otherwise facing disaster). Their premise is that the American family is in trouble. Many scholars have noted how the family is constantly described as in crisis throughout its historical development—with the calamity of the moment always reflecting contemporaneous sociopolitical tensions.[6] The idea of crisis has been used to justify family values debates, which usually involve public policy and political rhetoric that uses moral discourses to norm what counts as a healthy family.

In effect, family reality TV programs enter into their own family values debate. In their representation of family diversity (which different series laud or decry) and in their use of family crisis motifs, reality narratives capture a sense of apprehension and ambivalence about evolving family life in the United States. Reality TV markets themes about our current period of momentous social change: the shift from what sociologists term the modern family, the nuclear model that reached its full expression in the context of Victorian-era industrialization and peaked in the postwar 1950s, and the postmodern family, a diversity of forms that has emerged since then. Indeed, a key theme in reality TV depictions is that family is now perpetually in process or in flux, open to debate. Social historians define the modern family as a nuclear unit with a male breadwinner, female homemaker, and dependent children; its gendered division of labor was largely only an option historically for the white middle-class whose male heads of household had access to the family wage.[7] This form was presented as universal but was never the reality for a majority of people, even though it was upheld as a dominant cultural ideal.[8] A diversity of arrangements have openly appeared since the 1960s and 1970s, comprising what historian Edward Shorter termed the postmodern family.[9] New familial forms have emerged, spurred by increases in divorce rates and single-parent households, women's entrance into the labor force in large numbers after 1960, the decline of the family wage, and the pressures on labor caused by postindustrialism and by globalization.[10]

In chapters addressing this theme, I demonstrate that because family reality shows engage in their own family values debate, taken as a whole, the genre ultimately asserts that the family unit itself is still relevant to American social life. The programs launch competing visions, with some supporting a traditional modern nuclear family unit stereotype while others uphold a newer postmodern diversity of family forms. Thus the genre does not make a coherent claim for how the family might evolve in the future or for the so-called best family values, even as the family is becoming less central than other organizing units in society like the household (unmarried couples who cohabitate, for example). However, by spending so much time watching families and wrangling over family life tensions, reality TV does insist that family matters. Family reality series question some conventional familial norms while reinforcing others. I would agree with critics such as Tania Modleski and Sherrie A. Inness, who argue that popular culture texts that address issues like gendered roles and the real contradictions in women's lives often both challenge and reaffirm traditional values.[11] These reality programs picture some updated norms (frequently, the edited narratives validate wider definitions of what counts as family, or they support frazzled working mothers by urging husbands to undertake more domestic labor). But some also reinforce older modern nuclear family ideals. While the family reality shows do not all agree on these subjects, they nevertheless all fixate on family conflict and turn it into a spectacle, making fraught kinship issues a family circus in order to draw more viewers and advertising.

Fear of a Digital Planet

The way reality TV banks on tensions about social change also returns to the way the genre uses new media innovations. In addition to exploring fears about social change in families, reality shows also address anxieties about the very media innovations the genre uses, because they speak to larger worries about our digital era. While reality TV is banking on media trends, profiting from new media features that spark viewer interest and interaction, the genre also addresses anxieties about a period of intense media transformation. Indeed, many of the very media features reality TV incorporates can also generate concerns.

For example, recent media events offer us clues as to what reality TV means today. When interviewed about reality TV's impact on her own life in 2010 by *W* magazine, reality star Kim Kardashian insisted that while some saw reality programs as troubling exploitation and voyeurism in the past, now most audiences and participants see it as acceptable and nothing to be feared.[12] In her way of thinking, reality stardom is a way to make home movies of your life's experiences and share them with fans, to build a brand in the entertainment industry, and to be yourself in front of cameras and be applauded for it. While the rhetoric of careerism and the use of media to gain self-knowledge is familiar, what is striking is Kardashian's nothing to fear commentary. When asked specifically about *The Truman Show*, the dystopian satire of a man being unknowingly filmed for TV audience entertainment, with the TV producers controlling all the elements of a staged world, Kardashian claims that most people do not see that as a bad thing anymore. It is surprising that Kardashian does not register any kind of negative effects from reality culture, especially given how her reality stardom has evolved (with, more recently, her widely televised engagement and wedding followed by her much-criticized divorce after 72 days of marriage). Yet her embrace of reality TV is indicative of a key moment in reality TV's evolution, one in which for some, *The Truman Show* is a good thing, not a cautionary tale. This book examines the questions raised by such developments.

Indeed, in capturing the zeitgeist of our digital era, reality shows exploit an undercurrent of concern about the changing cultural landscape. More and more people are living parts of their lives on camera for audience consumption, while viewers question what is true about what they see on-screen. What does it mean to put yourself on camera for others to see? What are the ramifications of doing so? What does it mean to feel you know the real person you are seeing on-screen? These queries are complicated by the fact that the range of cameras and screens on which we see other people and ourselves is proliferating—spanning from surveillance footage or satellite feeds like Google Earth, to personal digital photos on Facebook or videos on YouTube, to broadcast or cable reality shows.

Watching a reality TV show and trying to ascertain what seems more genuine and what seems more manipulated can be a way of practicing one's survival skills in our digital age. Critics such as Jon Dovey and Arild Feitveit think reality TV meditates on how digital technology has led to greater manipulation of images and more questioning of truth claims, because audiences are trying to understand what reality means now that any image can be seamlessly altered on computers.[13] I would agree with this line of argumentation and believe that reality TV's popularity reflects our current fascination with the status of truth and reality in a digital context, in which it can be harder to distinguish between real and fake. While any act of representation is an act of mediation, digital texts amplify some of these issues. On reality TV, this problem of truthfulness is present in the visual image as well as in the loose scripting that leads castmembers to perform versions of themselves for the audience.

Audiences in search of media literacy need to know how to tell the difference between, for example, corporate advertisements masquerading as content versus user-generated content on YouTube. For reality TV, we might ask, for example, just how scripted is MTV's hit docusoap *The Real World* and to what extent is that part of the show's appeal, since most audiences will be aware of that dynamic from extensive media reports about it. We all know reality TV is "fake," as even reality celebutante Paris Hilton tells us (meaning it is edited, manipulated, and often lightly scripted). Yet one audience study found that viewers see reality programming as at least moderately real.[14]

Even if the difference is one of degree, these shows are presented as something realer than scripted television. Often that sense of reality involves castmembers performing their emotions or identity, explicitly drawing on the idea that being themselves as fully as possible on reality TV is the most "authentic" thing they can do and will garner viewers' sympathy (and even gain legions of devoted fans). Indeed, even though they know reality TV is highly edited, many viewers still look for what Ien Ang would term moments of "emotional realism," or psychological accuracy in the program, that is, people having believable reactions even if the situations are melodramatic ones (or, in the case of reality TV, faked or scripted ones).[15] Critic Annette Hill, in a large audience study, has documented how audiences seek out moments of "authenticity" while watching reality TV.[16] It is no mistake that the climactic moment of *Extreme Makeover: Home Edition* is the shot of the family weeping at the reveal of their palatial new home, courtesy of ABC. Fan devotion is evidenced by the show's high ratings over the years, but also by the thousands who volunteer to help build a home in their local neighborhood. Through such practices, reality TV spectacularly captures the opportunities and anxieties of the digital age. I will be exploring these issues more fully in Chapter 2, which focuses on the effects of reality TV's use of documentary mixed with fictional TV genres and on its use of emotional appeals to viewers.

Critics debate whether reality TV's use of new media is a move that exploits the democratic promise of the Internet's interactivity for corporate profit or that offers the hope and opportunity of greater fan access to and influence on media content. Mark Andrejevic, for example, argues that reality TV conditions audiences to accept mass customization marketing, greater surveillance of them, and that it hijacks new media's interactivity and democratic promise in order to serve corporate interests. In his view, the way reality TV harnesses the Internet merely gets viewers to generate their own content (from fan message boards to appearing on reality TV themselves) while companies profit from their free labor.[17] Jenkins, meanwhile, argues that even though the use of new media in trends like transmedia storytelling does serve corporate synergy interests, it nevertheless does offer audiences greater access to the media. For him, audiences can impact more content and make more of their own, precisely because these trends depend on participatory fan culture. He is optimistic about creating new models of interaction between fans and media companies that involve what he calls co-creation, although that kind of model would require new models for profit sharing.[18]

In my view, the dynamics of how much fan access and agency there is often depends on the specific context, that is, how the companies are marketing the product, how the text itself is set up and what its content is, and on how fans choose to respond, interact, and create for themselves in each instance. While I acknowledge the limits to how much power fans have, given the economic structures involved, I do side with approaches that are hopeful about active audiences. As I will discuss more in Chapter 1, the fact that audience responses and behaviors are unpredictable and cannot be controlled is vitally important.

Industry Context

In order to establish the context for reality TV as a media phenomenon, it is useful to outline how reality TV has evolved in the TV industry and built on existing norms and conventions. The emergence of reality TV as a genre and marketing category involves a movement from a fad to a growing critical mass of devoted fans to broad incorporation into television programming. This success has often been the result of large followings for particular reality franchises, as when *Survivor*'s summer 2000 high ratings sparked a reality boom.

Reality TV's hybrid genre mix includes the docusoap mixture of documentary and soap opera narrative and visual conventions. Other common examples include the incorporation of classic sitcom story lines into observational documentaries, such as in the reality sitcom *The Osbournes*.[19] The documentary form allows reality TV to make a sociological claim to document the people portrayed, while the conventions of fictional TV genres encourage audiences' emotional investment in the real people portrayed as characters on-screen.

Once considered an ephemeral trend, reality TV is now recognized as a staple of television that has thoroughly altered writing, production, and distribution practices.[20] It has swept across the major networks and a large number of cable channels, combining many genres, including the sitcom, prime-time drama, talk show, game show, travelogue, soap opera, and variety show. Several tentpole franchises have enjoyed record Nielsen ratings, notably Fox's *American Idol*, again, with each season averaging around 20 million viewers through 2011, and CBS's *Survivor*, whose first season finale in 2000 netted 52 million viewers.[21] *Survivor*'s high ratings spawned other reality successes, with a number of reality programs reaching the top 10 shows for each year; in the wake of the *Survivor* boom, during both the 2002–2003 and 2003–2004 seasons, five of the top 10 network shows were reality formats.[22] With reality formats thriving since, some industry executives see the genre maturing and achieving permanency, with one *Los Angeles Times* article arguing it has "mushroomed from a marginal trend to the brightest hope of the beleaguered broadcast TV business."[23] It has received Emmy categories from the Academy of Television Arts & Sciences, which offer a sign of industry acceptance.

Examples of how this programming has changed industry practices abound. The success of unscripted fare prompted television writers to worry about their jobs and to argue for writing credits, because of the story editing and often loose scripting involved.[24] Networks and production companies have pirated formats and sued unsuccessfully over copyright infringement.[25] Responding to summer reality hits, the schedule for network programming changed to more flexibly defined seasons, deemphasizing the old model of September premieres and 35-week seasons with summer reruns in favor of year-round, 52-week new programming. Instead of 22 episodes over a September to May season, they frequently feature 8 to 13 episodes in successive weeks as short-run series. In the summer of 2004, Fox and NBC began moving to year-round programming. Fox's parent company, News Corp., then launched its reality cable channel in 2005. The Fox Reality Channel has further institutionalized the genre, exemplifying the narrowcasting trend in which cable channels adopt a genre identity to promote viewer loyalty.[26]

The industry's political economy in the 1980s and 1990s, especially deregulation, cable competition, and the 1988 writer's strike, contributed to the genre's rise, as critics have detailed.[27] This trend of broadcast networks and cable channels turning to reality programming during a writer's strike or labor disputes continued with the 2007 Writers Guild of America strike. When production on some scripted shows was suspended during the strike, networks rushed new seasons of reality franchises to air, such as CBS's *Big Brother* and *The Amazing Race.*

Reality TV's formal elements and industry context have crucial ramifications for its content. Because reality TV can be produced and edited in weeks while scripted programs can take months, it can respond more quickly to sociocultural changes. Even though reality programs have story editors who cull story lines from hours of raw footage and some have light scripting and staged situations, the amount of scripting is much less than in fictional series. Reality TV raises key issues, including voyeurism, surveillance and social control, identity shaped through the media, the role of mass media in democracy, and the possibilities and limits for audience access and agency offered by new media forms, as scholars have been debating.[28] Critical attention to reality TV is important given not only the high number of viewers but also the passion of fan devotion. Witness the screaming fans jamming phone lines to vote for *American Idol, Survivor* viewing parties, or fans watching live Internet feeds of *Big Brother* or *The Real World* and flooding Internet forums.

In the chapters that follow, I analyze these media trends and the effects of their uses on reality TV. Chapter 1 analyzes transmedia storytelling, participatory fan culture, and how reality TV turns real people into characters (and the effects of these uses of narrative). Chapter 2 discusses the documentary-fictional TV genre hybrid mix and emotional appeals alongside how the genre banks on cultural fears about media change. Chapter 3 turns to how reality TV profits from anxieties about the family and why family themes are such an obsession in the genre. Chapter 4 details how the genre turns family themes into political arguments, engaging in its own family values debate. There, I address in particular reality shows that circulate a political rhetoric of neoliberalism. I also discuss how reality TV making itself a lightning rod for public controversy helps spark ratings and aid the genre's longevity. Witness how MTV's *Teen Mom* franchise, and the controversy over teen pregnancy, has made reality shows topics of public debate and even evidence in court cases about actual families. Chapter 5 looks at anxieties about changing gender roles in the context of these family themes, and it explores how wife swap and family switching programs express liberal pluralism. A conclusion predicts impending developments in reality TV, as the genre moves into brave new territories, invoking familiar themes with inventive media techniques. It draws on the earlier history of the genre, with the family documentary *An American Family* as the forerunner to current reality TV, and updates that history with projections of the future.

To begin elaborating the story of reality TV's evolution and success, my next chapter charts some of the most important new media elements the genre utilizes. From transmedia stories to novel ways of building characters, I examine how reality TV capitalizes on these elements. Here too, Kim Kardashian and her family have more to tell us than one might think.

Notes

1. "Nielsen Television TV Ratings for Primetime," *Zap2it,* December 25, 2011, http://www.zap2it.com/tv/ratings/zap-season-ratings,0,1937498.htmlstory.

2. Henry Jenkins, *Convergence Culture: Where Old and New Media Collide* (New York: New York University Press, 2006), 8.

3. Jennifer Gillan, *Television and New Media: Must-Click TV* (New York: Routledge, 2011), 2.

4. The date of the current reality trend's onset is a matter of critical debate. To cite representative examples, Kilborn dubs *America's Unsolved Mysteries* (1987), the original impetus for current reality TV, while Jermyn points to *Crimewatch UK* (1984–). Richard Kilborn, "How Real Can You Get?: Recent Developments in 'Reality' Television," *European Journal of Communications* 9 (1994): 421–439. Deborah Jermyn, " 'This *Is* About Real People!': Video Technologies, Actuality, and Affect in the Television Crime Appeal," *Understanding Reality Television,* ed. Su Holmes and Deborah Jermyn (London: Routledge, 2004), 75.

5. Lynn Spigel, *Make Room for TV: Television and the Family Ideal in Postwar America* (Chicago: University of Chicago Press, 1992).

6. Linda Gordon, *Heroes of Their Own Lives* (New York: Viking, 1988), 3.

7. Stephanie Coontz, *The Way We Never Were: American Families and the Nostalgia Trap* (New York: Basic Books, 1992), 12.

8. Two-parent households were the majority only from the 1920s to 1970s, and the modern nuclear family represented only a minority of those households. William H. Frey, Bill Abresch, and Jonathan Yeasting, *America By the Numbers: A Field Guide to the U.S. Population* (New York: New Press, 2001), 123–124.

9. Edward Shorter, *The Making of the Modern Family* (New York: Basic Books, 1975).

10. See sociologist Judith Stacey, *Brave New Families: Stories of Domestic Upheaval in Late Twentieth Century America* (New York: Basic Books, 1990), 3–19; Nancy F. Cott, *Public Vows: A History of Marriage and the Nation* (Cambridge, MA: Harvard University Press, 2000). Stacey notes that more children now live with single mothers than in modern nuclear families; married couples with kids comprise only a minority of U.S. households, and many of those couples are divorced and remarried. Stacey, *In The Name of the Family: Rethinking Family Values in the Postmodern Age* (Boston: Beacon Press, 1996), 45.

11. Tania Modleski, *Feminism Without Women: Culture and Criticism in a "Postfeminist" Age* (New York: Routledge, 1991), 7–9. Sherrie A. Inness, *Tough Girls* (Philadelphia: University of Pennsylvania Press, 1999), 178–179.

12. Lynn Hirschberg, "Kim Kardashian: The Art of Reality," *W* Magazine, November 2010.

13. Arild Fetveit, "Reality TV in the Digital Era: A Paradox in Visual Culture?" in *Reality Squared: Televisual Discourse on the Real,* ed. James Friedman (New Brunswick, NJ: Rutgers University Press, 2002), 119–137; Jon Dovey, "Reality TV," in *The Television Genre Book,* ed. Glen Creeber (London: British Film Institute, 2001), 134–137.

14. Robin L. Naby, Erica N. Biely, Sara J. Morgan, and Carmen R. Stitt, "Reality Based Television Programming and the Psychology of Its Appeal," *Media Psychology* 5 (2003): 303–330.

15. Ien Ang, *Watching Dallas: Television and the Melodramatic Imagination* (London: Routledge, 1985), 47.

16. Annette Hill, *Reality TV Audiences and Popular Factual Television* (London: Routledge, 2005).

17. Mark Andrejevic, *iSpy: Surveillance and Power in the Interactive Era* (Lawrence, KS: University Press of Kansas, 2007). Andrejevic, *Reality TV: The Work of Being Watched* (Lanham, MD: Rowman & Littlefield, 2004).

18. Jenkins, *Convergence Culture,* 168.

19. For an excellent discussion of reality TV and genre, see John Caldwell, "Prime-Time Fiction Theorizes the Docu-Real," in *Reality Squared: Televisual Discourse on the Real,* ed. James Friedman (New Brunswick, NJ: Rutgers University Press, 2002), 259–292. See also Caldwell, *Televisuality: Style, Crisis, and Authority in American Television* (New Brunswick, NJ: Rutgers University Press, 1995).

20. Bill Carter, "Reality TV Alters the Way TV Does Business," *New York Times,* January 25, 2003, A1.

21. Carter, "Reality TV Alters the Way TV Does Business," A1.

22. Alex Strachan, "Reality Check: Conventional Television Wisdom Turned on Its Ear," *The Star Phoenix* [Saskatoon, Saskatchewan], July 17, 2004, E1, final edition.

23. Scott Collins and Maria Elena Fernandez, "Life Imitates Reality TV When Execs Square Off," *Los Angeles Times: Electronic Edition,* July 16, 2004, http://www.calendarlive.com/tv/la-et-tvwar16jul16,0,6654375.story.

24. Statistics like networks running 14 percent of their schedules as reality shows in early 2003 prompted television writer Stephen Godchaux to state apocalyptically: "Scripted television is actually in peril," though that has not proven to be the case. Jenny Hontz, "Reality Is Harsh on TV's Creative Teams," *New York Times on the Web,* February 9, 2003, http://www.nytimes.com/2003/02/09/business/yourmoney/09TVTV.html?ex=1047286669&ei=1&en=7f296d3686edbd6a.

25. In 2003, CBS failed to convince judges that ABC's *I'm a Celebrity . . . Get Me Out of Here!* infringed on *Survivor,* and NBC aired another season of that franchise in 2009. Meanwhile, in 2004, ABC accused Fox of shoplifting the wife swap and nanny formats ABC acquired the rights to from British originals, while NBC accused Fox of scooping their boxing gamedoc format. Collins and Fernandez, "Life Imitates Reality TV."

26. On narrowcasting, see Graeme Turner, "The Uses and Limitations of Genre," in *The Television Genre Book,* ed. Glenn Creeber (London: British Film Institute, 2001), 4–6.

27. Chad Raphael notes that cable competition, fewer financial resources, the 1988 writer's strike, and other union battles initially sparked network interest in nonfiction formats such as *Cops.* Raphael, "The Political Economic Origins of Reali-TV," in *Reality TV: Remaking Television Culture,* eds. Susan Murray and Laurie Ouellette (New York: New York University Press, 2004), 119–136.

28. For solid overviews of the field, see: Laurie Ouellette and James Hay, *Better Living through Reality TV: Television and Post-welfare Citizenship* (Malden, MA: Blackwell, 2008); Jonathan Bignell, *Big Brother: Reality TV in the Twenty-First Century* (New York: Palgrave Macmillan, 2005); Susan Murray and Laurie Ouellette, eds., *Reality TV: Remaking Television Culture* (New York: New York University Press, 2004); Richard Kilborn, *Staging the Real: Factual TV Programming in the Age of Big Brother* (Manchester: Manchester University Press, 2003); Su Holmes and Deborah Jermyn, eds., *Understanding Reality Television* (London: Routledge, 2004); James Friedman, ed., *Reality Squared: Televisual Discourse on the Real* (New Brunswick, NJ: Rutgers University Press, 2002).

Chapter 1

Choose Your Own Adventure: Transmedia Storytelling, Reality Characters, and Fans

Reality shows bank on larger-than-life castmembers who draw in viewers with their emotional outbursts, conflicts, and melodramatic resolutions. Indeed, character is one of the main driving engines for the success of a reality show. Reality TV characters become the basis for entire brands as well as for transmedia storytelling, which depends on active fans. I would argue that a key factor in reality TV's success as a genre is its use of narrative techniques to turn real people into what I have elsewhere termed "character narratives," in which they are portrayed as story types starring in elaborate storylines shaped by the rhythms of fictional TV genres, such as sitcoms, soap operas, or dramas.[1] Reality TV reverses classic narrative. Instead of trying to make characters seem real, it turns real people into characters, using predictable and repetitive narrative frames.

This chapter examines how the reality genre capitalizes on three related media trends: transmedia storytelling, turning real people into characters, and participatory fan culture. Having established a strong character who encourages audience identification, reality programs can then take that character into stories that cross media platforms in a coordinated way. Successful shows prompt devoted fans who want to interact with those characters and plotlines to seek out the added content, trailing their favorite reality characters (often framed as heroes or villains) from TV to Web pages to mobile phone apps to books to music albums to book tours.

For example, cult figures such as Bethenny Frankel and NeNe Leakes from the Bravo *Real Housewives* franchise draw fans because they communicate

charismatic personalities. Sporting quick humor and sometimes outra-
geous behavior, they claim always to "be themselves" in front of the camera.
They insist that they will tell anyone exactly what they think, and their
viewers are encouraged to identify with their emotional roller-coaster rides,
what Ien Ang would call the "tragic structure of feeling" common in soap
operas.[2] Both women appear in the Bravo *Real Housewives*–related media
texts on different platforms, such as DVDs with extra commentary, companion books, reunion specials, numerous online games on the Bravo
website, mobile phone apps (like the "Housewives Hub," with news and
gossip about the cast), personal appearances by the cast, and interviews
with Bravo TV executive and talk show host Andy Cohen on his live talk
show, *Watch What Happens Live*.

Frankel in particular has used her reality stardom to become a media
mogul. She has starred on three different Bravo reality shows (the first
three seasons of *The Real Housewives of New York City* [2008–] and her
own *Bethenny Getting Married?* [2010] and *Bethenny Ever After* [2011–]
spin-offs). Her draw as a reality star is indicated by the fact that *Bethenny
Getting Married?*, which depicted her wedding to Jason Hoppy, had the
highest rated series premiere on Bravo at that time (with more than
2 million viewers).[3] Her media presence is based on her characterization
on reality TV as the witty, fast-talking, brash New Yorker with the heart of
gold. She is most often portrayed as using humor to deal with the chaos
of juggling her work with her new marriage and child. Her character narrative revolves around stories typical of family sitcoms (new parents try to
sleep through the night, in-laws hover, the wife rushes to put a holiday
dinner together with humorously disastrous results) or dramatic plotlines
(the husband and wife argue over what role religion will play in the child's
life, the couple grapple with business pressures, they deal with family
illnesses).

But what is most striking about Frankel is how she has parlayed that
reality stardom into her own entrepreneurial and media mogul efforts. In
building her character as brand, Frankel has appeared on two other reality
programs, both gamedocs: she was one of two finalists on *The Apprentice:
Martha Stewart* (2005), prior to her *Real Housewives* stint, and she was the
runner-up on *Skating With the Stars* (2011). She also launched her own talk
show, *Bethenny* (2012–). A natural foods chef, Frankel drew on her reality
stardom to release her own books, DVDs, online materials, diet products,
cosmetics, and clothing lines. All part of her Skinnygirl line of products,
they include items that span different media formats, such as a diet book

and audio accompaniment (*Naturally Thin* [2009] and *The Skinnygirl Rules* [2010]), a cookbook (*The Skinnygirl Dish* [2009]), exercise DVDs (*Body by Bethenny* [2010]), and an online personal trainer (*Skinnygirl Personal Trainer*). Most notably, she published a *New York Times* best-selling self-help book, *A Place of Yes: 10 Rules for Getting Everything You Want Out of Life* (2011). Developing her Skinnygirl line further, Frankel founded her own company, Skinnygirl Cocktails, and then sold her line of cocktails to a larger company, Fortune Brands's Beam Global, for an estimated $120 million (2011).[4] Frankel is currently continuing her transmedia branding of herself with a fictional novel she is writing, entitled *Skinnydipping,* which she advertises on her Twitter feed (to her over 730,000 followers) and her webpage (Bethenny.com). Many of her fans proved their devotion to her in person by attending her book tour, where she billed herself as an inspirational speaker, telling them humor-filled stories about how she found success as a woman business owner and author (with footage from the book tour featured on *Bethenny Ever After*).

Meanwhile, NeNe Leakes, from *The Real Housewives of Atlanta* (2008–), parlayed her reality stardom there into a role on *The Celebrity Apprentice* (in 2011). While she has not achieved the same level of media moguldom that Frankel has, she has become a cult figure similar to Frankel, and is known for being outspoken and confrontational. She declares loyalty to her friends but engages in highly melodramatic storylines in which she engages in volatile fights with them, even becoming estranged from them sometimes. Most famously, Leakes quit *The Celebrity Apprentice* during the season because she objected to how other celebrity castmembers, like Star Jones, were playing the game. In other dramatic storylines on *The Real Housewives,* Leakes searched for and met her biological father for the first time, advocated for domestic violence survivors like herself, and became separated from her current husband after on-going marital tensions and his financial troubles. In media ventures that bank on her reality show characterizations, Leakes has published her own autobiography, *Never Make the Same Mistake Twice: Lessons on Love and Life Learned the Hard Way* (2009). She also undertakes speaking tours and celebrity appearances.

More notably in terms of cultural responses to reality TV and fan culture, Leakes has become the favorite reality star of many media personalities. Cohen openly worships her on his *Watch What Happens Live,* journalist Anderson Cooper frequently declares his obsession with her, and the cast of *Glee* have emoted their stalker-level joy at her 2012 guest star turn on the Fox cult hit television series, and *Glee* creator Ryan Murphy has her appearing as Rocky, a charismatic personal assistant, on his new sitcom, *The New Normal* (2012–).[5] Bravo purposefully markets the fact that Leakes has become a fixation for other celebrities, like Sean "Diddy" Combs, who declares himself a NeNe fanatic. In an example of series-related sponsor content on their website, Bravo trumpeted the Diddy fan story alongside their advertising for the partnership between his Ciroc Vodka line and the *Real Housewives* franchise for a 2011 holiday sweepstakes competition (with the winner meeting some of the cast) and safe driving ad campaign.[6]

Thus, while both women appear in the tie-in media products about the *Real Housewives* franchise, each woman has also taken her own brand and character into other media areas (autobiographies, other reality shows that are not part of the *Real Housewives* franchise, Twitter feeds, etc.). My argument that character is key and becomes a branding feature is borne out by how these reality stars can move beyond the confines of their original reality show and take their character as brand into new media settings and stories (such as Frankel on *Skating With the Stars* and Leakes on *The Celebrity Apprentice*). While new editing and storylines in unrelated reality programs might portray them differently, these reality stars carefully fashion their own presentation of self in their interviews and in their communications with their fans via social networking sites like Twitter. They claim they are being authentically themselves in each context. The presentation of their character, both on edited reality shows and via their own media communications, depends on careful use of narrative and storytelling techniques.

Transmedia Storytelling, Reality Style

A key factor in creating reality TV stories and characters that audiences today care about is the use of transmedia storytelling. It is not a new development to combine different media forms to tell a story. Medieval illuminated manuscripts, for example, used the written word alongside gorgeous illustrations to communicate. Today, wildly popular graphic novels combine the mass-produced print culture of the written word with the visual culture of illustrations to capture a certain kind of artistic vision and convey it to eager readers. What is new, however, is the extensiveness of how current media texts tell a complex story across different media forms and the scale on which they are doing so. The specific features they use, and some recurring tendencies, are also indicative of current tendencies in our use of digital culture in the context of today's convergence culture.

Media scholar Henry Jenkins describes convergence culture as a new era of media in which various media systems coexist and content flows across multiple media platforms. Old media (like television, film, and books) and new media (defined as media that uses interactive digital technology, such as the Internet or smart mobile phones) interact in new ways. An obvious example is how companies take books online with electronic book readers, such as Amazon's Kindle or Barnes & Nobles' Nook readers. Consumers and producers interact in new ways as well. Key features include a rise in participatory fan culture, consumers becoming more active (seeking out entertainment they want across different media platforms), cooperation between various media industries, new media financing formats, and new and unpredictable interactions between grassroots and corporate media. Jenkins notes that developments such as digitization and new patterns of cross-media ownership beginning in the 1980s helped drive this convergence culture (with media conglomerates moving to own interests across the industry, in film, television, popular music, computer games, Web sites, toys, amusement park rides, books, newspapers, magazines, and comics).[7]

For television specifically, television companies have learned to incorporate new media developments, creating elements for their TV shows such as fan-centered websites, mobile phone apps, online games, and even music albums and tours, all conceived as features that help further the content. Television scholar Jennifer Gillan has demonstrated how networks monetized preexisting fandom practices (like fan websites) and mainstreamed them. She identifies two stages of TV development in this regard. In the 1990s, networks transformed TV series into platforms for promoting other media (like the Dawson's Desktop fan website for *Dawson's Creek* [1998–2003]). However, in the 2000s, new TV product is now conceptualized as a series of networked texts that prompt fans to track the content across multiple media platforms (like *Heroes* [2006–2010], which created a fan-centered website).[8]

This multiplatform content is now central to what TV does and how it will survive in our era of convergence culture. Television has to jockey for attention in the midst of other popular media platforms (like YouTube and other user-generated content websites, video games, and content for smart phones). Gillan argues that a model of multiplatform content also allows broadcast networks to target two audiences at once: the broader audience of the traditional broadcast platform, but now also the narrow-cast audience of the multiplatform (smaller niche audiences who might, for example, play video games related to the TV series). Hence the TV industry has a new model of a combination "narrowcast-broadcast" TV series, and advertisers have embraced this model by participating in branded entertainment deals.[9] This kind of model depends on attracting active fans who will become brand advocates who nurture fan networks, reposting content and links to their social networking sites (Facebook, Twitter, Tumblr, etc.).

Multiplatform texts, what Henry Jenkins terms transmedia storytelling, refer specifically to texts where content appears in a coordinated way across many different media formats (such as television, film, webisodes, mobile phone apps and mobisodes, and music albums).[10] Thus, for some popular web content, audiences increasingly expect to see it directly linked to a broader array of media texts. Innovative media formats have evolved in ways that speak to the cultural power of the Internet and to changing expectations of the entertainment content audiences seek there. The entertainment industry has also responded to this development. The Producer's Guild of America now recognizes transmedia producer as a category. A growing number of transmedia companies are appearing, often comprised of production units trying to generate transmedia content across film, games, TV, the Web, and mobile phones. Helios Entertainment, for example, bills itself as "a creative organization that conceives, develops and produces socially empowering entertainment properties that are designed to distribute across a wide variety of traditional and digital platforms including graphic novels, films, games, books, music and digital/interactive media" (which they advertise on their website, heliosentertainment.com).

Examples of the rise in multiplatform texts include the *Harry Potter* franchise, which began as novels by J. K. Rowling, expanding into a film series, web tie-ins, novelizations of the film versions, smart phone apps, and even a theme park (The Wizarding World of Harry Potter at Universal Orlando's Islands of Adventure). Again, the transmedia Potter text depends on active fans who will seek out, share that content, and also interact with it. Because of the highly active fan culture around the Potter franchise, and the large number of fan fiction websites, Rowling has created the Pottermore website to add more content to her series and to provide a space for further fan interaction. A fascinating development in the Harry

Potter fan culture is the existence of college Quidditch teams, comprised of fans who play the fictional Potter sport against other teams, both intramurally and intermurally, with players decked out in jerseys, wielding brooms, and living out their Potter universe fantasies.

A new development in terms of multiplatform storytelling involves fictional TV series that add a tied-in reality show. In the *Glee* example, as part of voluminous transmedia storytelling, the Fox series features numerous online music albums and singles on iTunes (many frequently placing in the iTunes best-seller lists), web tie-ins, a smart phone app (The Glee Experience) that lets you sing karaoke along with the *Glee* cast, and even a nationwide musical tour with castmembers performing in character. On the *Glee* YouTube channel, fans can watch sneak peeks that include scenes and musical numbers from upcoming episodes, plus behind the scenes videos. Fans can also receive text messages about *Glee* content, like hints about future plotlines. The transmedia storytelling of *Glee* continued with *Glee: The 3D Concert Movie* (2011). Most significantly, *Glee* added a reality TV gamedoc to involve fans more fully (in voting for a fan favorite to win a $10,000 prize) and to provide fans a chance to win a role on the series *Glee* itself. *The Glee Project* (Oxygen, 2011–) is designed to award the winner with a contract to be on *Glee* in a seven-episode character arc. The gamedoc provides marketing for *Glee* but also exists as a stand-alone text itself, meaning that viewers do not have to watch *Glee* to understand *The Glee Project.* Contestants sing and act and compete to win time with mentors from *Glee.* All appear in a weekly music video, which the judges evaluate and then pick the bottom three for a sing-off, which determines who will be sent home. For the separate fan favorite contest, viewers vote on the Oxygen website (at oxygen.com) and access additional videos with more content from *The Glee Project. Glee*'s transmedia storytelling has successfully generated an entire subculture of fans, dubbed Gleeks, who seek out and consume all *Glee* content across these various media platforms.

Jenkins describes transmedia texts as those that can create a rich, encyclopedic fictional universe with enough gaps in the open-ended narrative for different texts to fill in the spaces. Even more crucially, the narrative has to offer enough spaces for fans to want to fill them in, engaging with that entire fictional world in their own fan responses (including fan fiction). Each additional piece of planned content in the larger transmedia text is able to exist on its own but also contribute to the overall story. Each added item also draws on the strengths and features of each medium (such as television's ability to tell stories in on-going episodes and story arcs, film's capacity to be immersive, or a video game's power to let fans explore the world depicted). Meanwhile media companies also profit from their corporate synergy, with holdings in everything from movie studios to comic books. Jenkins argues that transmedia texts tend to focus on the overall fictional universe rather than on particular plotlines and characters, such that a changing cast of characters and their stories can inhabit different aspects of that fictional world.[11]

I would argue that in the case of reality TV, at least, character takes on increased importance in many reality transmedia texts. Applying the concept of transmedia storytelling to reality TV shows requires a few adjustments in the theory, since the programs are about actual people, rather than fictional worlds. Yet reality franchises can obviously be planned transmedia texts. Since reality shows depend on the storytelling codes drawn from fictional TV genres (like primetime dramas, sitcoms, and soap operas), their use of storytelling across multiple media platforms would qualify as an example of transmedia texts.

There are a number of examples of reality shows that focus on character narratives rather than on the subculture or even the larger world they inhabit. For example, in *Keeping Up With the Kardashians,* the show focuses on the Kardashians themselves, and the audience interest in each family member as a character is what drives the success or failure of spin-offs and storylines. Another good example is the E! reality series *The Girls Next Door,* which set out to depict the world of Hugh Hefner, the Playboy mansion, and his girlfriends. But because the women became more popular as characters themselves, spin-offs about them have had much greater success. *Kendra* follows the life of Kendra Wilkinson as she married NFL player Hank Baskett and had a son, and *Holly's World* follows Holly Madison's move to Las Vegas and her appearance in shows there. Audience interest followed specific characters more than the subculture depicted. Both women parlayed their reality stardom into spots on *Dancing With the Stars,* while Kendra Wilkinson also published a memoir.

Meanwhile, some other reality transmedia texts do fit the Jenkins transmedia description in the sense that the world they depict is most important, and the cast of people and plotlines can come and go. The *Real Housewives* franchise, which routinely switches out castmembers or switches narrative focus, is a good case in point, as it purports to capture the subculture of housewives in different locations, including Orange County, New York City, New Jersey, Atlanta, Miami, and Beverly Hills. Similarly, MTV's long-running *The Real World* features different settings and castmembers each season, foregrounding the idea of capturing the subcultures and conflicts of young 18- to 24-year-olds living together in a big city. Their gamedoc series *The Challenge* (formerly *The Real World/Road Rules Challenge,* which also drew on the *Road Rules* reality series) also changes out settings and many castmembers each season, focusing on that same youth culture in a competition format. The transmedia storytelling for those shows includes a film version of *The Real World,* numerous tie-in books, behind the scenes specials, reunion shows, DVDs with extra interviews and deleted scenes, online games, cast blogs, and even speaking tours with *Real World* castmembers travelling to college campuses. Thus, in reality shows, whether more focused on the world captured or on a specific character, such interlocking pieces of content can all exist on their own but also add to the larger multiplatform story.

A Kardashian World

One of the best examples of transmedia storytelling on reality TV is *Keeping Up With the Kardashians.* That reality franchise bears further scrutiny, not least because it is also a key instance of participatory fan culture and the reality show practice of turning real people into characters. The E! Kardashian franchise involves a planned multiplatform text in the sense that each additional text contributes to the whole but can stand alone, and each takes the story of this family's life into a specific media environment in order to further the story and communicate with fans. In a striking piece of transmedia storytelling, the E! network often uses their nightly entertainment news program, *E! News Live,* to interview Kardashian castmembers and to circulate entertainment news about the show, which functions as quite aggressive marketing for the program (with news host Ryan Seacrest, media mogul and prolific reality TV developer, notably serving as one of the program's executive producers). The reality show has generated successful spin-offs (*Khloé and Lamar,* and *Kourtney and Kim Take New York,* a continuation of *Kourtney and Khloé Take Miami*). It also became the basis for a related reality show about Kim Kardashian's public relations representatives (and close friends), Jonathan Chebon and Simon Huck, entitled *The Spin Crowd.* In addition to the spin-off shows, the Kardashian franchise also featured two different wedding specials, one depicting Khloé Kardashian's wedding to NBA player Lamar Odom, the other, *Kim's Fairytale Wedding: A Kardashian Event,* exhaustively chronicling Kim Kardashian's ill-fated wedding to NBA player Kris Humphries. In other reality roles, stepfather Bruce Jenner has appeared on reality shows previously (*I'm a Celebrity . . . Get Me Out of Here, Skating With Celebrities*), Kim and brother Rob Kardashian have both competed on *Dancing With the Stars,* and stepbrother Brody Jenner, who sometimes guest stars on *Keeping Up With the Kardashians,* has starred on several reality shows (MTV's *The Hills, Bromance,* and FOX's short-lived *The Princes of Malibu,* which was about two of Bruce Jenner's sons from a previous marriage).

In other transmedia features, the Kardashian books include Kris Jenner's autobiography (*Kris Jenner . . . And All Things Kardashian* [2011]) and the *New York Times* best seller, *Kardashian Konfidential* (2010), a book about how sisters Kim, Kourtney, and Khloé experience their reality stardom and their prestardom lives. Additional online content includes pitches for the products they promote on their shows. Their product integration includes a nail polish line, clothing lines (with various companies, including Sears and QVC), perfume lines, diet supplements (QuickTrim), cosmetics (Perfect Skin), and an ill-fated credit card endorsement that the Kardashians abandoned when there was a fan outcry over the card's exorbitant interest rates. Their product integration includes three locations of their own clothing boutique, Dash (with stores in Los Angeles, Miami, and New York).

The Kardashian sisters promote their various products with commercials that use their personae from their reality shows. In such appearances and in interviews, the three sisters often roll their eyes at their momager Kris Jenner, who is portrayed as overbearing, yet they also acknowledge her as the family media mogul and executive producer on the Kardashian-branded reality shows. Jenner provides one key guiding vision to how the family is portrayed, marketed, and branded.

The Kardashian shows have been polarizing, not least because of their obvious profit motive and manipulation, and all of the aggressive product integration, product endorsement, and branding. The family shares a six-figure payment for each reality episode, but their endorsements earn them much more, with the family pocketing $65 million in 2010 alone.[12] In perhaps the best example of narrative manipulation in the service of profits, with Kim's wedding special, the franchise turned a fairytale romance and wedding story into a multimillion dollar wedding. The televised special covering the wedding aired in two parts and garnered high ratings for E! (4.4 million viewers the first night and 4 million the second).[13] With the lavish, multimillion dollar wedding came media comparisons to the Prince William and Princess Catherine royal wedding (earning the Kardashians sometimes satirical analogies to American versions of celebrity as royalty). When Kim's media spectacle wedding to Kris Humphries ended in divorce 72 days later, many journalists and commentators criticized the opulent wedding and questioned whether the marriage had been a sham for the cameras. As part of the media backlash, one viewer even started a petition to ban the Kardashians from television because she felt they embodied empty, materialistic values and that the public had "had enough" of them. Addressed to E!, with over 165,000 signatures, the online petition states: "We are respectfully requesting that your network find other shows to air. *Keeping Up With the Kardashians* is just not viewing that we the public would like to see from your network. Enough is enough." When interviewed in the press, petition organizer Cyndy Snider explained:

> We feel that these shows are mostly staged and place an emphasis on vanity, greed, promiscuity, vulgarity and over-the-top conspicuous consumption. While some may have begun watching the spectacle as mindless entertainment or as a sort of "reality satire," it is a sad truth that many young people are looking up to this family and are modeling their appearance and behavior after them.[14]

However, the next season premiere of the reality show *Kourtney and Kim Take New York* (in November 2011), which promised to explain what happened in the marriage and why it ended in divorce, garnered the highest ratings for the series yet (3.2 million viewers, up from the show's January 2011 premiere of 3 million viewers).[15] The record ratings suggest that on one level, the negative publicity had only helped the Kardashian celebrity branding efforts.

On another level, though, what is striking about the Kardashian reality success is that it is all driven by the appeal of the familiar TV narratives the family embodies. Even if viewers felt cheated by the marriage fiasco, fans will return for a new narrative; that is, the story of how it all went wrong. The new story hook becomes Kim's reassessment of her idealistic true love concepts and her embrace of a more worldly view of relationships in today's society (in which over 50 percent of all marriages end in divorce), and then her relationship with her next boyfriend, singer Kanye West.

Even given all of the aggressive profit motives and branding involved, the engine that drives the connection to fans is the storytelling, especially the character narratives of reality sitcom and docusoap types, and the stories that cross different media platforms and with which fans interact. Kris Jenner appears as the overbearing matriarch to her children with her late first husband Robert Kardashian (famous as one of O.J. Simpson's attorneys). Daughter Kim is framed as the uptight perfectionist, Khloé as the irreverent funny sister, and Kourtney the laid-back sibling who finds herself a new mother contending with an alcoholic boyfriend. Rob has a storyline in which he struggles to break out of his character narrative as the lazy, aimless brother who lives off of his sisters. Even his *Dancing With the Stars* appearance furthers that storyline. There, Rob and other dancers declared in edited interviews on that show that he was finally "becoming a man" and "stepping out of the shadow of his sisters," while earning respect for dancing well enough to be the show's runner-up, as decided by a combination of judges' scores and fan votes. Young daughters Kendall and Kylie Jenner, children of Kris and Bruce Jenner and stepsisters to the Kardashians, are framed on the Kardashian reality shows as idealistic teens trying to enjoy their childhood in the midst of the pressures of family fame. Bruce Jenner is the doddering, powerless father and stepfather whom the brood find boring and overly strict but tolerate because he is well-intentioned.

The Kardashian shows' plotlines, some more obviously staged than others, plumb familiar sitcom narratives: teens learn to drive, jealous sisters bicker with each other, daughters rebel against their parents. Others mine docusoap and drama narratives: a son is rushed to the hospital, kids deal with grief from the earlier death of the family patriarch, adults attempt to overcome tensions in marriages and relationships. Some stories become metacommentaries on reality stardom: Kris worries about her appearance in front of cameras and gets plastic surgery, Kim and Khloé fight about who is more famous or more jealous of the other, Kourtney's boyfriend Scott Disick grows weary of always being placed in the villain role on TV.

The Kardashians thus combine storytelling across media platforms with extremely aggressive marketing and branding. Their branding practices have led industry magazines to conclude that the Kardashians are a building a new, highly influential business model based on the key elements of the success of their reality shows, social media interaction with fans, and profitable products and brand endorsements, all in the service of promoting the Kardashians as a brand. As Khloé Kardashian Odom notes: "These shows are a 30-minute commercial."[16] Even E! network executives report that it has altered the network's brand itself. According to Lisa Berger, E!'s executive vice president for original programming, "It has changed the face of E!. We were a place to report on celebrity; we weren't a place to break and make celebrity, which is now the whole idea of the E! brand."[17] Meanwhile, Kris Jenner argues for the show's appeal based on the family's relatability:

> We're just this big family with a lot of drama and a lot of issues, and there's someone here for everyone to relate to. I think if you've ever been embarrassed by your family—like your mother's a kook or your father's too strict—the show gives you hope. I've had so many people come over to me and say, "I remember the episode where you were crying over blah, blah, blah and it helped me so much and I got through my dad's death because of you."[18]

Her arguments about the success of their family life stories depend on the idea of them fitting into relatable family tropes, while presenting their large, boisterous family life as a spectacle and a family circus. *Keeping Up With the Kardashians* enjoys consistently high ratings (averaging over 3.5 million per week), while the season 4 finale set a record as the most-watched television episode on E!, with 4.8 million viewers.[19] Moving beyond the reality show into their transmedia presence, the Kardashian fanbase is quite large. Each Kardashian has at least two million Twitter followers, while Kim tops out at over 16 million, and the family as a whole has over 45 million followers. Their model of reality TV shows as the basis for multiplatform storytelling, particularly with features that brand the cast-members as characters, is clearly a bellwether for future media trends.

Authenticity Meets Frankenbiting

When Joaquin Phoenix made his hoax documentary, *I'm Still Here* (2010), in which he pretended to go crazy, descend into drug addiction, and try to leave his movie career for an ill-fated rap career, he was playing Joaquin Phoenix as a character in order to satirize how reality TV turns people into characters. The actor was ridiculing the media's superficial obsession with reality stars, suggesting that their reality personae are simply a put-on for the camera. On another level, he was asking, in effect, what are the risks and rewards of playing an exaggerated version of yourself on TV, a character type that fits into recurring story patterns and tropes? Phoenix's film critiques how mass media coverage in general tries to reduce actors and

artists to simple character narratives. That dynamic becomes more amplified and fraught on reality TV. After he went through his documentary
hoax experiment with his brother-in-law, director Casey Affleck, Phoenix
decided that playing a version of yourself as a character is akin to method
acting that never ends. He found it to be like a prison he could not escape (since he did not reveal the hoax until after the documentary was
released), and he was highly relieved when he could end his media stunt
experiment.[20]

A satire like Phoenix's raises key questions about the ramifications of
turning real people into characters on TV. What are the triumphs and tribulations entailed in embodying a TV narrative? Phoenix's film offers a dire
warning about the dehumanizing effects. In contrast, as I noted in my introduction, Kim Kardashian might signal a new attitude toward reality TV
when she insists that people no longer see the dystopian satire of *The Truman Show*, in which TV producers stage a man's world without his knowledge in order to film his life for viewer entertainment, as a bad thing. Yet
Kardashian might enjoy more control over her edited character narrative
than some reality show castmembers could ever achieve.

Anxiety about how real people are portrayed as characters is evident
on reality programs themselves, especially given the fraught presentation
of authenticity on these programs. In the *Real Housewives* examples of
Bethenny Frankel and NeNe Leakes, the factors at play in their success and
widespread media circulation include their emotional appeals to audiences
and how they formulate their own authenticity (a constructed idea of what
is genuine or organic) as part of their character portrayal. As I discussed
in my introduction, the emotional appeals can be seen as a kind of "emotional realism," what Ien Ang calls the believable and relatable emotional
response that seems psychologically consistent in television characters. For
reality castmembers, no matter how staged or scripted the situation might
seem, they appeal to viewers if they seem to be expressing a genuine emotional response that draws viewers in and encourages identification with
them. In terms of their construction of their own authenticity, the women
present a version of themselves that seems genuine (although it is of course
a performance of selfhood in the context of TV narratives, like any other
performance of selfhood, and it depends on how producers edit them into
storylines and character types).

Yet the editing of reality TV raises the question of how much castmembers can impact their character narratives. While producers sometimes
claim that they cannot make up a character out of whole cloth, since they

can only include footage of things characters actually said or events that actually happened, the widespread practice of Frankenbiting means that some producers actually do make up characterizations.[21] Frankenbiting refers to the editing practice of splicing two unrelated clips together to make it seem as if they are related, or editing a different audio track into a scene. Most famously, for example, producers on *Joe Millionaire* edited in a different audio clip to make it sound like bachelor Evan Marriott and contestant Sarah Kozler were having sex in the woods, when that was not true. As an example of other narrative and characterization practices, Jennifer Pozner has catalogued the way some reality producers look for stereotypes to cast, such as the so-called slut or the dumb jock.[22]

Reality Character Narratives: Lessons from Evil Dr. Will

Since a major factor that contributes to reality TV's appeal and fan following is how the genre utilizes narrative, it is useful to elaborate on the complex ways in which the genre turns real people's lives into media stories. While the use of stock tropes, such as hero or villain, relatable girl next door or everyman is prevalent, some shows take this narrative process one step further. In turning a castmember into a narrative trope, some reality formats actually allow people to perform TV narratives as if they are their own lives (witness *My Life Is a Sitcom,* where families pitched their lives as TV sitcoms, or *Scream Play,* where participants reenacted popular movie stunt scenes). The genre more generally pictures people enacting media fantasies in various ways; some programs have fans become contestants on the series they have just been watching (*Paradise Hotel*), some have casts enact new versions of old TV sitcoms (*The New Partridge Family, The Real Gilligan's Island*), while others have experts transform people into their favorite fictional characters or media celebrities, like movie character Rocky Balboa or country singer Loretta Lynn (*In Character*). Thus, reality shows often push for a collapse of the distance between a viewer at home and a character on the screen, because the viewer could become part of a reality show and effectively jump onscreen to become the character they see on television.

As reality series illuminate the process of identity formation through narrative, they raise larger issues about turning real people into characters or fashioning their real lives into stories for entertainment. Many of these programs imply that one can learn to find one's true self through media narratives. One result of this dynamic is that these series imply that social identity is an arbitrary performance—one can switch places with someone else and inhabit their social identity or decide to change who they are. The reality genre speaks to the appeal of storytelling, which in this case purports to make people's daily lives as compelling as fictional plotlines.

Indeed, reality TV presents itself as something new because it launches, in fuller form than ever before, the idea that viewers can not only interact with television series through connectivity such as Internet tie-ins and call-in voting shows, but also by literally entering into the stories and events pictured on the screen. It meditates on the role of television as a medium in the sense that it as it lets audiences watch people just like them enact their lives on shows structured like television plotlines. It speaks to some audience members' desire to live out TV scripts—for audiences to have their lives more closely resemble their favorite television tropes.

Big Brother has a striking example of a participant interacting with the show's narrative conventions when one castmember seized control of his own narrative. Contestant Will Kirby's strategy to win CBS's *Big Brother 2* implies that fictional narratives can be more compelling than supposedly real-life stories in this context. Kirby created a persona, an obnoxious puppetmaster referred to as Evil Dr. Will. Later describing the fictional characters he drew from to play this role, Kirby notes the plan he and his brother Ian developed: "We pulled from Christian Bale's character in *American Psycho* and Tyler Durden (Brad Pitt's character) from *Fight Club*. . . . We developed a character who was to be hated by everyone. He would appear weak at first and not considered a threat while he let everyone else pick each other apart. Then he would become a threat, doing anything he had to do to win. . . . By the end I was just making up lies right and left. It was crazy."[23] Kirby dubs himself the P.T. Barnum of reality TV.[24] He used his persona to win the gamedoc (and $500,000) and to garner spots on *Big Brother All-Stars* and *Dr. 90210*. His self-consciously produced literary persona becomes another level of narrative reality on these reality shows.

However, a participant's efforts to control their own reality narrative often lead to frustration and ambivalent results. Reality programs that have home viewers join shows already in progress constitute an extreme example. *Paradise Hotel* turned fans into contestants. The host selected several viewers from the studio audience, and producers flew them to the tropical location where the dating gamedoc was occurring. The new castmembers mistakenly believed they would be able to control how they were represented on television and win the game because they had just been watching the events unfolding from the TV camera's omniscient point of view. They responded with irritation when they realized that they did not have complete control over their entrance into the TV narratives they had been watching. Again, even though many reality TV producers insist that they cannot turn people into something they are not or completely create events, they nevertheless can choose to amplify events or emphasize existing character traits, and, indeed, some programs actually do make up events and characterizations by using Frankenbiting.[25] At the very least, the edited narrative is collaborative in a complex way, since producers take footage of the cast's actions and create story arcs. Reality castmembers sometimes bemoan the TV character they become, illuminating their own sometime ambivalence about being placed into TV narratives and turned into types. Witness *Survivor All-Star* castmember Jerri Manthey, who fled a studio audience interview, crying "we're real people too!," when hundreds of fans booed her for being the villain.[26]

Consequently, the way reality TV shapes identity through narrative is also fluctuating and ambivalent. One program has contestants live out a romance prewritten for them. In *The Dating Experiment*, adapted from a hit Japanese show, each episode followed two strangers who go on a series of blind dates together; they read a diary that outlines what they will do each day, describes their unfolding love story, and even says how they should be feeling. After the diary finishes its narrative, the two participants decide whether or not to continue dating. The story was supposed to induce so-called real love between the daters, with varying degrees of success.[27] The program implied that the act of living out a media romance narrative generates true emotions.

While not all reality programs take this narrative dynamic that far, most turn people into characters using common TV narrative tropes, like Ozzy Osbourne presented as a sitcom dad on *The Osbournes*. In so doing, they illuminate the appeal of TV narratives and the depth of audience identification with them. Likewise, reality TV's cult following speaks to how the genre successfully updates ideas of fame, now that anyone can become famous for playing themselves as a character on a reality show. But perhaps more powerfully, the genre captures the anxieties that come with this level of media interaction and with the idea that our lives are now lived digitally, on a range of cameras (whether on someone else's Facebook page or on a major network reality show), in images and stories that may circulate beyond our control.

Fan Culture Debates

Likewise, it is important to examine the dynamics of how fan participation is integrated into reality programming. This issue opens out onto a larger debate about the cultural politics and economics of the use of new media interactivity in general and in the context of reality TV in particular. As reality TV banks on participatory fan culture, what are the ramifications of that trend? Just as with the genre's use of real people as characters, the way in which reality TV incorporates new media developments can have a range of different effects. Many of these effects depend on how various audiences respond to the texts. It is often in the fan response that one can see the issues convergence culture raises, and fan behavior speaks to how reality TV reflects on those larger media trends.

For example, in transmedia storytelling, artists must work with others to help fashion these large textual universes with pieces of the story in lots of different mediums, or different units of a media company must work together as what Jenkins calls co-creators to develop this kind of transmedia material.[28] Online fan communities, meanwhile, share with each other all the information they can gather about the text, pooling their knowledge of a show like *Survivor* to predict outcomes. Pierre Lévy has argued that the Internet privileges what he calls "collective intelligence," where no one person knows all of the information being presented but rather each person contributes to a larger group knowledge, with the whole being greater than the sum of the parts. Lévy contrasts that model with an earlier model of "shared intelligence," where each member of a group possesses the same common knowledge.[29]

When fans go online to subscribe to a live feed of the *Big Brother* household or download the music they hear on *The Voice* reality singing competition, they are engaging with innovative media formats that have evolved in ways that speak to the cultural power of new media and the Internet and to changing expectations of the entertainment content audiences seek there. All of these developing formats depend vitally on audience interactivity. While again, transmedia storytelling itself predates the Internet, the power of the Internet as an entertainment medium is what has pushed multiplatform storytelling to the forefront of recent media culture. That kind of entertainment depends on active fans who will seek out their favorite content across any media platform, whether searching for the online clues to winners on *Survivor* or watching extra Internet footage of their favorite *American Idol* contestant. For Jenkins, only "spreadable media" survives, meaning media content that consumers actively interact with, transform, add value to, and pass along to others (as in the case of viral videos and Internet memes).[30]

Some of the beliefs driving this participatory fan culture trend, and indeed, the staggering rise in digital media usage more generally, involve visions of connectivity.[31] Many audiences thirst for immersive online content as well as community-building, based on the idea that digital interactions via social networking websites can make consumers feel part of larger affinity groups. Capitalizing on these kinds of beliefs and behaviors, online culture has deeply impacted how audiences interact with media in everyday life in our digital era, and a genre like reality TV makes use of these trends when it pulls in Internet-based interactive fan culture. The Internet has given consumers access to greater information more quickly and easily; it has altered the media production model by enabling far greater consumer interactivity; and it has created new paradigms for knowledge that depend on networks of people. It has also, however, sparked raging debates about the politics of that interactivity, especially where reality TV is concerned, given the potential for the exploitation of real people as castmembers as well as the audiences.

For example, inspired by the utopian possibilities of the Internet for organizing people and furthering intellectual discovery, Lévy insists that collective intelligence, exemplified by a user-generated content website such as Wikipedia, should be seen as a promising development rather than a problematic watering down or superficial dispersal of knowledge.[32] However, I would argue that while the Internet can clearly further knowledge and sharing, its effects depend crucially on the context. Consumers must actively shape what is valued on the Internet, because the medium can sometimes take on the feel of an incoherent, ungovernable Wild West landscape. While Wikipedia provides a much more democratic encyclopedia that perhaps covers more areas of human knowledge through pooled data, it also faces new dangers (for every accurate entry there are others with faulty data). Collective intelligence introduces the problem of synthesis. If, by definition, no one person or group understands all of the collective intelligence, and if information is so distributed and fragmentary, then how can there be effective quality control or oversight? Wikipedia depends on users to help police the quality of their content. If the Internet promises greater interactivity and democratic access, then users must take responsibility for helping to determine what is found there, for affecting what content is circulated and valued.

The rise of participatory fan culture also depends on digital interactivity and the greater access consumers can have to texts on the Internet. Recent media culture includes a number of innovative texts whose very format relies on interactive creation involving both producers and consumers. Television offers several cogent examples. *Bar Karma,* a show on Current TV, has fans vote for and contribute storylines online.[33] *Beckenfield,* a "mass participation television" science fiction show launched by online entertainment company Theatrics, has audiences pay a subscription fee and then allows them to contribute segments to the show (designed for aspiring actors to gain a platform for furthering their careers).[34] Producer McG's online TV show, *Aim High,* mass customizes by incorporating each viewer's name into the scenery and music from their iTunes library.

Another good case in point of participatory fan culture is crowdsourced music videos, a trend in which Internet users help generate the content for videos. This kind of media text exemplifies Lévy's collective intelligence knowledge model. The Johnny Cash Project is one exciting and lively example. In a global collective art project, filmmaker Chris Milk created a platform for fans to draw the frames of a music video for Cash's version of the song "Ain't No Grave."[35] The template takes images of Cash from earlier film documentaries, such as *Johnny Cash: The Man, His World, His Music* (Robert Elfstrom's 1969 documentary). Using a custom drawing program, users select a frame online and draw over it digitally. Once they submit their image, it is included in different versions of the video that play online. Each collection of frames is different, cycling and changing over time. Users can vote on the contributions they like best, and the site includes data such as the number of brush strokes used in any given frame. Internet consumers lured by a shared interest in a music icon can feel part of an online community generating tribute art together.

Reality TV has its own examples of crowdsourcing. MTV and E! routinely include viewer comments from their website message boards or from Facebook or Twitter posts as a scroll at the bottom of the screen, with viewers commenting on the reality shows being aired. The short-lived MC Hammer family reality show, *Hammertime,* included on-screen graphics of Hammer's tweets along with fan responses. In his discussion of multimedia branding efforts at an academic panel at Stanford, which aired on the premiere episode, Hammer notes that his incorporation of tweets was meant to make an emotional and interactive connection to viewers and to send them to his Twitter feed, which hawked more of his products, and to further his content creation for various media platforms.

The most striking example of reality show crowdsourcing is an Internet-based reality TV show that downplays the potential for exploitation involved in this audience interactivity. Actor Seth Green produced an online interactive reality TV show, *ControlTV*, in which viewers vote to determine what star Tristan Couvares will do, literally choosing what the young man starring on the show will do each day (from which young woman to date to what clothes to wear).[36] This young man's life becomes entertainment for viewers, and they are given the power to help him or harm him, all for the audience's viewing pleasure. While Green's website pitches the idea of audience community, the show itself also obviously entails some degree of exploitation, voyeurism, and public humiliation—the calling cards of many reality programs. Green pitched the show as the real-life *EDtv* (1999) in action. The *EDtv* film was itself both a comedy and a cautionary satire about the potentially degrading and debasing effects of reality TV. However, as we have seen, many of today's reality stars are more likely to turn earlier dystopian satires of reality TV into rallying cries for their own desire for stardom.

In another example of recent participatory fan culture media trends, some interactive videos use the technique of mass customization. This technique has become a dominant marketing strategy, in which an advertisement appears to be customized to each viewer, based on an aggregate of user information. An obvious example is the recommendations Amazon.com makes for you based on your past consumer behavior. Those recommendations might appear personal to you, but thousands of other users will receive the same personalized data, because it is personalized on a mass scale. In an example of a more creative use of this media trend, artist Chris Milk has used this mass customization technique in his online interactive music videos, such as a music video entitled "3 Dreams of Black" that functions like a video game, with the user clicking on images to open or choosing directions to take, guiding where the video goes. His interactive web film *The Wilderness Downtown* (a video for Arcade Fire's song "We Used to Wait") has users type in the address of their childhood home, and a Google Earth image of their home becomes one of the settings in the video (and the effect of seeing images of your childhood home in a music video can be unexpectedly poignant).[37]

Examples of mass customization on reality TV include the customization of reality websites for users once they register for the sites and express their interests (on a future visit to the site, you can be taken directly to your favorite reality show or castmember and their updates). MTV even advertises a new mobile phone app called WatchWith that sends you comments from other viewers in real time about the same show you are watching on MTV. They pitch to viewers by saying the WatchWith app will gossip with you about reality TV like *Jersey Shore* even when real-world friends will not. Emphasizing the liveness and the interactivity of this product, MTV depends on crowdsourcing (the comments of thousands of viewers) and mass customization (each person using the app has it customized for their show preferences). Unfortunately, the app feels like a fake digital friend meant to replace actual real-life friends, all formed through aggregating data.

Indeed, the technique of mass customization also has problematic uses. To elaborate on my brief discussion in my introduction, Mark Andrejevic and other critics have warned that the democratic promise of the Internet is dampened by commercial interests. He argues that when a consumer interacts with a text on the Internet, for example by voting online for their favorite singer on *American Idol* and posting their comments, that user is providing the Fox network with free labor by providing user-generated content for them on their website.[38] More crucially, that user is the product being sold to corporate advertisers, as when Fox tries to prove to an advertiser that they can deliver a certain demographic of viewers who will not only watch the television show but also visit the website and see the ad—or, increasingly, watch the show episode online.

Andrejevic has argued that reality TV in particular conditions viewers not only to accept but to desire surveillance of themselves. That surveillance comes not just in the form of TV cameras and webcams and fellow audiences but also corporate advertisers who will gather marketing data from what the viewers post or reveal about themselves.[39] Thus, users are being trained to perform the marketing research on themselves.

In contrast, critics such as Jenkins would argue that while corporate profit is certainly taking place, the interactive participatory fan culture nevertheless provides fans with greater access to the media and greater input in its content and form. One important point to underscore about many of these interactive, Internet-based media texts is that while they depend on user-generated content, the profits go to the company, a fact that raises other ethical issues. Though Jenkins has called for new models of profit-sharing in such cases, those models are not yet fully developed.[40] In many of these cases, the participants seem to be contributing their labor not simply because they are passionate fans but also because they want to gain professional success in the entertainment industry. Hence, they are using new media access to try and get jobs in old media, in some cases. Ironically, the new media user-generated content they themselves provide could potentially be undermining the existence of the professional careers they seek in old media.

In this debate, I side with the active audience's stance, which views popular culture as a site of negotiation and struggle in which market forces do impose a structure, yet audiences still exert some limited agency. The culture industries that produce commercial culture nevertheless cannot completely control the range of meanings consumers might derive from that culture. Corporate profit motives are powerful forces. However, since fan behavior is not predictable and is not fully controlled by market forces, some of the outcome here depends on fan behaviors, on how fans decide to use interactive media. I would argue that the cultural politics of usages of new media interactivity depend on the context, including the economics, textual content, and range of audience responses.

Audience behavior is wildly variable, and consumers put popular culture to their own uses. People's interaction with the media involves a deep range of creativity, community, and engagement that comes through popular culture. As George Lipsitz helpfully describes, popular culture texts are commodities, but at the same time they are also complex collective expressions and spaces for creating identity, sites where audiences can create substantive connections to the past.[41]

Audience members also create their own meaning out of the text, as critics in active audience studies would argue. An active audience approach differs from a mass culture definition of popular culture. For mass culture critics, audiences passively consume mass commodities that are standardized and formulaic. In this view, popular mass culture encourages consumers to accept a status quo of unequal power relations in society. In contrast, the active audience approach insists that one cannot predict what meanings an audience will derive from any given text. Drawn to popular culture with which they feel an affinity, even though the text is mass produced, audience members are often making their own disparate meanings out of the products they buy from the culture industry.

The multiple meanings audience members draw from texts differ widely. They might range from interpretations that would be in line with dominant readings or they might go against the grain and create new or subversive understandings. Some subcultural audiences might use a text in ways the producers never imagined (witness active subcultures that have formed around everything from punk rock to slash fan fiction). John Storey points out that one must question the idea of consumption as passive given that most popular culture products do not in fact turn a profit, thus it would be too reductive to say that audience members are only mindlessly following corporate advertising in their consumption choices.[42] Additionally, as Simon Frith notes, the vast majority of popular music loses money (traditionally, over 80 percent of albums and singles).[43]

Taking active audience stances a step further, some critics go so far as to argue that audiences are producing their own version of a text as they consume it. Michel de Certeau has argued that consumption is an act of "secondary production," in which consumers appropriate and use texts for their own purposes. For de Certeau, active audiences are textual "poachers," who scavenge among the culture industry products to make their own meaning and build their own identifications and communities out of them.[44]

However, while audiences have the agency to draw their own meanings and identifications from popular culture, it is also important to note that their agency is limited by the economic structures in which that culture is produced. While you can create your own YouTube videos for your friends to watch, your user-generated content still depends on access to YouTube, which that company provides. Thus, your ability to use the Web site depends on that corporation's own profit motives. Even in an era of greater interactivity that depends more and more on audience participation (the flash mob depends on the mob appearing, the Twitter celebrity depends on their followers reading their tweets), the audience only functions within a structure determined by the commodity producers and the economic model. Nevertheless, audiences have a significant impact on popular culture and their behavior cannot simply be controlled or predicted by the larger economic system or by the interests of media companies.

The behaviors of avid television fans provide a good case in point, such as fan spoiler behavior for reality TV. *Survivor* online communities have infamously conspired to predict the show's outcome and influence audience reception of that result. Active fans who watched live Internet feeds of *Big Brother* posted spoilers to message boards before the edited versions made it to the air. Some fans went so far as to try to disrupt and influence the game (flying a banner over the *Big Brother* compound, pulled behind an airplane, warning one contestant not to trust the other). *American Idol* fans have famously organized efforts via the Web to disrupt voting, either by voting for the worst singer or voting against contestants the judges support.

Ultimately, the Internet's audience interactivity can be put to both positive and negative uses. Scholars have shown how the Internet has shifted not only our knowledge models but also our understanding of our own identity, how we network and connect with others, how we build our own personas, and how we imagine ourselves fitting into larger communities. Michael Wesch has beautifully illustrated how the development of the Internet and of new media forms has involved changes in the way we relate to digital technology, encouraging us to interact through digital personas who are part of digital communities. In a measure of how our media expectations are evolving, Wesch has turned to YouTube to convey his scholarly ideas to a mass audience. He has made his arguments about how extensively Web 2.0 has changed our understanding of communication and of identity most powerfully via his own YouTube videos, such as "The Machine Is Us/ing Us," which has received over 11 million views.[45]

Yet one danger of this digital interaction is that some users can manipulate it for dishonest ends, like staging identity hoaxes. The intense obsession with character in this new media culture creates its own sets of problems. Indeed, even media hoaxes that show the vulnerability of social networking to impersonation emphasize the focus on character in new media culture. Noted celebrities such as Kanye West are angry that Twitter does not always shut down imposters' accounts.[46] The documentary *Catfish* (2010) told the shocking story of a woman who used Facebook to trick a savvy New York filmmaker into believing that she was the college-aged sister of a talented child artist, when in fact she was a mentally-ill middle-aged woman. She created a fake Facebook profile using other people's pictures, and she populated her fictional Facebook world with dozens of other fake people that she presented as real. The young filmmaker, Nev Schulman, thought he was in a months-long relationship with her that was happening entirely online and through texts. The fact that social networking site users could be tricked into thinking a fake person is a real one and, in fact, that they are dating that fake person without ever having met them offline, is stunning.

Such a hoax is only possible because of new social relations happening in social media. Anthropologist Mizuko Ito has studied the phenomenon of tele-cocooning, whereby couples may rarely or never see each other in person but yet carry on relationships online through constant texting and social networking communication.[47] Having taught the *Catfish* documentary in college classes, I can attest that the number of students who engage in such digital relationships is growing and that the number who have run into *Catfish*-style hoaxes is also on the rise. MTV has also teamed with filmmaker Schulman for a new reality TV show on the documentary; also called *Catfish* (2012–), the program follows real people who meet their online love in person for the first time. Some first connect via Facebook and then are shocked when they meet in person and uncover identity hoaxes. The original *Catfish* hoax worked because the woman created convincing characters that were compelling enough for a savvy audience to believe the storylines.

For reality TV, of course, this idea of becoming a new self via media interaction, or of creating fake people presented as real, has even bigger ramifications. Given how our Internet-based media culture impacts everything from people's sense of selfhood to their sense of community with others, it will be increasingly important for audiences to take active roles in this process. They must become active in shaping what is valued and circulated in that media culture. In terms of how viewers might choose to value reality TV, the genre would certainly necessitate on-going ethical debates. In my next chapter, I turn to a consideration of how reality TV creates its reality effects, assessing its use of documentary-fiction genre mashups and the ethics of how it uses documentary, and I also consider how it pitches emotional authenticity.

Notes

1. Leigh H. Edwards, "'What a Girl Wants': Gender Norming on Reality Game Shows," *Feminist Media Studies* 4, no. 2 (Summer 2004): 226–228.

2. Ien Ang, *Watching Dallas: Television and the Melodramatic Imagination* (London: Routledge, 1985), 47.

3. Kate Stanhope, "Ratings: Bethenny Getting Married? the Most-Watched Series Debut in Bravo History," *TVGuide.com*, July 11, 2010, http://www.tvguide.com/News/Bethenny-Married-Ratings-1019537.aspx.

4. "Forbes Magazine Looking Into Bethenny Frankel's Financials," *Huffington Post*, October 13, 2011, http://www.huffingtonpost.com/2011/10/13/bethenny-frankel-skinnygirl-120-million-lie-forbes-magazine_n_1008764.html.

5. Camille Mann, "'Real Housewives of Atlanta' Star NeNe Leakes to Guest Star on 'Glee,'" *CBS News*, December 20, 2011, http://www.cbsnews.com/8301-31749_162-57345727-10391698/real-housewives-of-atlanta-star-nene-leakes-to-guest-star-on-glee/.

6. Colleen Werthmann, "Why Diddy Hearts NeNe: The Major Mogul Shares His *Real Housewives* Fixation," *The Dish* blog, Bravotv.com, December 27, 2011, http://www.bravotv.com/blogs/the-dish/why-diddy-hearts-nene.

7. Henry Jenkins, *Convergence Culture: Where Old and New Media Collide* (New York: New York University Press, 2006), 4–16. Jenkins cites political scientist Ithiel de Sola Pool's book *Technologies of Freedom* [1983] as the first to discuss the media convergence concept.

8. Jennifer Gillan, *Television and New Media: Must-Click TV* (New York: Routledge, 2011), 2.

9. Gillan, *Television and New Media.*

10. Jenkins, *Convergence Culture,* 8.

11. Henry Jenkins, "Transmedia Storytelling 101," *Confessions of an Aca-Fan: The Official Weblog of Henry Jenkins,* March 22, 2007, http://www.henryjenkins.org/2007/03/transmedia_storytelling_101.html.

12. Judith Newman and Leslie Bruce, "How the Kardashians Made $65 Million Last Year," *The Hollywood Reporter,* February 16, 2011, http://www.hollywoodreporter.com/news/how-kardashians-made-65-million-100349.

13. Scott Collins, "Kim Kardashian's Wedding Special Toasts Giant Ratings," *Los Angeles Times,* October 11, 2011, http://latimesblogs.latimes.com/showtracker/2011/10/kim-kardashians-wedding-special-toasts-giant-ratings.html.

14. Chris Jancelewicz, "'Boycott Kim Kardashian' Petition Picks Up Steam Online," *HuffPost TV, The Huffington Post,* November 25, 2011, http://www.aoltv.com/2011/11/25/kim-kardashian-boycott-petition/.

15. Yvonne Villarreal, "'Kourtney & Kim Take New York' Scores Big Ratings," *Los Angeles Times,* November 28, 2011, http://latimesblogs.latimes.com/showtracker/2011/11/kim-kardashian-kourtney-kim-take-new-york-ratings.html.

16. Newman and Bruce, "How the Kardashians Made $65 Million."

17. Newman and Bruce, "How the Kardashians Made $65 Million."

18. Newman and Bruce, "How the Kardashians Made $65 Million."

19. Newman and Bruce, "How the Kardashians Made $65 Million."

20. *I'm Still Here,* dir. Casey Affleck (2010; Magnolia Home Entertainment, DVD).

21. *Reality of Reality,* Bravo, September 8–11, 2003.

22. Jennifer Pozner, *Reality Bites Back: The Troubling Truth about Guilty Pleasure TV* (Berkeley, CA: Seal Press, 2010).

23. Mark Hinson, "What You Don't Know About the Good Doctor. Really, He's Not So Bad. It Was All an Act, You See," *Tallahassee Democrat,* September 30, 2001, D1.

24. Lynette Rice, "The Q&A: 9021-Oh, Snap!," EW.com, August 2, 2007, http://www.ew.com/ew/article/0,20049601,00.html.

25. *Reality of Reality.*

26. *Survivor: All-Stars,* CBS, May 9, 2004.

27. ABC described the concept for the show as follows: "Complete strangers give up all control of their lives to be ruled by a mysterious diary, all in the hopes of finding true love, in a unique new reality romance series! The idea behind *The Dating Experiment:* If actors and actresses on movie sets fall in love because of heightened circumstances, can the same happen if real people are put in a similar situation?" "The Dating Experiment" (2003), ABC, December 12, 2004, http://abc. go.com/primetime/datingexperiment/.

28. Jenkins, "Transmedia Storytelling 101."

29. Jenkins, *Convergence Culture,* 4.

30. Henry Jenkins, "If It Doesn't Spread, It's Dead (Part One): Media Viruses and Memes," weblog, *Confessions of an Aca-Fan: The Official Weblog of Henry Jenkins,* February 11, 2009, http://www.henryjenkins.org/2009/02/if_it_doesnt_ spread_its_dead_p.html.

31. Internet users are now estimated to be 2 billion people worldwide, or around 30 percent of the world's population, with percentages varying by region (usage in North America is highest at 78 percent of the population). One study found that the growth in Internet usage worldwide between 2000 and 2011 was 480 percent. Internet World Stats, http://www.internetworldstats.com/stats.htm.

32. Jenkins, *Convergence Culture,* 4.

33. *Bar Karma,* Current TV, http://current.com/shows/bar-karma/.

34. *Beckinfield,* http://www.beckinfield.com.

35. Chris Milk, The Johnny Cash Project, http://www.thejohnnycashproject. com/#/about.

36. *ControlTV,* http://controltv.com.

37. Chris Milk, *The Wilderness Downtown,* http://www.thewildernessdown town.com/.

38. Mark Andrejevic, "Watching TV Without Pity," *FlowTV,* April 5, 2007, http://flowtv.org/2007/04/watching-tv-without-pity/.

39. Mark Andrejevic, *Reality TV: The Work of Being Watched* (Lanham, MD: Rowman & Littlefield, 2003).

40. Jenkins, *Convergence Culture,* 168.

41. George Lipsitz, *Time Passages: Collective Memory and American Popular Culture* (Minneapolis: University of Minnesota Press, 1990), 22.

42. John Storey, *Cultural Theory and Popular Culture: An Introduction,* 4th ed. (Athens: University of Georgia Press, 2006), 6.

43. Simon Frith, *Sound Effects: Youth, Leisure and the Politics of Rock* (London: Constable, 1983), 147.

44. Michel de Certeau, *The Practice of Everyday Life* (Berkeley: University of California Press, 1984), 174.

45. Michael Wesch, "The Machine Is Us/ing Us," YouTube video, http://www. youtube.com/watch?v=6gmP4nk0EOE.

46. Leigh H. Edwards, "Twitter: Democratizing the Media Versus Corporate Branding," *FlowTV* 9.14 (May 2009), http://flowtv.org/2009/05/twitter-democratizing-the-media-corporate-branding-leigh-h-edwards-florida-state-university/.

47. Jenkins, *Convergence Culture,* 17.

Chapter 2

Mashup: Hybrid Genres and Emotional Appeals

Television is well known for combining different genres to great success. The savvy mashup of the musical with the high-school teen drama has catapulted *Glee* to high ratings and a cult following of devoted Gleeks. A number of recent television hits merge the mockumentary with genres like the workplace sitcom (*The Office, Parks and Recreation*) or the family sitcom (*Modern Family*). But nowhere is the use of hybrid genres more evident than in reality TV. It is hybrid by definition, always combining documentary with a fictional TV genre, such as drama, sitcom, or soap opera, or with earlier factual TV genres like the game show or the talk show. In fact, reality TV has influenced the rest of television with the success and cultural impact of reality formats like the gamedoc (which merges documentary and game show elements, as in *Survivor, American Idol,* and *Dancing With the Stars*) and the docusoap (as in the documentary and soap opera mix of MTV's *The Real World*). Indeed, the rise of a program like *Modern Family,* as a mockumentary family sitcom, stems directly from the prevalence of family reality programs with their documentary and sitcom elements, such as earlier influential celebreality sitcoms like *The Osbournes.*

In this chapter, I examine two key media trends that reality TV banks on that contribute to this genre's success: the use of hybrid genres (here documentary mixed with fictional TV genres), and the use of emotional appeals to audiences. As I will demonstrate, reality TV uses the documentary–fiction genre mix to help market its product, whether that product is, for example, the scenes of celebrity life offered up for consumption on celebreality shows, or youth culture lifestyles on MTV shows. Reality TV uses the truth claims embedded in documentary as a form in order to convey realism. It combines that documentary effect with the fictional TV genres that help heighten the drama and conflicts.

The genre also uses the documentary–fiction genre mix to amplify its emotional appeal to viewers, finding new ways to make emotional connections with audiences. Reality series use documentary techniques to generate emotional accuracy; that is, the sense that these people are showing you their true emotions or are behaving in psychologically convincing ways, even if the events they are reacting to are obviously staged. If a castmember weeps convincingly enough or appears to be overcome with joy (or any other emotion) in a believable way, the show uses the documentary effect of making a higher truth claim; that is, because real people are pictured, it makes the emotional content even more persuasive to audiences. Again, Annette Hill's audience research has shown that even though audiences know much reality TV is faked or staged, they still look for moments of emotional authenticity and they find them believable, like the moments in which castmembers break down and cry. Fictional genre techniques from sitcoms, dramas, and soap operas also help make emotional connections to the audience because they garner audience sympathy with characters. For example, soap operas generate emotional authenticity even in the midst of melodrama, because audiences identify with characters and go on their emotional journey with them.

Another key factor in how the genre makes emotional connections to audiences is how it creates new versions of celebrity and stardom, adapting older models of stardom. It draws audiences in by placing new emphasis on the ordinariness of reality celebrities. Many reality shows offer the sense that it could be the viewer themselves on screen, since these reality stars are famous for simply appearing as themselves on camera.

Thus, this chapter assesses reality TV's documentary–fiction genre mix, particularly how that mix helps shows market their products and also helps make emotional appeals to viewers. On the second media trend, the affective economics involved, I examine how, in addition to the hybrid genre effects, the genre also makes emotional appeals through creating new versions of celebrity and stardom. Reality TV's emphasis on emotion and on engaging the emotion of viewers is part of a larger media trend in which media producers try to get audiences emotionally invested in their stories or products, because the emotional link is what research indicates drives consumer purchases and viewer loyalty, a process Henry Jenkins calls affective economics.[1]

Hybrid Genre Mix

When I say that reality TV uses a hybrid genre mix to produce certain effects, by genre conventions, I mean customary practices that are in some measure shared by producers and consumers and constitute a relatively stable, but always changing, set of interpretive and economic assumptions. As stylistic and ideological categories, genres shape and reflect cultural values and provide a way of characterizing audiences' relationships to representation. John Caldwell has demonstrated how fictional television has always used documentary techniques to critique the fiction/nonfiction distinction.[2] My interest here is in how reality TV's mixture of genres interacts with changing genre conventions and expectations as part of the cultural and political economy of television's production, distribution, and reception. Jane Feuer's pioneering work has established that TV genres evolve cyclically, rather than being static or linear in their progression, and that they depend on cultural and industrial changes as much as on textual and audience preferences.[3] Jason Mittel has outlined his model of TV genres as cultural categories that emerge out of specific historical contexts and organize cultural practices in the media industry, audience, public policy, and critical reception, reflecting the larger practice of shaping the social world through category differences and hierarchies. For Mittel, genres are sites of cultural struggle over contesting assumptions.[4] Noting that genre mixing is one of reality TV's essential production strategies, almost always involving merging documentary with fictional genres, he asserts that when TV series mix genre categories to great public controversy and debate, they ultimately reinforce "the central role of genres in media."[5]

Just as the sitcom and soap opera do, reality TV creates a marketing and institutional effect as a genre term; it mobilizes a range of expectations and forms and generates cultural work out of their interaction. It is important to note that program makers explicitly term their own texts hybrid forms, from *The Real World* producers' explicit attempts to mix soap opera and documentary to *The Osbournes* producers' description of their series as the first reality sitcom.[6] As reality TV combines generic forms, one effect it achieves is to create a hierarchy of visual realism, a dynamic common to visual representation systems. As I will discuss more fully later in this chapter, reality TV's visual hierarchy presents itself as aware of its own construction and mediation, yet it still offers, for example, surveillance footage of an event as more "authentic" through juxtaposing it with other visual technologies, like interpretive interview sequences where casts argue over what really happened.

I will focus most of my attention on how documentary functions in this genre mixture. Among the TV genres reality programming adapts, including the teen drama, talk show, variety show, travelogue, game show, dating show, and crime drama, the two key genres for my purposes here are the sitcom and the soap opera. These two genres of fictional television are of particular importance to my discussion because of how often reality programs invoke their generic conventions (expectations of narrative, theme, form, industry context, political economy, and cultural value associated with those genres at any given time, depending on the strains of sitcom and soap opera that reality programs reference).

Observational documentaries tend to make the individuals they depict stand in for larger social institutions, making them symptomatic of the status of particular issues and trends in society. On the common theme of family life, for example, the PBS documentary series *An American Love Story* (1999) charts a year in the life of an interracial family in Queens, New York (comprised of an Anglo-American wife, African American husband, and their two daughters). As it records the tensions the family members negotiate, particularly their historical experience of changing miscegenation views, the documentary makes this family a symbol for the state of interracial marriage and family throughout U.S. society.[7] Similarly, Richard Leacock's film, *Happy Mother's Day* (1965), an exemplary observational documentary, records a South Dakota mother who in 1963 gave birth to the first U.S. quintuplets to survive. The film comments on what a multiple birth family comes to signify more generally—how they are often seen as exceptional cases of family vitality and the health of the American family. Leacock captures the town's wish to turn the family into an emblem of civic pride and a source of commercial exploitation while the parents fear the media spotlight—in stark contrast to today's reality TV broods frantic to live their lives on camera.

Meanwhile, fictional TV genres are focused on garnering audience sympathy and identification. Sitcoms make characters consistent and developed over the course of a series in order to encourage audience bonding with those characters. Some, as Feuer has detailed, make flat characters into vehicles for social critiques.[8] Alternatively, the soap opera manages audience identification with its characters through its manipulation of serial narrative. In addition to its sensationalism and melodrama, the soap opera makes claims to psychological realism, again, what Ien Ang calls

TV's emotional realism, an audience's sense of accuracy in the treatment of psychological situations, even in the midst of hyberbolic dynamics; viewers are aware this emotional realism emerges out of the artifice of fictional narrative genre patterns.[9] The most famous forerunner to reality TV exhibits this hybrid mix. *An American Family* (1973) is the key precursor for reality TV because the filmmakers adapted documentary expectations to television drama as well as to soap opera structures and narratives, making a claim to document changes to American family life in the 1970s but also generating sensationalistic, soap opera-style storylines about these real people's lives.[10] *An American Family* likewise inspired the British TV series, *The Family* (1974), often cited as a precursor to later reality genres like the 1990s British "docusoap" (a pejorative term coined by journalists to condemn new factual TV as downgrading documentary seriousness into soap opera superficiality).

In reality TV, this generic combination yields striking results. For instance, as *The Osbournes* offers typical family sitcom narratives of daily domestic troubles resolved and reassuring moral lessons reached, yet combines them with a broader documentary claim, the implication is that it depicts the real-life Osbournes both to entertain and to educate. The series frames the Osbournes as emblematic of celebrity families. It teaches us something about what fame and mass mediation do to the family unit. Family switching shows like *Wife Swap* and *Trading Spouses* and nanny programs like *Nanny 911* and *Supernanny* adopt soap opera narrative techniques along with documentary insights. While *Nanny 911* (adapted from a British format) focuses on one-off episodic narratives with closure and resolution, the nanny team is consistent in each episode and has its own serial narrative. Shot from British "Nanny Central" (the exterior of an English thatched cottage), the nannies decide who will go out to fix parenting problems in America each week. The narratives for every household focus, as in the soap opera, on melodramatic cliffhangers solved after commercial breaks, character reversals, and last-minute plot twists, melodramatic claims of family emergencies that the nanny must solve to avert absolute disaster, redundancy and summary of preceding events so viewers can watch the program sporadically and not miss important information, and the open-ended conflict of always having more desperate families who need help. At the same time, such programs adopt a documentary pedagogical tone whereby the problems each household faces are typical and indicative of the larger social status of the family in the United States. We are to understand, for instance, that permissive U.S. mothers and fathers do not know how to set appropriate boundaries and that they need a healthy shot in the arm of good British discipline to prop up their miserable parenting skills.

Reality Documentary

The genre's specific uses of documentary styles allow it to make claims to realism, or what critic James Friedman has described as televisual neorealism.[11] As they depend heavily on observational documentary's attempts to capture the rhythms of daily life, reality series use both schools of observational documentary developed and debated in the 1960s: cinéma vérité (where the filmmaker interacts with the subjects and acknowledges that interaction frequently) and direct cinema (the conceit of an invisible fly on the wall). Those forms, and their subsequent offshoots, are often collapsed into the one rubric, observational documentary. Reality producers adapting such documentary forms frequently provoke the action and set up situations, drawing extensively on the paradox documentary historian Erik Barnouw identifies in cinéma vérité, the idea that "artificial circumstances could bring hidden truth to the surface."[12] These programs also intermix techniques from expository documentary, like talking head set-up interviews or voice of God authoritative voice-overs that establish an omniscient perspective judging the scene. Reality programming is obviously not the only television genre to adapt documentary elements, but it does make its own unique, elaborate truth claims.

My concern here is to question how reality TV programs use these embedded truth claims in documentary to position themselves as authentic representations of reality. Reality TV takes the problem of documentary's claim to represent truth and the real world to a logical extreme, pressuring its fiction versus nonfiction distinction, what Stella Bruzzi calls the conundrum of the factual image.[13] As reality TV's visual forms become standardized, they reflect our era's definitions of the real, as well as our own representational strategies and technologies for visual approximations of authenticity. Observational documentaries emerged in the 1960s in the technological context of new lightweight 16 mm cameras and portable, synch-sound recorders (though scholars disagree about whether the technology sparked the documentary style or vice versa).[14] For the reality TV boom of the 1990s, newer technological innovations affect what visual styles are possible; the lightweight digital hand-held cameras and quick, accessible, and extremely cost-effective editing software have marked these shows with specific optical tropes. Jon Dovey notes that the very definition of reality TV as a genre has become linked to its particular visual documentary style, and the visual style itself has become a marker for truth:

> "Reality TV" is now used as a genre description of any factual programme based on an aesthetic style of apparent "zero-degree realism"—in other words a direct, unmediated account of events, often associated with the use of video and surveillance-imaging technologies. During the 1990s, the low-gauge video image, grainy, under-lit and often unsteady, became the preeminent televisual signifier of truthfulness.[15]

Similarly, Bruzzi notes that both factual and fictional TV use "the shorthand of wobbly cam, blurred shots, crash-zooms and inaudible dialogue to signify greater truthfulness."[16] Caldwell argues that when "reality soap" programs like *The Real World* use documentary techniques, they only ever reveal the fictional construction of the genre; that is, the shows do not record the verity of "seven people picked to live together and have their lives taped," they document, rather, the fabrication of the series, replete with story-boarding, editing into narrative arcs, and sometimes loose scripting.[17] I agree with Caldwell, but I also see another important dynamic at play, one that deserves more inquiry.

Reality TV cannibalizes documentary. But most interesting is that it tries to reendow documentary with the status of truth. While theorists and filmmakers have long remarked on the inevitable merger of fact and fiction, witnessing and interpretation in the nonfiction film form, reality TV wants to change course and make documentary synonymous with authenticity. Audiences join filmmakers in the knowledge that a filmmaker changes a system as they observe it, and that observational expression as always motivated, coming from a particular perspective. Richard Kilborn and John Izod contextualize the shift in how viewers relate to documentaries in terms of the postmodern turn since the 1960s and 1970s, noting that a gradual abandonment of belief in referential truth has destabilized documentary's claim to a special, close relationship to the socio-historical world, just as there are more faked documentaries causing scandals.[18]

In the case of reality TV, viewers realize that the actual content of these programs consists of, at best, what Barnouw would term "provoked action" and, at worst, scripted situations performed poorly by nonprofessional actors.[19] But reality TV wants to downplay that knowledge, at least for the sake of marketing. And perhaps their success in merchandizing reveals more about some degree of nostalgia for the truth claims of film and video as visual forms than anything else. Again, emerging audience studies give us empirical evidence that viewers know many reality shows are loosely scripted but they still consider reality programming as at least moderately real. By staging their own version of "documentary," where blockbuster shows mime formal techniques such as single-camera interviews and black and white surveillance sequences, these programs pretend to deliver on the marketing promise of their reality moniker. Instead of asking viewers to believe in the content, reality programming asks audiences to believe in the form, i.e., the use of documentary techniques themselves is supposed to symbolize realism, even when the content is obviously staged or fake.

Indeed, I would argue that when reality TV mobilizes documentary and combines it with fiction forms, it captures a nostalgia for the idea that images simply convey the full truth of anything they are depicting in the real world. This idea, what Marita Sturken and Lisa Cartwright term the myth of photographic truth, has been put under greater question than ever before in our digital era of CGI and Photoshop-altered images. A complex new mix of TV's long-running concerns, reality TV reflects the medium's ever more complicated interrogation of truth and the role of mediated representation in our daily lives. When it self-reflexively uses documentary forms, reality TV playfully recycles documentary styles along with self-consciously wishful beliefs about the ability of any representation to portray accurately lived experience. Reality TV's hybrid form thus records nostalgia for the outmoded idea that visual technologies transparently capture the real world (when we know that they are instead pieces of representation that are inherently mediated, and that the artist selects and frames those images in certain ways from certain points of view). At the same time, reality TV acknowledges and registers the constructedness of that photographic truth, because of its self-awareness about how shows involve staging and fakeness (a fact the genre expects audiences to be aware of too).

However, audiences enjoy suspending their disbelief, at least partially, in order to consume the spectacle of these reality show interviews, confessionals, and surveillance footage scenes as if they are actuality, even when everyone knows the content is loosely scripted, staged, or even faked. As the genre takes documentary's truth claims and uses them in a sensationalized new context, reality TV has sparked important critical debates about its effect on the evolution and future of documentary—precisely because it manipulates documentary's cultural authority. Scholars fiercely argue over whether reality TV debases documentary's public service mission (making unsuspecting viewers believe false truth claims) or if it instead increases venues and viewers for documentary forms. Some also worry that reality TV's use of documentary in so many different formats and contexts means that documentary as a term is losing some of its meaning, becoming a catch-all category that could lose some of its impact, as part of what John Corner calls a "post-documentary" culture where reality TV has expanded documentary's values and motives.[20] I would side with critics who insist that reality TV simply generates new models and new contexts for some of these documentary techniques, and that viewers are smart enough to see the mix of fact and fiction in reality TV that has also always been a part of documentary itself (what Corner calls their "sliding scale of fakery").[21]

The Products of a Hybrid Genre

If, then, reality TV uses documentary to signal the real, to what effect? How does reality TV make use of this complicated documentary realism? Many programs use documentary forms to reinforce their product. That product ranges from being the program itself, or an image—such as a celebrity's private life offered for public consumption, or the viewer-as-product to be sold to corporate advertisers. I focus particular attention on the strategies reality TV uses with marked frequency, like direct address, interviews, surveillance footage, and observational documentary's study of people's daily lives.

For example, reality TV uses the direct address technique of speaking to the camera in ways that mimic documentary's frequent deployment of that technique, whether in expository documentary's voice-over narration and set-up interviews or in cinéma vérité's on-camera interviews. Indeed, the two main ways reality programs use direct address are (1) voice-over narration (in the mode of direct address documentary style off-screen narration) and (2) castmembers talking directly to the camera. Here, speaking directly to camera happens in three main ways: (1) in on-camera interviews in the midst of events being recorded observationally (a cinéma vérité technique resembling the journalistic interview, but most often with the interviewer edited out); (2) spontaneously, when castmembers suddenly talk to the camera during observational sequences (where the direct address comments sometimes disrupt the invisible camera conceit if the sequence had been operating in direct cinema mode); (3) or in set-up talking head single-camera interviews (where the subject looks directly into the camera while speaking, and the interviewer and their questions are edited out).

While newscasts and even fictional TV programs use direct address in related ways, reality TV may be distinguished by its specific mimicry of documentary uses. For example, reality shows often intercut observational documentary scenes with footage from later direct address set-up interviews where casts comment on those very events being seen (a mix of direct cinema and expository documentary styles). MTV's youth shows such as *The Real World,* meanwhile, have perfected a confessional mode of direct address (widely copied by other series) where castmembers go into the confessional, a room with a stationary camera the castmember activates. Then the youth speaks directly to the lens, in a mode somewhat akin to the diaristic or first-person documentary style. Many an MTV castmember has walked into the room and collapsed into tears while gazing into the camera. The technique is nothing if not squirm-inducing as it gleefully places audiences in the position of a Foucauldian confessor. And it certainly traffics in heavy doses of the therapeutic discourse that Mimi White isolates as a dominant rhetoric shaping identity on talk shows and on television in general.[22] Likewise, some programs give participants their own hand-held digital video camera in order to film and comment on events (*Things I Hate About You*). Producers often ask the castmembers to speak in the present tense while discussing events filmed days or even months earlier. Some interviews include sociological or pedagogical claims while others enter into a therapeutic discourse. This technique, in which participants comment on their daily lives as we watch them unfold, not only puts reality TV in a hybrid documentary universe, in which some documentary techniques appear real through their contrast with others that seem interpretive, but it also has the documentary effect of insisting that normal people's daily lives are a valid subject for public scrutiny.

We know that visual representation systems establish hierarchies of realism, and as critics such as Annette Hill and Justin Lewis have noted, reality TV offers elaborate codes of realism that viewers then parse.[23] I would argue that reality TV's visual realism depends on these shifting documentary forms; their combination generates different effects. For example, when an episode intercuts observational footage of daily events with interviews, the observational footage takes on a higher status of authenticity because the interviews are commentary—they are interpretive, therapeutic, sometimes full of sociological debates. The observational documentary footage takes on the status of direct realism (while surveillance footage often achieves the highest truth value). The interview footage, in contrast, prompts emotional realism, much like the soap opera. Here, we see someone's authentic feelings—we get a window onto their subjective sense of reality, their affective reaction to events. The intercut interview is the place where reality TV also asserts its mode of sociological inquiry. The competing interviews, for example, frame family values as a debate with no single answer but rather multiple deeply felt viewpoints of the same issues. Within reality TV's hierarchy of visual realism, the direct address interview establishes emotional intimacy, sympathy toward the speaker, a sense of their interiority, what Jon Dovey calls the effect of first person media.[24] Another type of interview, in contrast, involves the speaker staring at an off-screen interviewer (someone who we never hear speak or appear but we know is there), as if over the camera's shoulder. That visual effect projects a slightly more sociological situation. It is not as intimate as the direct address technique. Instead, we get a more objective spin, as if the fact that people have gathered to discuss these events means they are sociologically important, and our unseen interlocutor signals expository documentary's claims to objectivity.

Direct address serves varied purposes here. For example, celebrity reality shows use direct address to reinforce the trappings of fame in their televisual world, using documentary techniques, as stars talk to their audience or push the cameras away, to replicate the performance and form of camera-mediated stardom. MTV's youth shows, meanwhile, use the technique in their confessionals and set-up interviews (with MTV's very directive prompts edited out) to help establish a particular ideology in their castmembers—an ideology of personal growth toward liberal pluralist consensus, creating a subjectivity for cast and viewers that allows MTV to deliver a specific kind of audience-as-product to their corporate advertisers. In the first case, where direct address showcases celebrity, the form establishes the cultural value of an image as the show's product. In the second case, where direct address enacts pluralist consensus on youth shows, the form helps establish an ideology as a way to fashion the viewer as product.

As the reality programs purport to deliver reality through their visual vocabulary, they imply they will even sometimes be absolved from doing so through their content. For example, often the form of the single-camera direct address interview suggests reality rather than the actual content of that interview. Sometimes a castmember might deliver a particularly moving speech full of content that induces viewer sympathy for what seems an accurate representation of that person's life. But more often than not, if that interview is unconvincing or even boring, the visual frame of the subject in a chair delivering a direct address message to the audience will imply to viewers that what they are watching is real life, not completely fake, even given the mediation and editing viewers know is part of the image they see.

There are abundant examples of reality programs using documentary formats to make truth claims even when the episode's plot or dialogue is obviously fabricated. On the one hand, televangelist Tammy Faye Messner (formerly Bakker), starring in *The Surreal Life,* gives a moving direct address interview about how her religion saved her from suicide. Her emotional words and delivery frame her as a candid truth-teller and the WB Network's message boards light up with praise for what a down to earth, believable person she is.[25] Yet, on the other hand, Paris Hilton, in season one of *The Simple Life,* sits at the kitchen table of the Arkansas family hosting her (the premise for this reverse Beverly Hillbillies, fish-out-of-water story of a celebrity party girl living with rural Southerners), and says "What is Wal-Mart? Do they sell wall stuff?"[26] We know she is delivering a put-on. In a later print interview, she admitted she knew what Wal-Mart was, saying "I was just playing a part. If I knew what everything was, it wouldn't be funny."[27] Hilton discloses that she was enacting an interesting persona for the camera rather than expressing her actual reactions to real-life situations. But her televisual world is presented in cinéma vérité style. The cameras follow her around the table, picturing the family from her perspective and vice versa with several shot/reverse shot images, all intercut with footage from Hilton's later set-up talking head interview commenting on the action and explaining her difficulty in understanding her hosts. Thus, we get to experience pleasure in the visual forms that in documentary claim truth value, even when the content cannot approximate the real half as well itself.

Documenting Celebrity

One way reality TV uses the hybrid genre mix is to document a newer version of fame and celebrity, just as it uses that version of reality stardom to create emotional appeals to viewers. In celebrity reality programs, U.S. culture's obsession with fame has found a new way to satiate itself. What would it be like to be a superstar? We have our vicarious answer. A camera locks its gaze on luminaries, and we get to follow them beyond the velvet ropes, into the VIP area, to scrutinize their daily lives behind the idol façade. But as we are invited to look under the media construction, to see the man behind the Oz-like curtain, we do not so much abandon our belief in celebrity as find new ways to reinforce it; when a program offers to display to audiences the private person beneath the constructed public persona, it reinforces the very existence and cultural capital of that public persona (particularly when the private persona is equally constructed).

Direct address functions as part of the central framework of such series, encoding celebrity as a visual performance involving an intricate ballet of cameras, microphones, booms, wires, and a semireluctant, semiwilling, semifamous star. The subgenre emphasizes observational cinema approaches to suggest immediate access to the stars. Not surprisingly, the celebrities usually get to speak for themselves too, meditating on the minutiae of their lives. Single-camera interviews let them comment on the events pictured, sometimes accompanied by black and white flashbacks of earlier sequences—which are accorded the status of confirmed visual evidence. NBC's *The Apprentice* offers a good example of voice-over narration in the subgenre. Slamming hapless contestants, hawking products, or intoning business philosophies, Donald Trump narrates the show as castmembers compete to run one of his companies, and his voice-over identifies the show with his celebrity point of view.

Notably, celebrities break reality genre taboos. Witness spontaneous direct address moments during the action sequences (versus clearly delineated interview sequences), where stars interrupt the action to talk to the camera, insistently drawing attention to the crew or the videotaping, sometimes breaking the fourth wall by referencing the audience explicitly. Other reality subgenres render that behavior strictly forbidden. Castmembers on shows such as *The Real World* or *Survivor* are instructed not to interact with the camera crew or speak directly to the lens except during set-up interviews. I would argue that celebrity shows encourage their casts to violate the invisibility conceit because those moments confirm celebrity by having the castmembers perform it. The stars are at pains to reestablish the contours of their natural mediated habitat, which consists of dodging film crews, reporters, and paparazzi, embodying the object of the camera's gaze, being the center of media attention. When castmembers tell the television cameras to go away or insist that the producers turn the camera off, they reassuringly enact celebrity identity.

Reality Fame

As the reality genre both responds to and shapes the television industry, the way it alters the normative categories of fame and narrative is central to the success of reality formats. On the issue of fame, what does it mean to make people famous for being themselves on TV? How does a celebrity's fame change when they let viewers see their private home life, behind closed doors? Will everyone eventually have their own reality show, whether they self-broadcast it on YouTube or they participate in a reality TV program? The way reality TV offers the prospect of fame to everyday viewers contributes greatly to it becoming a cult following with legions of devoted followers (who express their enthusiasm on websites such as realitytvworld.com).

Reality programs provide more people access to fame and audiences more access to the inner workings of stars. Critics have long argued that the rhetoric of stardom involves a split between the public and the private and a relationship between what critic John Ellis calls the ordinary and the extraordinary.[28] Stars must be extraordinary (some talent or quality makes them exceptional, unreachable, thus seen in glamorous, larger-than-life surroundings). Yet they must also be ordinary (relatable, in close proximity to the viewer because they want the same things everyday people want, often described in terms of the personal: home, family, marriage, happiness for their kids).

Reality TV puts the interaction of the public and private and the ordinary and extraordinary on greater display than ever before. When a noncelebrity becomes famous simply for performing a version of themselves on reality TV, the genre offers us the spectacle of an ordinary person being placed in extraordinary circumstances. A program like MTV's long-running franchise, *The Real World*, masterfully puts 18- to 24-year-old castmembers on display as they perform the lifestyle programming MTV uses to sell products to its target audience. While they are extraordinary for being on TV and gaining reality stardom, these castmembers retain their ordinary connection to the viewers at home, because viewers could audition to be on the show's next season. Meanwhile, when a celebrity has a reality show, they offer audiences greater

access to the private person or their ordinary life behind their extraordinary stardom. MTV's *The Osbournes* (starring heavy metal icon Ozzy
Osbourne) and *Run's House* (featuring Joseph "Reverend Run" Simmons
from pioneering rap group Run-DMC) publicize the stars' relatable
family life.

I would argue that as reality programming becomes ubiquitous, reality
formats place more pressure on the ordinary side of the extraordinary–
ordinary balance in the rhetoric of stardom. If an average Joe becomes
famous for being himself on TV but then begins to behave pretentiously,
inserts his celebrity status too aggressively into his reality show, or becomes
too obvious in his search for fame, audiences can turn against such stars
for leaving the relatable ordinary too far behind. Or if a celebrity suffers
a scandal that makes her private life impossible to appear ordinary, the reality show narrative breaks down. A case in point is when famous bounty
hunter Duane "Dog" Chapman, of A&E's *Dog the Bounty Hunter,* had his
show suspended briefly after he made racist comments in 2007 and then
tried to renovate his public image.

Indeed, for either celebreality shows or programs about noncelebri-
ties, abandoning the ordinary seems to violate the conventions of reality
TV fame. A spectacular case in point is the backlash against Jon and Kate
Gosselin, stars of TLC's *Jon & Kate Plus 8.* The program enjoyed ratings
success as it followed the couple raising their two sets of multiples; that is,
twin girls and sextuplets. While the premise of raising such a large family
and the unusual situation of two multiples provided an extraordinary setting, the show's narrative focused on how ordinary this family really was,
as they tried to replicate a stereotypical modern nuclear family unit of
breadwinner father and dependent mother and children.

Yet in 2008, the show's fourth season began focusing on product place-
ment tie-ins and lavish vacations provided gratis by resorts looking for
advertising. This dynamic created a narrative tension that escalated in
the program's fifth season in 2009, when tabloids accused Jon of cheating
on Kate, Kate of desperately seeking fame and fortune, with the children
caught in the middle. In response to a media firestorm, the couple actually
addressed the rumors in one episode, announcing their divorce and de-
crying the toll the media scrutiny had taken on them, while insisting that
they never put fame or fortune above their family.[29] The fact that they found
it necessary to respond to media allegations directly, within the narrative of
their show (in direct address interviews and in shots of paparazzi camped
outside their home), indicates the degree to which they were perceived

as violating codes of fame as well as the normative family codes they had earlier reproduced.

Celebrity reality programs in particular invite audiences to see the star's authentic personality even in the midst of a mediated show where stars could be understood as playing the role of themselves. Richard Dyer and Richard deCordova have shown that in Hollywood film, when a star gives media access to their private life, that supporting material actually reinforces their public star persona. The star's publicly available private life—splashed across tabloids and promotional materials—and their film roles mutually inform each other, as if a star's performance in a film appears to reveal something about their personality (even though the film scenario has nothing to do with their actual life).[30] The process of manufacturing the star image glamorously becomes part of the image itself, as Dyer puts it, "like a conjuror showing you how a trick is done."[31] Yet audiences continually look for traces of the star's authentic self in their performance.

Reality TV twists this formula. As I noted earlier, Annette Hill observes that reality audiences know people act differently when a camera is watching, yet they still look for authentic moments of self beneath the performance.[32] Just as in society more generally, we still search for some version of an authentic self even while knowing most identity is constant performance. On reality programs about celebrities, we see multiple layers of performance, as the stars navigate their public persona, their private persona, and different kinds of selfhood. Viewers are encouraged to parse out which moments are "authentic." If, as Dyer argued, the classic Hollywood film star served as an exemplar of individualism in a capitalist society, an exceptional person who becomes famous for some quality or talent, what does it mean if anyone can be a star now for being themselves on reality TV?[33] Critic Su Holmes argues persuasively that reality stars who play themselves on camera speak to an anxiety about changing models of selfhood—a postmodern view of identity as constantly changing performance versus an older, premodern notion of stable identity. Holmes insists that the fear now is about how to have an authentic selfhood in an era in which identity is mass mediated.[34] If a star's performances are in a feedback loop with supporting media (fanzines, biographies), reality series redefine stardom by trying to be all-encompassing, covering all aspects of stars through Web tie-ins, material incorporated into the program, and even behind-the-scenes specials.[35]

In order to more fully establish how reality TV puts the hybrid genre mix to use, and how it generates emotional connections to viewers, I will now turn to a discussion of three specific shows as test cases for these issues: MTV's *The Osbournes,* VH1's *The Surreal Life,* and MTV's *The Real World. The Osbournes* demonstrates how MTV markets documentary truth claims alongside a sitcom plotline, all while culling emotional connections to the relatable, ordinary side of the stars. *The Surreal Life* amps up the emotional, confessional dynamic of the hybrid genre alongside the claims to stardom. Meanwhile, *The Real World* tries to pull the target audience in by modeling a lifestyle they are asked to feel an emotional connection with and to emulate, as if they could become reality stars too.

The Osbournes as Reality Stars

The Osbournes mixes documentary and sitcom techniques not only to establish the pop idol status of their objects of study and to propose that viewers are gaining access to their private reality, but also to verify the cultural cachet of the series itself, bringing *The Osbournes* into the realm of celebrity object while also making the claim of documenting the show on a meta level. The series was a smash hit for MTV precisely because it ironically juxtaposes Ozzy's bat-biting Prince of Darkness public rock star image with a private persona, one MTV narrativizes as the addled domestic sitcom patriarch of "America's favorite dysfunctional family." *The Osbournes* offers a paradigmatic case of reality TV adapting older media models of the American family in a new historical and cultural context. Jennifer Gillan has illustrated how *The Osbournes* actually updates the 1950s star sitcom format (Lucille Ball and Desi Arnaz, George Burns and Gracie Allen, Ozzie and Harriet Nelson), while Derek Kompare has proven that it redeploys the documentary styles that *An American Family* used.[36]

The program constantly merges documentary techniques, like observational documentary's constant 24/7 coverage of the subjects over months and years, with sitcom tropes and structures. It turns the family members into sitcom character types like rebellious teens, doddering dad, or caring mom. The show often ironizes sitcom expectations as it invokes them, because the Osbournes both fit those expectations and depart from them. Much of the show's humor depends on the playful juxtaposition of, for instance, the dad trying to discipline his children in one scene and then screaming onstage at his heavy metal concert in the next. The program fits typical sitcom structures in that it is a half-hour program that foregrounds humor and comedic snafus, rapid pacing, a main plot and a subplot that get resolved in each weekly episode, the family sitcom's domestic focus and character types, and a return to the situational status quo each week. At the same time, it pushes the boundaries of topics treated in the sitcom frame, realisitically addressing actual-life drug abuse by the father and teenage children and the mother's cancer treatments. The series treats those moments with emotional realism but without melodrama, and it places them within a reassuring sitcom frame of humor, even if it is sometimes gallows humor, like Sharon joking about her chemotherapy.

The premiere episode establishes the show's invocation of sitcom conventions and its ironic treatment of them (a feature typical to many so-called postmodern sitcoms of the late 1990s and early 2000s, like *The Simpsons* or *Malcolm in the Middle*). A voice-over intones "meet the perfect American family" as we see a montage of the family at home and at entertainment-industry events intercut with amusing clips of the family members cursing or saying something incendiary in set-up interviews. The voice-over cues clips with "there's the Mom," "the son," "the daughter," "and of course, the Dad" (to introduce an image of a wild-eyed Ozzy yelling "rock and roll!" as he boards a plane while on tour).[37] Graphic title cards introduce different segments with sitcom scenarios like "There Goes the Neighborhood," as the Osbournes move into their new home, decorating it with devil's horns and crucifixes, and greet their neighbors in Beverly Hills, or "Fight Club," as teen siblings Jack and Kelly constantly bicker. The program's counterpointing between the domestic and Ozzy's public heavy metal career is often enacted structurally. This episode's A story line involves the family chaotically moving into their new home while the B story line involves Ozzy going on *The Tonight Show with Jay Leno* to promote his new solo heavy metal album. The specific sitcom-documentary merger becomes clear in this episode in moments such as when Kelly hits Jack and he points to the camera, breaking the invisibility conceit that had been operating in the scene to that point, and says in direct address "That's on camera, Kelly!" Like the typical sitcom teen, he wants to complain to his mother that his sister is hitting him. Unlike the standard sitcom brother, Jack can plead his case by showing MTV's observational documentary to his mother as visual proof.

From this documentary-sitcom hybrid, we learn our "character narrative" lessons: the father is loveable but poignantly disoriented and barely functional, partly from years of drug abuse and the heavy metal lifestyle; the mother is in charge and manages their business interests with a mafioso's iron fist; the teenage kids run amok, trying to find themselves amidst a series of family tragedies and escapades; they are all now celebrities. They are at once typical and exceptional. When the series shows Ozzy talking to the camera or crew when he should not, we are to believe he does so because of his characteristic confusion. He must ask the crew where he lives or he would never find his way home. But more than that, the spontaneous direct address moments bestow the fetish of fame on both the family and the show. An on-camera direct address interview with Sharon launches the program's second season, disrupting the series' dominant mode of direct cinema invisibility. She gleefully exhibits all the magazine covers and press attention their show garnered during its first season.[38] The episode shifts from documenting this media sensation through direct address back to following Sharon and her children around music industry events using direct cinema style. The truth claims of the direct address scene attempt to blanket the rest of that episode's footage, and the series itself, in authenticity as well as confirmed celebrity.

By contrasting *The Osbournes* to other televisual representations of this family, we can see precisely how the program uses its own version of documentary to sell its product. A notorious episode in season three that features very startling footage of Ozzy immediately after a motorized all-terrain vehicle (ATV) accident that almost killed him.[39] More than Ozzy's near-death experience, this episode dramatizes MTV's ability to capture real-life events on camera because of its reality format. MTV jams documentary footage into its domestic sitcom narrative, combining black and white shots of the event with direct address clips of Ozzy joking about the accident later. Again, the episode's narrative frame situates him as affable father in the family tragicomedy, or the sitcom dad laughing about another family disaster comically averted. The light sitcom tone draws attention to itself given the gravity of the real-life incidents in question. In contrast, ABC's *Primetime Thursday* newsmagazine contemporaneously aired a Diane Sawyer interview with Sharon and Ozzy.[40] This interview is obviously part of a newsmagazine, not a documentary, but it also differs markedly from *The Osbournes'* representation in that it uses a much more serious, traumatized tone to focus on how severe the accident was. It tries to achieve journalistic credibility by adding on-camera interviews with Ozzy's doctors and shots of his X-rays. Both shows are constructed narratives. But *The Osbournes* lays claim to a higher level of actuality. The newsmagazine attempts to verify the facts of what happened with expert testimony and reportage, yet significantly, it uses MTV's clips as visual evidence of the accident itself. The reality show, meanwhile, tries to capture the actual experience—and explain how Ozzy really felt about it—since their marketing promise involves their potential to document the entire lives of their subjects on video.

Advertisements for this episode imply that MTV will show Ozzy almost dying on camera. However, the episode does not show the moment of his crash but rather it implies that it could have. The sequence moves from a comical shot of Ozzy haphazardly steering his ATV around a field to an intercut, sped-up aerial shot of his bike racing across the terrain, to a jerky black and white shot of Ozzy's prone body on the ground, his body guard desperately trying to revive him as other ATVs race to the scene. The crash occurs offscreen. The image of Ozzy on the ground is a hand-held video camera moving frame shot from the point of view of someone following on an ATV. In the next shot, the program draws attention to itself, breaking the direct cinema invisibility conceit by having the camera man speak, recorded by the in-camera microphone, as he puts his camera down on the ground to run for help. Here, MTV wants viewers to know they abandoned taping to help Ozzy, contrasting themselves with other reality programs criticized for their ethics, as when a camera crew shoots the action rather than helping the hurt castmember (as *Survivor* creator Mark Burnett infamously instructed his crew to do).[41] This shot of Ozzy is from the camera man's subjective point of view, whereas the program elsewhere uses a limited omniscient point of view. The camera keeps rolling, silently watching, giving us a canted frame image of Ozzy lying unconscious on the ground. Hearing the camera man's agitation is another marker of authentic proof that this event really happened. The camera saw it, as did its operator. The absence of a crash picture as well as the sudden shift to a subjective point of view highlights the program's more omniscient gaze elsewhere. This sequence suggests the panoptic power of MTV's cameras. They can give you access to the ocular proof and then take it away. They can retain the power to picture a near-death accident as well as the moral position of not doing so. Here, reality TV's documentary techniques signal truth claim ability.

These documentary techniques promote the show just as they promote Ozzy's public/private star image. Moments of direct address encourage the viewer to feel a part of their domestic universe, drawing audiences into family bonding, emphasizing the ordinary and the personal side of the star image. In one episode, daughter Kelly looks to the camera while speaking of her friend Robert, soon to be adopted by the family: "You think I like him, don't you? You're so dirty!" She is talking to the crew and then to the camera operator through the lens, but the direct address includes the home viewers in her gaze, drawing them in as interlocutors asked to comment on her relationship with her imminent sibling.

Meanwhile, other documentary techniques concurrently reinforce the extraordinary, celebrity side of the Osbourne family star image. One controversial surveillance camera scene in season one features a family meeting Sharon calls so the parents can urge Jack and Kelly to curb their wild partying and drug use. Both teens eventually ended up in drug rehabilitation clinics. At one point, MTV ran an interview special with Jack where he urged viewers to avoid drugs. The teens respond to this meeting in a way that highlights the mix of ordinary and extraordinary in their star family life. Kelly details the hardships of fame, such as a childhood raised on the road during rock tours and being ridiculed at school. Taped in black and white with a stationary unattended camera, the scene's surveillance visual style implies that viewers have been allowed into a private family meeting in an upstairs room not usually shown to the public. Jack and Kelly later claimed they did not know the planted camera was there and that MTV staged the scene, while Sharon insisted MTV did not stage it. The fact that Sharon knows the cameras are there while the teenagers claim they did not suggests that she and the producers are attempting to get a less mediated reaction from the kids. Producers lend this scene narrative and visual weight, running it as a direct cinema style long take uninterrupted by cuts. The scene's claims to realism stand in formal contrast to the hyperrealism of some other moments in the series.

The fact that the show offers a supposedly more authentic moment to the viewer, and that the moment is a family meeting, illustrates two key points. First, the program insists that it gives you access to the Osbournes' real lives, yet it offers you moments that are even realer. It extends the possibility that there is purer entrée to be had. The visual vocabulary of this family meeting scene both undercuts the authenticity of other scenes and reinforces the idea that this scene is less mediated than others, when, of course, it is all mediated and edited. Here we get the ever-vanishing real, the promise of newer vistas of reality to be consumed. Second, this scene suggests that if one could get behind the Osbourne celebrity, the camera mediation, and the hype, one would find them in ordinary moments like this family meeting, as family becomes a symbol for the personal or the private, yet this family can never escape stardom, hence the extraordinary, public features are always there, as Kelly bemoans them.

In response to criticism about this scene in particular, the Osbournes and the producers collaborated to make the season three finale a mockumentary. There, the Osbournes realistically pretend that Jack had accidentally killed Sharon's favorite dog and Sharon had left the family.[42] The episode ends with a man-behind-the-curtain shot of the Osbournes gathered laughing with the camera crew in the kitchen, the dog safely among them. Sharon wanted to ridicule press reports that some events were contrived by MTV, so they orchestrated a parody of that charge. But as in Dyer's formulation of film, once we see how the conjuror performs the trick, we do not have any less fascination with the performance of that trick. Indeed, Internet message boards lit up with viewers arguing over whether to appreciate the self-reflexive joke or feel betrayed by it, with some fans so invested in the show's truth claims they worried whether the dog was actually alive.[43] Ultimately, as the show merges documentary and fiction techniques, the reality sitcom markets celebrity alongside an emotional appeal for audiences still to relate to them and feel bonded to them as a supposedly ordinary family too.

Other celebrity family programs similarly struggle to maintain a delicate ordinary/extraordinary mix. In MTV's *Run's House,* "Reverend Run," like Ozzy before him, markets his domesticom through ironic juxtaposition: the rapper lives the star life but has a normal family life and is even a minister.[44] Deeply intertwining commerce and family, Run presides over a growing business empire that includes his music, clothing lines with his mogul brother, Russell Simmons, and various media and business endeavors his children launch. While the program follows their jetsetter lifestyles, it must balance that dynamic with domestic scenes of Run and his second wife Justine parenting their blended family of six kids.

Similarly, A&E's *Gene Simmons Family Jewels* balances the extraordinary with the ordinary in depicting KISS rock star Simmons's daily family life, marketed as a "real-life A&E family series."[45] While Simmons and his partner, model Shannon Tweed, question family norms by emphasizing their unmarried state, the program nevertheless applies a modern nuclear family framework (and the two eventually marry and televise their wedding). Using *The Osbournes'* blueprint, the show implies savvy audiences steeped in rock marketing practices will be fascinated to see Simmons the domesticated father behind the fire-breathing image. Since his rock star image is so iconic, so immediately recognizable, and so incessantly consumed by fans eager for more (or nostalgic for their favorite band's heyday), the next logical step in branding that image is to give fans behind-the-scenes access to Simmons's daily life.

Far from undercutting his rocker demon stage persona, the reality sitcom account of Simmons out of his black leather and puttering around the house only fuels his media image. Fans see the extraordinary rock star living a glamorous life, but they see that balanced with footage of the ordinary, goofy father overly invested in his kids' lives. They are encouraged to envy the star yet identify with the man behind the curtain, maintaining an equilibrium lest the star seem too remote or the ordinary man seem too familiar.

The Surreal Life as Celebreality Paradigm

The Surreal Life is another popular reality series that verifies the celebrity of its product through visual and narrative forms taken from documentary. The program warrants extensive analysis because it explicitly meditates on fame as well as the rituals of camera-mediated stardom, illuminating how its celebrity product is produced by using the documentary form, and provides a catalogue of techniques in the celebreality TV subgenre. A self-conscious program like *The Surreal Life* interrogates what visual evidence has come to mean in this context, often questioning then partially reasserting the idea that the visual image is equivalent to actuality; as such, it sometimes draws on the experimental style of reflexive documentary, which explicitly questions what is fact and what is fiction. Programs like this one register a deep awareness of how media construction of images works, and they uncover some profound ambivalences about this procedure, particularly concerning audience identification with the celebrities and the process of turning an image into a commodity.

The program uses sitcom conventions for humor and to mine the ordinary side of the extraordinary/ordinary star binary. The second season, for example, focuses attention on Tammy Faye Messner (who was diagnosed with cancer soon after the show aired and was very public in her discussion of her own illness leading up to her death from the disease in 2007). On the program, Messner cares for Trishelle Cannatella (former MTV *Real World* castmember) when she is upset, in what both women call a mother–daughter relationship in their intercut interviews. Messner comforts Cannatella during typical domestic sitcom plotlines, as when

Cannatella develops an unrequited crush or she has conflicts with her peers in the house. Similarly, the series follows former TV star Erik Estrada as he continually tries to soothe 1990s rapper Rob "Vanilla Ice" Van Winkle. As Van Winkle throws tantrums or furniture and then calms down when Estrada reasons with him, the show tropes him as a rebellious sitcom teen and includes clips of him calling Estrada the older brother he always wished he could have, while cast interviews frame Messner and Estrada as the house mother and father.

The Surreal Life also intermixes soap opera conventions. It mines melodrama (such as the highly emotional response it gets from the religious Messner when she is supposed to go on a group trip to a nudist colony or to interact with castmate Ron Jeremy's friends from the adult film world). It focuses on interpersonal relationships even in the midst of outlandish situations, and it treats the real lives of the castmembers as open-ended serials with gaps in meaning (as when it jumps around chronologically, or when it creates a spin-off series like *Strange Love* to follow the continuing exploits of certain castmembers without filling in all the plot gaps). *The Surreal Life* also exhibits soap opera's repetition, summary, redundancy, gossip, and previewing functions. Robert C. Allen notes that soap operas create a fluctuating community of characters that result in shifting audience attention.[46] *The Surreal Life* franchise was an open-ended serial in the sense that always had new celebrities moving into a Surreal Life house in Hollywood, using the demi-monde of stardom as the recurring setting. During season three, the series went from an hour-long time slot to a half-hour slot, thus emphasizing the sitcom's time slot and format of domestic dilemmas resolved each week, yet it still retained key elements of the soap opera too.

In the analysis that follows, I will focus on how this franchise elucidates reality documentary and celebrity. The dance of identification and disidentification in celebrity reality programs is an elaborate one, because viewers must identify with the celebrities but not too closely, otherwise the cast's star status is lost. *The Surreal Life*'s premise establishes its documentary setting and its method for enacting celebrity: cameras track a flock of B-list stars brought together to live in a house in a fine example of Barnouw's provoked action. In each episode, the stars are asked to perform tasks, such as putting on talent shows or flipping burgers at a fast food restaurant. In an episode during season one, erstwhile child star Corey Feldman instigates a fight with his costars on a tour bus and suddenly demands that the crew stop filming, brushing the microphones and cameras aside. Feldman suddenly breaks the documentary conceit of direct cinema invisibility, making you aware of the camera in order to establish the forms of stardom on which the franchise depends.[47] In case some viewers were worried, perhaps understandably, that Feldman could no longer claim movie idol status, these moments perform celebrity for him, distinguishing him from the viewers.

As it pictures stardom, this subgenre stages both the lure and the frustration of entering what Sut Jhally terms the "commodity-image system," where the mass media fetishizes visual commodities, flattening out a person into an icon.[48] The reality genre accelerates the process of image commodification, even as it creates new celebrities. Several *Surreal Life* castmembers' only claim to fame is that they appeared on a previous reality series (Cannatella, from *Real World: Las Vegas,* season three's Ryan Starr from *American Idol,* season four's Adrianne Curry from *America's Next Top Model*). The series critiques how the media in general and reality programming in particular create those commodity images precisely by reducing a person to a single trait. As *Joe Millionaire* contestant Sarah Kozer complains of reality TV's fake editing, "I've been to law school, traveled the world, but now I'm the girl in the bushes" with Joe Millionaire.[49] Likewise, *The Surreal Life* frames people as types, introducing Estrada with a graphic reading: "The '70s Heart Throb," while Cannatella's graphic reads "The Reality Vixen," and Jeremy's says "The Porn King."

The Surreal Life thus ironizes how media images work, yet it banks off the titillation of reality TV conventions. The series' conceit is that celebrity itself is surreal in the age of mass-mediated hyperreality. It ridicules how television produces stars. In the second season, the group house includes Warhol-style portraits of each media personality in their heyday, effectively satirizing a 1970s television actor like Estrada trying to recapture his youthful glory years or white rapper Rob Van Winkle trying to escape his trite Vanilla Ice image from the 1990s. The camera follows him as he spray paints over his Vanilla Ice portrait, saying "I'm sick of being perceived as that image that wasn't even me."[50] But *The Surreal Life* continues to sell that image, since it is the basis for his fame. As he tries to reject his old media image, the show simply gives him a new narrative—he is no longer just the talentless white rapper, he is the washed-up singer angry about his media image. The series turns the celebrities' discomfort with controlled media images into a marketing vehicle, as when it pictures the self-reflexivity of fame in each episode by having the cast read about what they will be doing that day in a fake tabloid newspaper.

We know "Porn King" Jeremy is there to titillate, the pairing of him and "Televangelist" Tammy Faye a walking punch line, though the series fails to provoke conflict in its headliner odd couple, who establish a lingua franca of tolerance, becoming fast friends. But in its portrayal of Jeremy, *The Surreal Life* makes a larger point about voyeurism and genre. It analogizes the voyeurism of viewing pornography with that of watching reality TV, again deconstructing reality TV conventions while also using them for marketing. Jeremy's rapid title sequence montage mixes partial shots from his adult films with his footage from *The Surreal Life,* and its graphic overlays create an image of the same animated camera shooting both. It suggests the audience at a porn film is like the audience watching *The Surreal Life,* just as it draws an analogy between pornographic filmmakers and reality TV producers. As the program registers the pornographic nature of the pleasure of looking in the reality TV genre, it ironizes that structure of seeing and making. At the same time, the series also banks on these kinds of images, advertising such plot twists as a trip to a nudist colony and a pool party with Jeremy's adult film cohort, then gazing on their pixilated naked bodies.

In spite of elements that self-ironize televisual images and media stardom, *The Surreal Life* also makes truth claims that it is showing you the supposedly real person beneath the celebrity persona, and it asks you to sympathize with those stars. For a psychic visit and séance, action sequences are intercut with lengthy talking head cast interviews, eliciting viewer sympathy for each person's point of view about those events. These monologues, done one-on-one in their bedrooms, are offered as sober, confessional actuality as opposed to the kitschy séance.[51] Similarly, the season finale pictures a staged Sally Jessy Raphael talk show in the house, replete with a studio audience. Grandstanding, the talk show host screens *Surreal Life* clip reels and trashes the stars' morals. We then see behind-the-scenes footage of angry castmembers and a matter-of-fact Sally Jessy, whose attitude is that the cast should accept the exploitative circumstances, since they agreed to be on reality TV. As it deconstructs the fake talk show, the program implies that these on-camera direct address interview and observational documentary moments (of stars fleeing the studio audience set) after the staged talk show are authentic reactions.[52] Now for further insight let us turn to Tammy Faye's crying eyes, the true stars of the talk show. There as elsewhere in the series, Tammy Faye moves her castmembers to tears, her emotional testimonials ringing like a Pavlovian bell, here one that makes her peers hungry to confess.

The Eyes of Tammy Faye

From her leopard-print dresses and impossibly thick makeup to her emotional breakdowns, on this program, Tammy Faye is a spectacle. And *The Surreal Life* positively devours her. It at once ridicules her persona, a charming version of a church lady stereotype, and it also tries to elicit viewer sympathy for her moral views and what it presents as the purportedly true-to-life Tammy Faye. The series' clearest depiction of celebrity through a documentary–reality hybrid form comes in its fixation on her. The show mimes earlier documentary and journalistic footage of her when it focuses on images of her in tears. In this context, it is Tammy Faye's crying eyes that have become a media fetish, and both she and *The Surreal Life* producers know it. TV viewers will likely be able to recall video journalistic coverage of her then-husband Jim Bakker's Praise the Lord (PTL) ministry embezzlement scandal in 1989 and the infamy of his affair with his secretary, Jessica Hahn. There were endless reels of Tammy Faye sobbing, her mascara running down her face, transforming it into a garish mask of pain. Accused of embezzling $158 million from PTL, Jim Bakker went to jail. Tammy Faye went to the Betty Ford Clinic. Tammy Faye herself made a living by creating her own media self-representations, helping build the three largest Christian television networks and hosting several television programs.[53]

Its direct-address interviews with her while she is weeping work to establish both documentary-style truth claims for the show and her status as a celebrity hounded by cameras in her moments of authentic suffering. The program is self-conscious about how it achieves its mixture of fact and fiction by juxtaposing old and new media images—old television show and movie images enjoy the status of fact because they are part of our collective pop culture consciousness. A 1970s image of Estrada from *CHiPs* takes on the same status as a journalistic shot from Tammy Faye's scandal days. But the show depends on those hybrid images even as it ironizes them. Though we would not categorize news as documentary, it is nevertheless relevant to note that the show mixes news footage shots recombined with reality documentary styles in order to further its truth claims.

By mixing earlier journalistic footage of Tammy Faye with its own reality documentary footage, *The Surreal Life* wants to achieve the status of accurate reportage too, translated into the terms of reality show mimesis. In her title sequence, an old scandal-era image of Tammy Faye appears, Kleenex in hand, bedecked in blonde hair, a huge diamond ring, and tears tinged with mascara. This still video image is superimposed in front of a graphic of a church with an animated red sky, while a graphic reading "The Televangelist" appears in the bottom left of the frame. We pan right to an animated cross and graphics of three angels with the face of Tammy Faye (ca. 1989) fly into the sky, one after the other. Next, recent video footage from the current show appears, picturing her with red hair and large black sunglasses. She raises her hand to her sunglasses, then tilts them down to peer over them with a knowing glance and a smile, a movement the sequence comically repeats at high speed. As the current Tammy Faye (at the time of the reality show) tilts her sunglasses, the last of the three angel figures rises on the screen as if emerging from her hand. The montage suggests that *The Surreal Life* Tammy Faye can summon the angels of her past at will.

The sonic and visual landscape of the show thus draws direct parallels between the old and new Tammy Faye, the journalism coverage and *The Surreal Life* coverage, the footage of her recorded responses to historical events and the program's own documentary forms. *The Surreal Life* invokes those earlier journalism images as visual truth. Both sets of images, the sequence implies, have the status of accurate reportage. In fact, the audio track encourages viewers to collapse those images with its use of two sound clips. The first plays while the old image of Tammy Faye is on the screen, and we hear her say in voice-over: "God has gotten ahold of my heart," the second accompanies the new Tammy Faye: "I said I'd never cry on TV again, well so you made me cry." Although the sequence implies that the first audio clip is from her PTL days, both are actually drawn from *The Surreal Life,* from spontaneous direct address speeches she makes by interrupting events being filmed and speaking to the camera. The first clip comes when she refuses to consult the visiting psychic. The never-cry-on-TV-again audio clip is from the episode that sends the celebrities to a nudist camp, at which point Tammy Faye balks and weeps, an historically significant act, as she notes—one implying that *The Surreal Life* is documenting a moment in television and pop culture history similar to the journalism coverage of Bakker's embezzlement scandal. In a direct address set-up interview, Tammy Faye herself claims to be "the original reality TV star" because of her talk shows and scandal coverage.[54]

Those crying eyes have warranted their own documentary, *The Eyes of Tammy Faye* (2000).[55] Comparing that film with *The Surreal Life,* we can see how the television series does not problematize the truth claims of the documentary techniques it scavenges and retools, even though many documentary films do so themselves. In the documentary, film-makers Fenton Bailey and Randy Barbato explore Tammy Faye's status as a gay icon and her camp appeal, replete with voice-over narration by celebrity drag queen RuPaul. The film is a situated cultural argument that admits it wants to make a sympathetic intervention on her behalf; it claims that televangelist Jerry Falwell betrayed the couple, stealing their ministry, and that the embezzlement accusations were false. Pondering her visual iconography, the film pictures Tammy Faye self-awarely revealing: "Without my eyelashes, I wouldn't be Tammy Faye. I don't know who I'd be, but it wouldn't be me." The documentary presents itself as a mixture of fact and fiction that can only make qualified, contextualized truth claims. While Bailey and Barbato's reality series efforts like *Showbiz Moms and Dads* try to bring in an element of self-reflexivity, most reality programs avoid too much self-analysis. For all its unique self-awareness, *The Surreal Life* stops short of admitting that it is itself a cultural argument and instead deploys stock documentary techniques to make its own truth claims.

During the psychic episode, intercut interviews with Tammy Faye establish the show's ridicule as well as its embrace of her, a knotty mixture of identification and disidentification. The documentary techniques here organize her celebrity persona, the folksy religious diva who is outlandish but nevertheless trustworthy and of high moral character. Calling to mind Dana Carvey's earlier madcap satire of a church lady stereotype on *Saturday Night Live, The Surreal Life* deliberately eroticizes their televangelist, trying for a jolt of scandalous energy. The series objectifies her, with close-up body shots, clips of other castmembers telling her she "has a great body," and viewer posts on the WB website that concur.[56] The psychic sequence begins with a shot intercut from Tammy Faye's later set-up direct address interview in which she disparages psychics and séances. Her interview continues in voice-over narration as we watch the action sequence begin, and the form consequently encourages audiences to share her viewpoints. When asked to go meet with the psychic, Tammy Faye has an emotional breakdown in the house living room, depicted in an unusual direct cinema-style long take:

God has gotten ahold of my heart. And he has kept me from committing suicide. Has kept me from . . . from things that could have killed me. And has given me peace in spite of the horrible circumstances I've faced. And I like that lady, she's a nice lady, but I'm not going to her for advice. I'm going to get on my knees for advice and ask God to tell me, because he can tell me anything she's going to tell me if he wants me to know it.[57]

The scene begins with a medium shot of Tammy Faye; as she begins to cry during her speech about turning to Christianity rather than to psychics for revelations, we cut to a close-up of her face, intercut with reaction shots of her castmates, all looking serious and supportive, like an adoring audience gathered around her. After the séance, the episode transitions to a scene where the cast is partying and drinking into the night, but it intercuts a grainy high-angle surveillance camera shot of Tammy Faye going to bed, and the editing sympathizes with her genial moral avoidance of the party. Her testimonials have the effect of bringing her castmates and audience into cathartic sympathy with her and her viewpoints. Indeed, a protective Jeremy is so moved by Tammy Faye's testimonials that he angrily tells Sally Jessy he would "kill anyone who tried to take [Tammy Faye's] Bible from her."[58] These scenes with Tammy Faye obviously invoke the generic conventions of the talk show, the witnessing, personal testimony of televangelism, and the intense melodrama of the soap opera (particularly as the episode previews later scenes of her weeping). But it is in how the series combines those conventions with documentary that it achieves its own particular cultural effects, here its creation of authenticity for Tammy Faye.

Throughout this series, Tammy Faye explains her appeal in direct address interviews by saying she is "a real person who tells it like it is." Such moments provoke viewer sympathy even as they consistently frame her as a media icon. One fan posting on the WB's discussion boards notes she "used to view Tammy Faye as a caricature," but after watching the show has "so much respect and admiration" for this "sweet, tolerant lady" who is "the first one you'd think would be a diva and she's actually the most agreeable person in that house."[59] In a clear paradigm of how celebrity documentary works in this subgenre, the show thus encourages viewers to accept their direct address interviews as well as surveillance footage as accurate depictions of reality, a reality that merges Tammy Faye's public image with her purportedly true self—a straight-talking authentic woman.

MTV Youth Shows and Ideology

MTV's *The Real World* puts a cast of attractive 18- to 24-year-olds in a house-as-sound-stage setting and asks them to bare their hearts for the camera. Here, direct address helps deliver a different kind of product: the 18- to 29-year-old viewer demographic (sometimes defined more broadly as a 13- to 35-year-old demographic) drawn to MTV's visions of consumerism.[60] *The Real World* features two kinds of direct address interviews: a diary confessional room where castmembers enter and activate a static camera themselves, and interviews conducted by a producer or director (who is some seasons has also been a clinical psychologist), taped as direct address to the camera with the staff and their questions edited out. Savvy about how to hail both their young cast and their viewers, creators Jonathan Murray and the late Mary-Ellis Bunim noted how they wanted it to appear as though the castmembers "were talking directly to . . . the viewer at home."[61] In the video diary segments, explicitly termed "confessionals," castmembers embark on a Foucauldian journey in which they internalize their own discipline by adapting to the program's dominant ideologies. The audience is their confessor. The staff-conducted interviews, meanwhile, shape Bildungsroman narratives that trace the castmembers' psychological development and how their identity is being formed by the show and its staged experiences. Fashioning the audience as their product by drawing on the appeal of this complex narrative process, *The Real World* pulls viewers in by playing on a desire to fetishize narrative, to reify the process of imagining one's life as a story. A show like *The Real World* delivers an image of the model viewer on the screen; that is, castmembers who participate in a saturated MTV consumer reality situation and mirror home viewer desires. Audiences can identify with the casts they see on-screen. Founder Robert Pittman created the channel in 1981 as an on-screen "pure environment" for his commercial messages with a "zero-based" programming strategy—he profiled his market and then tried to recreate their lifestyle desires in his channel's content.[62]

The text constructs this screen surrogate by creating MTV's ideology of liberal pluralist consensus, one that sells the viewer group to corporate advertisers. The franchise focuses on interpersonal conflicts and social tensions, the fights and fits that fuel its ratings, yet its overriding narrative encourages castmembers to arrive at a pluralist resolution. The show's plotline frequently follows a teenager who learns to abandon views such as racism and homophobia, but their change is often superficial. They learn to feel their roommate's individual pain at racist comments without critiquing the institutional structures that support and promulgate racism. This superficiality serves what critics have termed "corporate multiculturalism," or liberal pluralism that purports to deliver diversity but fails to do so in any substantive way, thus maintaining existing social hierarchies of race and class; corporations make diversity or difference into a product to sell to consumers. In the show's version of pluralism, it upholds a vision of American culture in which minority groups are included and represented, but only at the margins. *The Real World* casts a balance of men and women but includes a clear majority of white characters and tokenizes the people of color on the cast. The franchise's model reflects the kind of pluralism Lisa Lowe has critiqued for masking "the existence of exclusions by recuperating dissent, conflict, and otherness through the promise of inclusion."[63] Indeed, the series is an instance of what Robert Stam would term a liberal-pluralist form of multiculturalism, which "develops a patronizing etiquette of tolerance and inclusiveness, a paternalistic exhortation to 'be nice to minorities,' what Peter Sellers once satirized as the spirit of 'Take an Indian to lunch this week.' "[64]

Reality TV Meets Bell Hooks

What would bell hooks say if she were appearing in a reality TV show? MTV pretends to find out. In an episode that advertises itself as pedagogy by flashing a title card at the beginning warning viewers of a "frank" discussion of race, *The Real World* uses a visual image of a bell hooks book as a stand-in for a structural critique of racism, all on their way to establishing their liberal pluralist ideology based on possessive individualism rather than the kind of wide-ranging critique of institutional racism hooks actually gives us.[65]

On the first season of *The Real World: San Diego,* the lone black male castmember, Jacquese, finds himself having to confront Robin, a white female castmember who uses the "N word" during a bar fight. The episode establishes Jacquese's personal pain in a sympathetic framing of him in direct address interviews. In both diary direct address footage and later interview footage, Jacquese expresses how troubling it is for his roommate not to understand that the racial epithet is offensive and painful. In jump cuts of the action, Jacquese confronts a drunk Robin at the bar as she argues she should be able to use the epithet, then the show intercuts a later direct address interview with fellow castmate Brad (from a staff-conducted set-up interview), a white man, saying he does not think it is ever right to use that word. We then see shots of the housemates returning home and comforting an upset Robin, leaving Jacquese to call his mother for support. His mother tells him he cannot turn into "a stereotype of an angry black man" and should instead have patience with them because they simply do not know or understand how racism works.

Jacquese consults the Internet for information about racism and the camera pans over quick shots of the stacked spines of his books on his shelves, including bell hooks's *Talking Back* and Angela Davis's *Women, Race, & Class.* Jacquese has a house meeting with everyone, explaining his hurt feelings, but the meeting dissolves when Robin becomes distraught, saying she has emotional issues about racial identity because a black man raped her, but she never meant to hurt anyone's feelings. Jacquese comforts her and they both bond about their mutual understanding of shared pain.

As the editors intercut the action sequences with direct address interviews, the program encourages the viewers to empathize with a reading of the situation that rejects racial epithets because they hurt the individual's feelings. The episode does not include any verbal account of structural racism, only gesturing toward such analysis by picturing books or Internet pages, very brief images of them. Thus a shot of a bell hooks book is a substitute for the structural critique the show does not make. Similarly, in the first season of *The Real World: New Orleans,* an episode devoted to the "N-word" pictures a white man, Jamie, learning to question his own racism when a castmate who is a woman of color, Melissa, explains why the word hurts her feelings, and his character development is staged in direct address interviews.[66] The program insisted on this story arc even when Jamie himself objected to it in interviews after the season aired, feeling he had been misrepresented as being racist and homophobic.[67]

Direct address here tries to relate castmembers and audiences, encouraging viewers to identify and sympathize with the cast talking directly to them, modeling behavior, and hailing audiences to join their particular kind of imagined pluralist community. *The Real World,* along with many other reality shows, turns this documentary form into a truth claim meant to fashion ideologies with which viewers can identify. The program also makes further truth claims through tie-in products, such as behind the scenes documentary-style footage that asserts it will let you in on: "the real world you never saw," or "the really, real world." Buy these docu-style videos and you can chase the ever-evaporating real. These specials are similar to the original reality show, produced by the same networks and companies, a piece of meta-reality TV, carving out a new space for an even realer, more authentic documentary. For example, MTV's sister company, VH1, also owned by Viacom, billed their documentary, *Reality T.V. Secrets Revealed,* as an exposé of how "producers, editors, and contestants use clever methods to get big ratings."[68] Thus the documentary form keeps getting positioned as the real, even able to comment on itself with the accuracy of an exposé meant to change viewer's minds about what reality TV is.

Reality TV's use of documentary techniques reveals multifaceted and sometimes competing agendas in the genre. These programs use the purported authenticity of documentary to work through specific cultural problems, such as the relationship between celebrity and identity, and the way popular culture helps construct personhood. They also try to model a consumer identity, a viewer-as-product to be sold to their corporate advertisers.

Staged Spectacles

Different documentary forms help reality TV make different realist claims, because the forms deliver specific kinds of information. Tammy Faye's on-camera direct address interview when she talks about religion saving her from suicide generates a truth effect because that form helps achieve emotional sincerity, particularly when it is combined with soap opera conventions of melodrama. Meanwhile, the shaky camera shots of Ozzy Osbourne's motor accident deliver a different kind of realism effect, the kind of immediate access of what it would look like if you had been standing there—the jiggled visual images you see before your eyes, the blurriness of actual ocular proof as our weak eyesight attempts to decipher the world around us. Producers combine that with the sitcom narrative of doddering dad, as Ozzy appears in intercut on-camera interviews later joking about his own ineptness—how he gave the family a real scare this time but evaded a scrape. The show produces fictional TV genre entertainment merged with documentary's sociological claims to comment on family life.

Ultimately, reality TV provokes situations that become spaces for identity construction. Young star Cannatella, for example, told interviewers she appeared twice on reality TV, joining the cast for *The Surreal Life* after having been on MTV's *Real World: Las Vegas,* because: "Being followed around by cameras and people in white vans is strange, but after living [on camera] in Vegas, it was kind of weird not having that constant companionship. I was almost lonely."[69] In his analysis of reality TV, Andrejevic offers a wealth of evidence from his interviews with castmembers that young reality stars say they think they are "finding themselves" or gaining self-knowledge through appearing on reality TV. Again, he interprets this dynamic in terms of how ever more sophisticated marketing strategies encourage consumers to accept constant surveillance as a way of finding selfhood.[70]

It is particularly striking that these portraits of domestic identity achieve a level of sociological validity because the genre appropriates documentary styles to signal reality and cultural authority. Audience know that the documentary situation is staged, mediated, and constructed. But we perhaps nurture some wistful feelings about visual truth. In a perfect example of reality TV's fact-fiction mix, ABC's coverage of Ryan and Trista Sutter's wedding for *The Bachelorette* includes surveillance footage and interviews about an incident at Ryan's bachelor party. Producers put on the wedding and were able to frame the events, though Trista and Ryan were consulted. Editing implies a drunken Ryan might be leaving to hook up with the female dancers from his bachelor party. Surveillance footage shows him stumbling off down the beach with them, and the shaky, grainy night cam footage implies by its very form that something illicit is happening that the all-seeing eye of the camera will expose. But Ryan instead leaves the women and finds a worried Trista, who has been desperately searching for him, and they embrace, asserting their bond. The episode intercuts a later direct address interview with Ryan where he castigates producers for trying to trap him. In these scenes, the program claims a meta-documentary status for itself—it presents itself as supposedly "objectively" reporting Ryan's frustration as he comments on what the show itself did to him. Trista and Ryan appear together in another direct address interview to, again, affirm their love no matter the obstacle.

Thus the show stages an obstacle in order to create narrative tension and conflict, but also in order to affirm Trista and Ryan's romance story for millions of viewers. The plot comes from sitcom narrative tropes (their romantic stasis interrupted by a conflict laughingly resolved, their bonds reaffirmed and a return to the status quo, as the light comic tone is reestablished by the end) and from soap opera (previews of potential disaster, narratively framed as melodramatic crises, the wedding as scene of emotional spectacle, the suggestion that the next serial event to follow in their lives will be their successful quest for a baby). Nevertheless, while the wedding ceremony embraces traditional family ideals, the way these two got there is anything but. The couple was created by and for reality TV, the woman chose her mate from among over two dozen men she was dating at the same time, and their entire relationship is mediated by fame. Even while family is being redefined, this program (and other reality shows) asks viewers to join together in consuming the spectacle of family itself as central to American life. My next chapter explores how such a family spectacle functions on reality TV.

Notes

1. Henry Jenkins, *Convergence Culture: Where Old and New Media Collide* (New York: New York University Press, 2006), 27.

2. John Caldwell, "Prime-Time Fiction Theorizes the Docu-Real," *Reality Squared: Televisual Discourse on the Real,* ed. James Friedman (New Brunswick, NJ: Rutgers University Press, 2002) 259–292. See also Caldwell, *Televisuality: Style, Crisis, and Authority in American Television* (New Brunswick, NJ: Rutgers University Press, 1995).

3. Jane Feuer, "Genre Study and Television," *Channels of Discourse, Reassembled: Television and Contemporary Criticism,* ed. Robert C. Allen, 2nd ed. (1987; Chapel Hill: University of North Carolina Press, 1992), 138–159. See also Jane Feuer, Paul Kerr, and Tise Vahimagi, *MTM: "Quality Television"* (London: British Film Institute, 1984).

4. Jason Mittel, *Genre and Television: From Cop Shows to Cartoons in American Culture* (New York: Routledge, 2004). *The Television Genre Book,* ed. Glen Creeber (London: British Film Institute, 2001). Robert C. Allen, *Speaking of Soap Operas* (Chapel Hill: University of North Carolina Press, 1985).

5. Mittel, *Genre and Television,* 197.

6. Brian Graden, interview with Leon Harris, *CNN Live Today,* CNN, March 5, 2002; Nancy Miller, "American Goth: How the Osbournes, a Simple, Headbanging British Family, Became Our Nation's Latest Reality-TV Addiction," *Entertainment Weekly,* April 19, 2002: 25.

7. *An American Love Story,* dir. Jennifer Fox, New Video Group, 1999.

8. Feuer, "Genre Study and Television," 146–158.

9. Ien Ang, *Watching Dallas: Television and the Melodramatic Imagination* (London: Routledge, 1985), 47.

10. Jeffrey Ruoff, *An American Family: A Televised Life* (Minneapolis: University of Minnesota Press, 2002), 53.

11. James Friedman, *Reality Squared: Televisual Discourse on the Real* (New Brunswick, NJ: Rutgers University Press, 2002), 7.

12. Erik Barnouw, *Documentary: A History of the Non-Fiction Film,* 2nd rev. ed. (New York: Oxford University Press, 1993), 255.

13. Stella Bruzzi, "'Accidental Footage,'" *The Television Genre Book,* ed. Glen Creeber (London: British Film Institute, 2001), 133.

14. Bruzzi argues the technology sparks the formal innovation and cites Kuhn as an example of the counterargument. Bruzzi, "'Accidental Footage,'"

129. Annette Kuhn, "The Camera I: Observations on Documentary," *Screen* 19, no. 2 (1978): 75.

15. Jon Dovey, "Reality TV," Creeber, *The Television Genre Book,* 135, 137.

16. Bruzzi, " 'Accidental Footage,' " 133.

17. Caldwell, "Prime-Time Fiction Theorizes the Docu-Real," 272–276.

18. Similarly, Jon Dovey sees the boom in "first person media" in factual television as evidence of anxiety over truth claims and an effort to locate truth in the subjective accounts of individual speakers. Jon Dovey, *Freakshow: First Person Media and Factual Television* (London: Pluto, 2000), 7. Richard Kilborn and John Izod, *An Introduction to Television Documentary* (Manchester: Manchester University Press, 1997), 10–11.

19. Barnouw, *Documentary,* 254.

20. John Corner, "Afterword: Framing the New," *Understanding Reality Television,* eds. Su Holmes and Deborah Jermyn (London: Routledge, 2004), 297.

21. John Corner, "Documentary Fakes," *The Television Genre Book,* ed. Glen Creeber (London: British Film Institute, 2001), 128. Bruzzi, " 'Accidental Footage,' " Creeber, *The Television Genre Book,* 133. Bill Nichols, *Representing Reality: Issues and Concepts in Documentary* (Bloomington and Indianapolis: Indiana University Press, 1991), see also Nichols, *Introduction to Documentary* (Bloomington and Indianapolis: Indiana University Press, 2001), 39, 54–55. Susan Murray asserts that documentary truth claims were always a marketing claim and that reality TV uses the educate and entertain directive of documentary, not just the entertainment side, albeit in different contexts and for different marketing purposes. Susan Murray, " 'I Think We Need a New Name for It': The Meeting of Documentary and Reality TV," *Reality TV: Remaking Television Culture,* eds. Susan Murray and Laurie Ouellette (New York: New York University Press, 2004), 43–44.

22. Mimi White, "Television, Therapy, and the Social Subject; or, The TV Therapy Machine," *Reality Squared: Televisual Discourse on the Real,* ed. James Friedman (New Brunswick, NJ: Rutgers University Press, 2002), 313–322. See also White, *Tele-Advising: Therapeutic Discourse in American Television* (Chapel Hill: University of North Carolina Press, 1992).

23. Justin Lewis, "The Meaning of Real Life," Murray and Ouelette, *Reality TV,* 288–302. Annette Hill, "*Big Brother*: The Real Audience," *Television and New Media* 3(3): 323–325. See also Hill, *Reality TV: Factual Entertainment and Television Audiences* (London: Routledge, 2005).

24. Dovey, *Freakshow.*

25. "Return of the One-Eyed Monster," *The Surreal Life,* WB, January 25, 2004. Fan posting from "Feedback," online postings, February 3, 2004, The WB Home Page, February 4, 2004, http://www.thewb.com/Faces/CastBio/0,7930,146600,00.html.

26. "Ro-Day-O vs. Ro-Dee-O," *The Simple Life,* Fox, December 2, 2003.

27. Interview with *USA Today*, quoted in Michael A. Lipton and Steve Barnes, "Girls Gone Hog Wild," *People*, December 15, 2003: 66–68.

28. John Ellis, *Visible Fictions: Cinema, Television, Video*, 2nd ed. (London: Routledge, 1992).

29. "Houses and Changes," *Jon & Kate Plus 8*, TLC, June 22, 2009.

30. Richard Dyer, *Stars* (London: British Film Institute, 1998); Dyer, *Heavenly Bodies: Film Stars and Society* (Basingstoke: Macmillan, 1986); Richard deCordova, *Personalities: The Emergence of the Star System in America* (Urbana: University of Illinois Press, 1990).

31. Richard Dyer, "Four Films of Lana Turner," in *Star Texts: Image and Performance in Film and Television*, ed. Jeremy G. Butler (Detroit: Wayne State University Press, 1991), 228.

32. Hill, *"Big Brother," Reality TV*.

33. Dyer, "Four Films of Lana Turner," 226–228.

34. Su Holmes, "'All You've Got to Worry About Is the Task, Having a Cup of Tea, and Doing a Bit of Sunbathing': Approaching Celebrity in Big Brother," in *Understanding Reality Television*, eds. Su Holmes and Deborah Jermyn (London: Routledge, 2004), 128, 132.

35. John Ellis, "Stars as a Cinematic Phenomenon," in *Star Texts: Image and Performance in Film and Television*, ed. Jeremy G. Butler (Detroit: Wayne State University Press, 1991), 302.

36. Jennifer Gillan, "From Ozzie Nelson to Ozzy Osbourne: The Genesis and Development of the Reality (Star) Sitcom," Holmes and Jermyn, eds., *Understanding Reality Television*, 54–70. Derek Kompare, "Extraordinarily Ordinary: *The Osbournes* as 'An American Family,'" Murray and Ouellette, eds., *Reality TV*, 97–116.

37. "A House Divided," *The Osbournes*, MTV, March 5, 2002.

38. "Catching Up with the Osbournes," *The Osbournes*, MTV, November 19, 2002.

39. "The Accidental Tourist," *The Osbournes*, MTV, February 24, 2004.

40. *Primetime Thursday*, ABC, February 19, 2004.

41. "Survivor," *VH1 Goes Inside*, VH1, September 13, 2003.

42. "Ozz Well That Ends Well," *The Osbournes*, MTV, August 12, 2003.

43. Jeannette Walls, "*The Osbournes* Goes to the Dogs: Some Fans of *The Osbournes* Are Not Amused by the Latest Episode," *Jeannette Walls Delivers the Scoop*, MSNBC.com, August 16, 2003, http://www.msnbc.com/modules/exports/ct_email.asp?/news/943880.asp.

44. *Run's House: Complete Seasons 1 & 2*, DVD, Paramount, 2007.

45. *Gene Simmons Family Jewels: The Complete Season 1*, DVD, A&E, 2006.

46. Robert C. Allen, "Making Sense of Soaps," *The Television Studies Reader*, eds. Robert C. Allen and Annette Hill (London: Routledge, 2004), 242–257.

47. "Vegas/Church," *The Surreal Life*, WB, January 30, 2003.

48. Sut Jhally, "Image-Based Culture: Advertising and Popular Culture," *Gender, Race, and Class in Media: A Text-Reader,* eds. Gail Dines and Jean M. Humez, 2nd ed. (Thousand Oaks, CA: Sage Publications, 2003), 249–257.

49. *Reality TV Secrets Revealed,* VH1, January 2, 2004.

50. "Return of the One-Eyed Monster," *The Surreal Life.*

51. "Return of the One-Eyed Monster," *The Surreal Life.*

52. "Dirty Laundry," *The Surreal Life,* WB, February 22, 2004.

53. The Christian Broadcasting Network (CBN, with Pat Robertson), The Trinity Broadcasting Network (TBN, with Paul Crouch), and PTL with Bakker, which included a theme park, Heritage USA. "Cast Bio: Tammy Faye Messner," *The WB Home Page,* February 4, 2004, http://www.thewb.com/Faces/CastBio/0,7930,146600,00.html.

54. "Back in the Saddle," *The Surreal Life,* NBC, November 4, 2004. The program notes her television show with Jim Bakker had, at its peak, 14.5 million viewers.

55. *The Eyes of Tammy Faye,* dir. Fenton Bailey and Randy Barbato, Lions Gate Films, 2000.

56. "Feedback," *The Surreal Life.*

57. "Dirty Laundry," *The Surreal Life.*

58. "Dirty Laundry," *The Surreal Life.*

59. "Feedback," *The Surreal Life.*

60. John Pettegrew, "A Post-Modernist Moment: 1980s Commercial Culture and the Founding of MTV," *Gender, Race, and Class in Media: A Text-Reader,* eds. Gail Dines and Jean M. Humez, 1st ed. (Thousand Oaks, CA: Sage Publications, 1995), 490.

61. Amy Keyishian and Sarah Malarkey, eds., *MTV's The Real World Diaries* (New York: MTV Books/Pocket Books/Melcher Media, 1996), 5.

62. Pettegrew, *Gender, Race, and Class in Media,* 489.

63. Lisa Lowe, "Imagining Los Angeles in the Production of Multiculturalism," *Mapping Multiculturalism,* eds. Avery F. Gordon and Christopher Newfield (Minneapolis: University of Minnesota Press, 1996), 415.

64. Robert Stam, "Multiculturalism and the Neoconservatives," *Dangerous Liaisons: Gender, Nation, and Postcolonial Perspectives,* eds. Anne McClintock, Aamir Mufti, and Ella Shohat (Minneapolis: University of Minneapolis Press, 1997), 188–203.

65. "Human Race," *The Real World: San Diego,* MTV, January 13, 2004.

66. "Racism is Bad," *The Real World: New Orleans,* MTV, August 1, 2000.

67. Alison Pollet, *The Real World New Orleans Unmasked* (New York: MTV Books/Pocket Books, 2000), 18.

68. *Reality TV Secrets Revealed,* VH1, January 2, 2004.

69. "Interview with … The Surreal Life Cast," *The WB Home Page,* June 10, 2004, http://www.thewb.com/Faces/Interview/0,8114,148035%7C%7C,00.html.

70. Mark Andrejevic, *Reality TV: The Work of Being Watched* (Lanham, MD: Rowman & Littlefield, 2004).

Chapter 3

Picturing Social Change: Reality TV's Family Circus

Reality TV has been wildly successful at capturing the cultural zeitgeist of the moment, seizing on hot topics in American culture and then revealing compelling scenes of real people making their way through momentous issues. The genre's special fondness for the family means that viewers are treated to spectacles of rebellious children, quarreling spouses, and falling-down houses. But underneath the sensationalism, the genre does portray substantive issues (even though it does not solve them), which speaks to the success of some reality programs, however melodramatic they are. On the family theme, the reality genre stages its own family values debate, pitting an older modern nuclear family ideal against a newer postmodern family diversity of forms.

As I will detail in this chapter, I would argue that there are four key narrative stances toward social change that occur frequently across this programming: nostalgia for the traditional modern nuclear family; promotion of a new modified nuclear family norm in which husband and wife both work outside the home; a tentative, superficial embrace of family pluralism in the context of liberal pluralism; and an open-ended questioning of norms that might include a more extensive sense of family diversity. Thus, when reality TV gazes upon the family, some programs make a rhetorical space for a new diversity of family forms. Others return to an earlier stereotype of a traditional modern nuclear family and reinforce it.

Reality TV hones in on a key social theme at a time of social change and tension about it, and it turns that attention into conflict to seize ratings and buzz. In the case of family themes, reality TV becomes a cultural site at which contemporary family politics are being negotiated. The ways in which these shows comment on their sociohistorical contexts in this regard deserves a more in-depth study here. Critics have shown how the family unit itself becoming less central to social life than, say, the household (as with cohabitating couples) as an organizing unit in today's society. Yet, as family historians have noted, even as it has become less prominent in demographic fact, what Beck and Beck-Gernshein call a "zombie category" because it is dying out but continues to walk among us, the family has become even more important ideologically, as a charged symbol in U.S. culture.[1] The large number of reality shows obsessed with the family, again, by picturing real people in their family lives, speak to this symbolic importance as well as to larger cultural anxieties about family change and the lessening influence of the family unit in general.

Family Documentary

Linking this family theme back to my previous chapter's discussion of reality TV's hybrid documentary–fiction mix and its emotional appeals, I would argue that when reality TV combines documentary and TV genres to explore family life, it meditates on several of television's recurring concerns as well as larger questions about cultural representation and its affect on identity. Reality TV rethinks television's status as a domestic medium that can realistically both portray and shape daily life. It complicates TV's usual ways of relating public and private, exceptional and typical, representation and self. The genre also opens for consideration the link between the family as a central social institution through which we structure domestic space, and TV's similar insistence on the family as its target audience and favorite topic (down to how networks organize programming schedules and "family viewing" hours). It is reasonable to expect that the formal strategies of realism for any given era reflect the prevailing ideologies of what constitutes "the real" for that period, and in this way too reality TV's formal combination proves revealing. With particular clarity, this genre presents the family unit itself as an arbiter of mass media's real, a space of reception for media images, an idealized social unit program makers, public policy architects, and audiences alike use to evaluate the cultural value and appropriateness of media representations. Many reality programs display a sophisticated awareness of how the media and the family are mutually informing institutions. We watch actual families becoming famous through interacting with TV genre conventions as their lives are turned into sitcom tropes, their members depicted as stock characters like the nurturing mom or the rebellious teen. Using the hybrid genre, again, the documentary form lets reality TV make a sociological claim to document the family as an institution, while the conventions of fictional TV genres such as the sitcom or the soap opera mobilize audiences' affective investment in and identification with the real people portrayed as characters on the screen.

The family switching subgenre offers an apt example of how reality TV seizes documentary authority to weigh in on the debates surrounding family values. In the parent swap subgenre, viewers see the inside workings of someone else's family from a visitor's point of view, as the new temporary mother or father becomes our screen surrogate. Like the visitor, audiences are encouraged to judge what they see. *Wife Swap* and *Trading Spouses* make extensive use of direct address, single-camera interviews where a parent, child, or the visitor discusses their own behaviors, habits, and beliefs about how families should be. Reality programs become pedagogical narratives in which teams of experts or the castmembers themselves evaluate domestic life, advising home viewers in family matters (often with contradictory conclusions) as they anxiously gauge new household forms. This instructional tone suggests that the home viewer can be both an expert passing judgment and a sympathetic participant observer who might measure their own life against what they see evaluated on the screen. Thus, reality series that come in and improve a family each week, like *Renovate My Family* or the nanny shows, take their place in a long line of domestic advisors, from nineteenth-century domestic science to Dr. Benjamin Spock in the 1950s to Dr. Phil today. Because we hear multiple points of view, however, these shows undercut the idea of one single model of an ideal family, even though they often try to privilege putatively more reasonable viewpoints over others through their narrative editing. When ABC's *Wife Swap* drew attention to the fact that one of their episodes "for the first time" swapped a single mother with the wife in a nuclear family, the resulting media attention for these families suggested that more family models were possible, although it simultaneously identified the single-mother household as outside of the norm.[2] That episode epitomized how many reality family programs thus both query and reestablish conventional familial norms.

Defining Family

The term family itself has highly contested, unstable definitions. Obviously a social unit that is socially constructed and based on ideologies that change across cultures and time periods, the very definition of family leads to a highly political argument. The Census Bureau defines a family as two or more people living in the same household and related by blood, marriage, or adoption. Western nations in general have had a norm of a conjugal family of husband, wife, and children living in the same household (while in contrast, other nations might emphasize extended families more, for example). However, the U.S. trends of high rates of divorce have altered kinship ties and challenged that norm. With over half of U.S. marriages ending in divorce, the country has the highest divorce rate for any developed nation, and these changing demographics have led to families shaped by cohabitation (including parents with children from previous marriages), remarriage, and stepfamilies. The Census conflation of family and household no longer holds. As historian Andrew Cherlin notes, that family–household naturalized link is breaking down with the rise of forms like complex families, which can extend across several households of stepfamilies, and with the increasing importance of what he calls created kinship (such as gay and lesbian families of choice, or stepfamily relations without blood ties).[3]

Because of the major changes to family life since the 1970s, dominant definitions of family are in question in the United States. These changes have involved the shift from a modern nuclear family unit ideal (again, the breadwinner-homemaker form that was idealized and established a norm but was never the dominant form in reality) to a postmodern diversity of forms (including blended families or stepfamilies, single-parent families, cohabitation, gay and lesbian families of choice, gay marriage and parenthood).[4] The rise of divorce (at fast rates, which doubled between 1960 and 1980) and cohabitation has led some conservative politicians and activists to argue that there is a family crisis in the United States, and that the family unit itself is in decline and under threat.[5] Yet because of the large number of rights and benefits marriage grants by the state (over 100), it retains a position of privilege in relation to other family or household forms (such as domestic partnerships, cohabitation, single-parent households, extended families, kinship networks, gay and lesbian families, and families of choice).[6] While six states and Washington, D.C., have now legalized same-sex marriage, more than half of U.S. states have passed constitutional amendments restricting marriage to the union of one man and one woman. The family values debate is reflected in family policy laws and government policies, and the sense of rapid family change is reflected in anxious family themes in the media.

TV Contexts

The links between TV and the family are foundational. Television historian Lynn Spigel has demonstrated how early TV developed coextensively with the postwar suburban middle-class families the medium made into its favored topic and target audience.[7] Historian Stephanie Coontz has noted how current nostalgia for the nuclear family ideal is filtered through 1950s domestic sitcoms like *Leave It to Beaver.*[8] As such work makes clear, family shows not only comment on society's basic organizing unit but also on demographic transformations by tracing their impact on the family. Ella Taylor traces a family crisis motif in 1970s series such as *All in the Family, The Jeffersons,* and *One Day at a Time,* noting network efforts to generate socially relevant programming in order to attract a targeted middle-class demographic as well as to respond to social changes prompted by the women's and civil rights movements.[9] Herman Gray, likewise, has detailed assimilationist messages, reflecting prevailing social trends of the time, in portraits of African American families in the 1980s, like *The Cosby Show.*[10]

I demonstrate how reality TV opens a fresh chapter in TV's long-running love affair with the family—a new genre that grapples with the postmodern family condition. Ultimately, these shows convey a kind of emotional realism regarding changes in family structures in the United States, capturing a recent shift in middle-class attitudes toward the American family, a change in what Raymond Williams would call that group's collective beliefs or "structure of feeling."[11] These programs watch middle-class average joes, perhaps the viewer's friends and neighbors, navigate the shoals of domesticity, grappling with cultural problems like the tension between kinship and chosen bonds, the impact of media on the family, and the state's efforts to define family as a matter of national concern and to determine who enjoys access to the rights and economic privileges of marriage.

The genre explores angst about what "the American family" is in the first place. Reality TV illuminates the sociocultural tensions underlying disputes about the family, such as the contested nature of the family as a U.S. institution that legitimates social identities, confers legal and property rights, and models the nation imagined as a family, whether a "house united" or a "house divided." Part of the genre's vast ratings appeal stems from the fact that it portrays real people struggling with long-running cultural problems with no easy answer: tensions in the ties that bind, between kinship and chosen bonds, tradition and change, personal versus social identity, and competing moralities. Such widespread worries are not surprising, given that this unit has historically encoded gendered roles and hierarchies of class, race, and sexuality that define ideas of social acceptance, a crucible for selfhood and nationhood. Critics have shown the regulatory nature of the modern nuclear family model, with official discourse traditionally framing that unit as a white, middle-class, heterosexual norm citizens should aspire to approximate.[12]

Different reality programs do not explicitly solve those family values disputes. Instead, many concentrate on mining the conflict between the older modern nuclear family norm and the newer postmodern family diversity. Rather than answering what the postmodern family will become, the reality genre, taken as a whole, rehearses sundry arguments about how the familial unit is getting exposed, built up, torn down, and redefined. Some programs offer wish fulfillment fantasies, smoothing over rancorous public squabbles and social changes but not resolving those tensions.

Reflecting this panoply, for example, Bravo's *Things I Hate About You* turns domesticity into a sport, where snarky judges determine which member of a couple is more annoying to live with and partners happily air their dirty laundry on TV (sometimes literally). One week we see an unmarried heterosexual couple with no children, the next a gay domestic partnership. No one model dominates. The series fits all of these groupings into the same narrative framework: a story about family and the daily irritations of domesticity. Other reality programs chart a fading modern nuclear family ideal. The dating show subgenre continues to spawn a vast number of formats and high audience ratings. While series like *The Bachelor* romanticize young people trying to find a mate, marry, have children, and embody the traditional family ideals of their parents' generation, they also implicitly register the shifting of those norms, not least because the castmembers also see the overwhelming majority of these arranged TV couplings and engagements dissolve, just as over 50 percent of marriages in the United States end in divorce.[13]

The TV network context is also relevant here. Different reality shows and networks market their family values debates differently, with the network target demographic playing a role, sometimes taking on the tenor of a red-state–blue-state fight. One tendency is for reality shows to embrace the dual-career couple as a new norm but still contextualize it in terms of traditional modern nuclear family ideals—a way of engaging with the new social changes and trends but making them more palatable, less potentially threatening to viewers who might be anxious about these social changes and how they have impacted people's sense of their world. This kind of portrayal might critique how the woman is doing more domestic labor than the man, for example, but the show frames it as a personal problem rather than a structural critique (it becomes a problem of having the individual husband choose to pitch in more).

Similarly, some shows might portray tensions between career moms and stay-at-home moms as personal choices, when in fact those depictions have a relationship to a broader context: what Susan Douglas and Meredith Michaels term the "Mommy Wars," a media-generated war between working mothers and stay-at-home mothers that is part of a backlash against feminist advances in women's rights.[14] Douglas and Michaels critique what they call the "new momism," which tries to make both working mothers and stay-at-home mothers subsume themselves to the anxious care of their children and feel guilty that they cannot achieve a supermom ideal. They date this idealized version of motherhood to a postfeminist backlash since the 1970s, identifying it as an upper-middle class white, corporate model in which women choose to stay home and be the perfect mom, or if they do work, to pull a second shift at home and have to be perfect at all things (competitive at work, the ultimate nurturer at home). It involves mommy wars, or demonizing so-called bad mothers, usually welfare moms or working moms, who fail to uphold the "intensive mothering" ideal, a stereotype that ignores larger structural social problems. It is postfeminist in the sense that it claims women won the right to be in the workforce but decided they prefer the kitchen. Motherhood becomes a privatized, individualized responsibility to perfection. Part of the new momism is to want and expect equality with men but not to expect men to do equal domestic labor, in part because women decide they do it better and faster. As I will detail in Chapter 5, many family reality shows fit this model.

The broadcast network shows have tended in particular toward a safe but slightly edgy dynamic in their appeal to a mass audience. They market the topicality of what their shows are portraying, banking on their discussion of taboos, but they carefully couch the incendiary themes in terms of familiar, traditionally normative tropes. Hence, they both explore anxieties about changing family life in America and yet buffer those anxieties.

Meanwhile, reality shows on cable networks that target a specific demographic have tended to be less middle-of-the-road in their portrayals, with, for example, a conservative show like *World's Strictest Parents* (2009–) (authoritarian traditionalist family values) targeting a more conservative demographic of country music fans on CMT. In contrast, a more progressive show like Bravo's *Things I Hate About You* presents gay and lesbian couples alongside straight couples. Bravo thus appeals to their affluent, liberal, urban-minded target demographic. Similarly, LOGO's *The A-List* (2010–) depicts an interracial gay male married couple who are having a child together using a surrogate, appealing to their target demographic.

Overall, the different reality family shows profit from family values anxieties. Moreover, these reality series themselves often become part of the debate (as in the press debates over whether MTV's *Teen Mom* franchise glorifies teen pregnancy and causes more of it, even though teen pregnancy rates are down). Their themes of family change both grow out of and participate in the family values debates particular to this era (gay marriage, single moms, teen pregnancy), as can be seen in some of the specific trends I analyze below.

Trends in Reality TV's Textual Representations of the Family

In picturing the hot topic of family themes, what is striking about reality family TV is how directly it speaks to prevailing trends and beliefs concerning the changing American family, as a discussion of how recurring tropes manifest themselves across the genre will serve to illustrate. The way reality serials address familial life illuminates an uneasy shift from modern nuclear family ideals to the postmodern reality of diverse practices. As the genre explores the modern and postmodern family in various ways, it often explicitly engages with public policy and media discussions. Drawing on the sociopolitical and media history of the family values debates, reality TV offers viewers the voyeuristic chance to peer into other people's households to see how all this cultural ruckus is affecting actual families.

One main trend in reality programming is for series to look backward with a recuperative nostalgia for the modern nuclear family, revealing the instability of that model. Some series revert to older concepts like sociologist Talcott Parsons's mid-twentieth-century theories of functional and dysfunctional family forms. He argued that the modern nuclear family's function under industrialized capitalism was to reproduce and socialize children into dominant moral codes, as well as to norm sexual behavior and ideas of affective bonds associated with companionate marriage. He argued for functionalism as a sociological theory that determines the functions of social structures and organization. His research in the 1950s implied that the breadwinner-homemaker family idealized in that period was the most desirable form or functional form because it was well-organized to fulfill social tasks. For Parsons, the family group worked best with the husband as instrumental leader (who organized the unit to achieve tasks) and the wife as expressive or socioemotional leader (who provided necessary emotional support to all other family members). With those gendered roles, this family model, in Parson's view, fulfilled the social roles of raising children and providing labor successfully.[15] The desperate housewives trend of the 1950s, the women that historian Elaine Tyler May notes were turning to alcohol out of frustration with their home-bound and dependent roles, might beg to differ with Parsons.[16] Dysfunctional families that deviated from norms were functionalism's defining "Other," and some critics argue that this paradigm still problematically influences sociological research on family life.[17]

Pop psychology concepts of functionalism and dysfunctionalism certainly circulate widely in current mass media, and they are clearly present on reality shows. A particularly apt example is the spouse swapping subgenre, with shows like ABC's *Wife Swap.* The show documents strangers who switch households and parenting duties for a short period. Similarly, on Fox's *Trading Spouses: Meet Your New Mommy,* two parents each occupy the other's home for several days. Both series focus on the conflict between households, revealing a fierce debate among participants as to whose family is healthier, more normal, or more functional.

On *Trading Spouses,* one two-part episode swaps mothers from white suburban nuclear families, each comprised of a husband, wife, two kids, and a dog.[18] Both clans want to claim modern nuclear family functionality for themselves, but economic tensions ensue, even though each woman describes her family as middle class. A California mom with the opulent beach house judges her Massachusetts hosts with their modest home and verbal fisticuffs as unkempt, while her outspoken counterpart deems the beach household materialistic and emotionally disconnected. Both women characterize the other family as dysfunctional. Their conflict reveals not only the degree to which many people still use these older ideals as their own measuring stick, here staged as issues like tidiness or appropriate levels of emotional closeness, but also the tenuousness of those ideals, given the intense contradictions between two supposedly functional families.

Through the premise of swapping households or roles for several days, these programs explore Otherness by having participants step into someone else's performance of kinship behaviors. In so doing, they illuminate identity categories as performed through the family, perhaps most notably on the FX series *Black.White.*, which used makeup to switch a white and black family for several weeks and staged racial tensions between them. In this subgenre more generally, participants reproduce a version of their counterpart's social identity. Thus the switch highlights the arbitrariness of such identity performances. Since the shows allow the participants to judge each other (rather than turning to expert judges), family appears as a topic of open-ended debate.

These programs depend on conflict generated by social hierarchies of race, class, gender, and sexuality, and they privilege white male heteronormativity, in which they present households headed by straight white men as the norm. Their narratives often focus on gender, encouraging men to take on more childcare and domestic chores. Yet they still rely on ideologies of gender difference to explain household units and to reaffirm the mother's role as nurturer-caregiver. By absenting the mother, the wife swap series imply that husbands and kids will learn to appreciate the woman of the house more.

These series also encourage a liberal pluralist resolution to conflicts, one which upholds an easy humanist consensus or corporate multiculturalism. The framing narratives resolve competing ideas, most often by norming a modified modern nuclear family (two working parents). In shows about alternative households, for example, the narratives sympathize with the single mother or the gay couple but uphold the intact nuclear family as more rational and functional. Yet at the same time, the narratives also often critique overly intense nostalgia for the old modern nuclear ideal in participants and they sometimes allow for some validation of alternative models, such as an African American extended family.

This open warfare over functional and dysfunctional families includes a huge helping of nostalgia, as epitomized by a series like MTV's *The Osbournes*. This hit show supports the sense that if the modern nuclear ideal has been replaced by a diversity of family forms, U.S. culture still has an intense nostalgia for the older norm. Is nostalgia for the fantasy nuclear unit actually a defining characteristic of the postmodern family? It is for *The Osbournes*. Viewers flocked to the show because it juxtaposes a famously hard-living heavy metal family with classic sitcom family plotlines, edited to emphasize the irony of seeing the cursing, drug-abusing rock star Ozzy and his brood hilariously butchering *Ozzie and Harriet*–style narratives.

The entertainment press dubbed them "America's favorite family," and a series of high-profile magazine cover stories tried to explain the show's wild popularity by pointing to how the Osbournes "put the fun in dys-

functional." The show garnered MTV's highest-rated debut at that time
and enjoyed some of the strongest ratings in the channel's history during
its airing.[19] Part of the appeal lies in how the Osbournes seem to capture
on video tape a more accurate sense of the pressures of current family life,
ranging from sibling rivalry to teen sex and drug use to a serious illness
(such as matriarch Sharon's cancer diagnosis and treatment). Although
their fame and fortune make them unlike home viewers, the family is relatable for target young (aged 18–34) viewers because of the struggles they
confront openly. Likewise, they reflect current family diversity because
they are a blended family; their brood includes their son and two daughters (one of whom declined to appear on the series), Ozzy's son from his
first marriage, and their children's teen friend whom they adopted during
the show after his mother died of cancer. Ozzy himself suggested that he
did the series in order to expand understandings of the family: "What is
a functional family? I know I'm dysfunctional by a long shot, but what
guidelines do we all have to go by? *The Waltons*?"[20] Ozzy here is both arbiter and agent; he notes TV's power to define a range of meanings for the
family, whether through the Waltons or the Osbournes.

Yet even while the program's narrative meditates on entertaining dysfunctionality and new family realities, it also continuously tries to recuperate the Osbournes as a functional nuclear family. Story arcs are edited to
frame them as dysfunctional (cursing parents, wild fights, teenage drug
use), but also rescue them as functional, with sentimental shots of the family gathered together in their kitchen or clips of them expressing their love
and loyalty despite the titillating fights. Even though Ozzy tells his family
they are "all f***-ing mad," in the same breath, he says he "loves them more
than life itself."[21] The edited narrative purposefully emphasizes the bonds
of hearth and home, sometimes trying to establish functionality by cutting
out serious family events that would have made Parsons blanch: Ozzy's
drug relapse, severe mental illness, and nervous breakdown during taping;
son Jack and daughter Kelly's trips to drug rehab; and Sharon's temporary
separation from Ozzy over these issues.

Press coverage of the show and fan response likewise emphasized a recuperative dynamic, looking for the loveable, reassuring nuclear family beneath the rough exterior. As an *Entertainment Weekly* cover story noted,
Ozzy Osbourne went from being boycotted by parents' groups in the 1980s
for bat-biting and supposedly Satanic lyrics to being asked for parenting
advice from men's magazines.[22] Thus, even while registering the limitations of Parsons' model, the series still tries to rehabilitate this celebrity

family as functional. As a result, this program and others like it explore the postmodern family, but at the same time they look back wistfully on the old modern nuclear paradigm.

The Osbournes is also a prime example of a program that explicitly comments on the impact of television on family ideals. Part of the show's insight comes from registering how much the media, whether the popular music industry or television, has shaped this family unit. Brian Graden, then president of MTV Entertainment, described the program's draw as "the juxtaposition of the fantastical rock-star life with the ordinary and the everyday"; summarizing one episode, he laughed, "Am I really seeing Ozzy Osbourne trying to turn on the vacuum cleaner?" Graden noted that after they collected footage on the Osbournes, producers realized "that a lot of these story lines mirrored classic domestic sitcom story lines, yet with a twist of outrageousness that you wouldn't believe."[23]

Watching footage of their daily experiences, Graden immediately views them through the lens of earlier TV sitcoms; everywhere he looks, he sees the Cleavers on speed. Likewise, the program Graden's company makes of this family's life might one day comprise the plotlines other viewers use to interpret their own experiences in some way. After their highly successful and much-publicized first season, the Osbournes were feted at the White House Correspondents' dinner and managed to parlay such national attention into more entertainment career opportunities, with a new MTV show, *Battle for Ozzfest* (2004), hosted by Sharon and Ozzy, featuring bands competing to join their summer tour, Sharon's own syndicated talk show (2003–2004) and later stints on *America's Got Talent* and *The Talk,* Kelly's role on *Dancing With the Stars,* and the children's numerous television, film, and music ventures growing out of their exposure from the reality program.

While most families could not follow the Osbournes into celebrity, what many do share with the rockers is the knowledge that TV significantly shapes familial ideals. This media awareness marks a parenting trend. In their recent audience study of family television viewing practices, Stewart M. Hoover, Lynn Schofield Clark, and Diane F. Alters found that parents had a highly self-reflexive attitude toward the media. They were well conscious of how the mass media both reflects and shapes social beliefs, and expressed worry at the daily influence of television in their children's lives. Hoover et al. identified this media anxiety as part of what they term "self-reflexive parenting" behaviors stemming from increased concerns about childrearing since the 1960s. They see this model of parenting as part of what Anthony Giddens calls the project of self-reflexivity in modernity, in which people have to perform the task of developing personal identity, making identity choices based on their reflections about their interaction with the social world as they continually incorporate mediated experiences into their sense of self.[24]

Meanwhile, other programs amplify the friction between older and newer family models. The two most prominent parenting shows, *Nanny 911* and *Supernanny,* portray a severe tension between modern nuclear ideals and postmodern variations. They suggest that threats from within and outside the American family are destabilizing it to the extent that it must be saved by the no-nonsense childrearing philosophies of its colonial parent, dispatched in the form of a Mary Poppins–style nanny. They implicitly recur to nineteenth-century domestic science ideals as well as mid-twentieth-century sociological theories such as Parsons's schema of functionalism and dysfunctionalism.

As a case study, these shows clarify how anxiety about expertise and professionalism contributes to consumer behavior (hire a nanny to fix your unruly children, buy the series' tie-in books as magic talismans). They relate to other programs, such as The Learning Channel's suite of shows about parenting and childbirth (such as *A Baby Story* and *A Wedding Story*), all of which, as Rebecca Stephens notes, resort to expert advice and affirm conventional modern nuclear family forms.[25] They demonstrate how reality programming can be framed as a pedagogical narrative. Again, as Annette Hill has found, many viewers see reality TV as an opportunity for social learning.[26] As Ron Becker argues, these nanny programs also display neoliberal rhetoric because they focus on the need for the family to be autonomous to help legitimate the shift to post-welfare-state governance in contemporary America.[27]

By way of contrast, there is a more marginal satire of parenting found in Bravo's suite of shows, *Showbiz Moms and Dads* (2004), *Sportskids Moms and Dads* (2005–2006), and *Showdog Moms and Dads* (2005). These programs follow parents whom the edited narratives present as overly protective or controlling. They spend too much on consumer goods, live their dreams vicariously through their kids, suffer from intractable generational tensions, and sometimes treat their pets like children to a rather extreme extent. The shows denaturalize parenting behaviors and elucidate them as performative roles, and such an ironic treatment also dovetails with a marketing imperative, because it fits into Bravo's marketing to the channel's target audiences of highly educated viewers seeking "quality television."

Encapsulating a different element of domestic science rhetoric, home makeover shows establish an ideological tie between a rationalized home and a healthy family, a connection that reveals further blurring of the traditional public–private split. In the long-running blockbuster, ABC's *Extreme Makeover: Home Edition* and its short-lived imitator, Fox's *Renovate My Family*, teams of experts evaluate family life, advising participants and home viewers alike in family values as they anxiously gauge new household forms. On both series, it is families that depart from the modern nuclear norm that need assistance (whether single-parent, blended, impoverished, or orphaned households).

Instead of advocating government aid in the form of low-income housing or social welfare safety nets, these series perform a kind of neoliberal privatization and outsourcing, which speaks to a diminishing public sphere. Through the largesse of their corporate advertisers, these programs will provide needy families with domestic palaces and consumer goods that will supposedly effortlessly heal any family troubles. In the case of *Renovate My Family*, the program uses pop psychology to counsel families on problems as various as alcoholism, threats of divorce, or withdrawn children. It is no surprise that the host is Jay McGraw, son of famous TV life coach Dr. Phil McGraw, tough love guru, because the show becomes part of McGraw's branding of his own therapeutic television empire. In this reality format, as critics have shown, the moment of revealing the new home is supposed to spark emotional realism in the family, the weeping moments of purported authenticity that viewers seek. As I will discuss in my next chapter, neoliberalism reaches new heights in *Extreme Makeover* when former First Lady Laura Bush appeared on one episode to laud their work, and a series of other episodes sent the design team to hurricane-ravaged Gulf Coast areas to "help out" where the government had not.

Another main trend in reality TV is a push forward to an uncertain present and future, an exploration of emergent models of the postmodern family, following single-parent and patchwork households as they try to negotiate interpersonal relationships and constant redefinitions of the family. A program like Bravo's *Showbiz Moms and Dads* follows several single moms (along with other nontraditional family types) as they pursue the dream of fame and celebrity for their children, somewhat enacted for these families by being on the series.

As part of a similar critique of older family ideals, some programs simply meditate on threats to the continued survival of the nuclear family, tapping into fears for the sake of ratings. These programs imagine the threat to the nuclear ideal in terms of divorce (programs pairing divorcees for another tilt at the marriage wheel, such as *Who Wants to Marry My Dad?*, and *Who Wants to Marry My Mom?*), infidelity (*Temptation Island, The Ultimate Love Test*), lack of commitment (*Paradise Hotel, Forever Eden, Love Cruise*), the lure of money over romantic entanglement or family bonds (*For Love or Money, Joe Millionaire, Mr. Personality, The Family*), or the pressures of fame (*Newlyweds: Nick and Jessica, 'Til Death Do Us Part: Carmen and Dave, Meet the Barkers, Diary Presents Brandy: Special Delivery*).

Some programs turn the instability of the nuclear family into sensationalized plot twists. One season of *Big Brother* included the surprise ploy of having a half-brother and half-sister as contestants in the house together; the two did not know of each other's existence, since the sister grew up with their father and the brother had never met him. Producers, upon realizing their connection when both applied to the show, put them in the house together, then used the new-found blood bond to generate high drama in the Machiavellian competition game, as the two discovered they were siblings. Fox turned the search for one's birth parent into reality fodder with *Who's Your Daddy?*, which had an adopted daughter attempt to pick out her biological father from a group of men. That program incited protests from adoption groups for trivializing the process, while in CBS's *The Will* (2004) cutthroat relatives competed for a patriarch's inheritance, which also sparked protests for insensitivity and was cancelled after one episode.[28]

Addressing the long history of family forms, several key reality programs historicize the development of familial ideals and their inequities. Historical experience programs till this ground. Linking family history to a broader framework of U.S. history, this subgenre sends participants back in time to reenact earlier lifestyles and pinpoints the exclusionary nature of white patriarchal family models and the social institutions founded on them.

On PBS's House series, for example, many of the female, African American, or gay and lesbian participants become frustrated with the historical roles they must fit into on *Colonial House* (2004) or the Victorian-era *Frontier House* (2002) (as they materially register in some way what it would have been like to be disenfranchised women, enslaved blacks, or sexual dissidents facing a penalty of death). As they explore a different epoch and its material conditions, these series often examine how the family unit came to be seen as the fundamental unit of social organization, an instrument for colonization and imperialism, or a model for the modern nation-state (witness CBC's *Pioneer Quest* in Canada as well BBC/PBS House programs set in England: *Manor House, 1900 House* and *The 1940s House*).

Cultural Histories and Family Values Media Debates

I have been arguing that the family values debate is an important cultural context for this new blockbuster TV format. Why reality TV and why the family? Let me delve further into how the genre's family tropes fit into this specific sociopolitical and media history. It is worthwhile to elaborate on relevant cultural and sociohistorical frameworks for reality TV in terms of the family values debates because it helps clarify how family reality TV comprises a new chapter in television's history as a domestic medium that has always focused on the family.

Popular culture has long been a battleground for arguments about familial forms. Pundits, politicians, media critics, and psychologists alike have insisted that television helps define the modern family and contributes to that social unit's evolution or decline, depending on one's point of view. Indeed, from Focus on the Family–led campaigns against televised sex and violence to their ACLU sparring partners' cries against censorship, arguments about television continue to hinge on what it does to and for the family. High-profile examples include then-President George H. W. Bush's diatribe against cartoon character Bart Simpson for supposedly encouraging juvenile delinquency (1992), and Jerry Falwell's much-derided outing of Teletubby Tinky Winky as contributing to the moral decay of children by supposedly promoting a homosexual lifestyle (1999; animated character SpongeBob SquarePants was the topic of similar controversy in 2005). An FCC investigation after Janet Jackson's "wardrobe malfunction" nudity incident disrupted the 2004 Super Bowl halftime show during family viewing hours resulted in the FCC threatening CBS with hefty fines. These kinds of media events are examples of what John Fiske has termed media spectacles, hyperreal moments in which the difference between representation and reality has been collapsed. For Fiske, such moments reflect social changes but also shape and produce them.[29]

To unpack further the values rhetoric from the early 1990s to the present, let me return to the two bookends I mentioned earlier: Dan Quayle then and gay marriage now. Quayle's infamous attack was based on the idea that Murphy Brown could contribute to a crisis in family values by portraying single motherhood in anything other than negative terms (and former presidential candidate Mike Huckabee made a similar comment about celebrity Natalie Portman in 2011). Stacey notes that while many then laughed at Quayle's potato/potatoe inability to distinguish between fantasy characters and reality, he managed to parlay his assault on television

content into a groundswell of political support from family values advo-
cacy groups, adding fuel to a fundamentalist effort to recuperate a nostalgic model of the 1950s nuclear family ideal. Coontz, in fact, compares the
1990s idealization of the nuclear family with a similar trend a century ago.
She argues that conspicuous consumption in what she calls both a first
and a second Gilded Age (the mid-1870s to early 1890s, and then the mid-
1970s to the early 1990s) of unbridled greed led to a romanticization of the
nuclear family, which in both cases was used to justify economic inequity
and to repudiate preceding eras of social reform.[30]

Demographic trends during our current period also mark significant
changes in family patterns, and these alterations have spurred charges that
the media prompts so-called bad families and dysfunctionality. The crisis
rhetoric reality TV picks up on is in part a response to the postmodern
family. The U.S. Census in 2000 and 2010 registered significant alterations in family life since 1970: the number of married couples with children dropped almost by half (from 40 percent of all households in 1970 to
24 percent in 2000 to 20 percent in 2010); single-parent households more
than doubled (single-mother families grew to 26 percent in 2000, up from
12 percent in 1970, and single-father families grew to 5 percent in 2000
from 1 percent in 1970); the number of unmarried couples cohabitating
grew (3.7 percent of all households in 2000); the median age at first marriage increased (from 20.8 years in 1970 to 25.1 in 2000 for women, from
23.2 to 26.8 years for men). Births to unmarried women increased; and
household and family size declined (the average number of people per
household was 3.14 in 1970 and 2.62 in 2000). Divorce rates have risen since
the 1970s, leveling off in the 1990s, and the proportion of never married and
divorced men and women has nearly doubled since 1970 (48 percent in 2000
versus 28 percent in 1970). The percentage of both women and men who
were currently married in 2000 was down from 1970 (in 2000, for women,
52 percent versus 60 percent earlier). Nonfamily households have also
grown more common over the last 30 years (by 2000, family households
made up 69 percent of all households, down from 81 percent in 1970; in
2010, that number was 66 percent).[31]

Shorter coined the term "postmodern family" in 1975, using it to refer
to three momentous changes in Western families: higher divorce and instability in marriages, more women leaving the home, and greater peer
(versus parental) influence on children. More recently, Stacey has defined
the term as the rejection of any one norm or ideal of family, instead accept-
ing family forms as being in a constant state of diversity and redefinition.[32]

Cultural theorist Dana Heller traces a similar dynamic when she argues that family is no longer a symbol of cultural unity but rather a narrative of perpetual cultural redescription.[33]

Meanwhile, the recent gay dating shows illuminate how reality TV engages with family debates in particular sociohistorical contexts. Reality programs take the fact that the gay marriage debate has been highly politicized and use that to generate viewer interest in the issue. For example, Bravo's gay dating show, *Boy Meets Boy* (2003), aired at the same time as increasing public debates over gay marriage were underway. In 2003 and 2004, a push to legalize same-sex marriage had some initial success at the state level but was met with resistance in the form of a proposed federal Constitutional Amendment defining marriage as heterosexual and by 11 states passing a ban on same-sex marriage in the elections of November 2004. The proposed federal amendment, unlikely ever to pass, would write a ban on same-sex marriage into the Constitution. It would build on but significantly extend the 1996 Defense of Marriage Act, which denied federal and state-to-state recognition of same-sex unions but did not amend the Constitution. Arguing in support of the amendment, then-President George W. Bush insisted: "The union of a man and woman in marriage is the most enduring and important human institution."[34] He went on to link the family to the nation when arguing for the historic importance of the issue: "An amendment to the Constitution is never to be undertaken lightly. The amendment process has addressed many serious matters of national concern. And the preservation of marriage rises to this level of national importance."[35] Public opinion polling on the issue indicates that a majority of Americans do not favor legalizing gay marriage but they also do not favor the idea of writing a ban into the federal Constitution.[36]

Stances like Quayle's and Bush's speak to the politicization of the family. The state has a stake in this process because through the family, the state confers legal, economic, and property rights. The family has been the social unit seen as undergirding the nation, replete with all the corrosive social hierarchies long haunting U.S. democracy, with laws deciding who could marry and who could not (the could-nots historically being interracial and same-sex couples). Coontz has proven that the family has been seen as the moral guide for the nation ever since the late nineteenth century, from Theodore Roosevelt's insistence that the nation's future rested on the "right kind of home life," to Ronald Reagan's assertion that "strong families are the foundation of society."[37] As media studies critic Laura Kipnis notes in her witty polemic against modern coupledom, alternative models of organization trouble the social contract, so it is no mistake that "the citizenship-as-marriage analogy has been a recurring theme in liberal-democratic political theory for the last couple of hundred years or so, from Rousseau on."[38]

The highly politicized family values debates, beginning in the 1970s with the women's liberation movement's gains (including more women working outside of the home and a spike in divorce rates), have intensified since the 1980s and Ronald Reagan's insistence on his definition of family (the modern nuclear family version) as being the cornerstone of a strong nation. Reagan argued for the family's centrality to the nation even while he stigmatized welfare mothers, cut funding for family support services, deregulated and placed an emphasis on neoliberal privatization rather than public support for families as the social unit supposedly so important to a strong nation. Likewise, the 1996 welfare reform law encourages marriage. Congress passed a welfare bill in 2006 that put $150 million annually into marriage promotion efforts (in an effort to increase marriage rates), for research and projects that promote "healthy marriage and responsible fatherhood" (ranging from high school educational programs to ad campaigns). The links between family and nation go back to political ideology informing the early Republican period in the United States, when the founders were influenced by French philosopher Montesquieu's argument that marriage was key to a successful republic.[39]

The most recent iteration of family values debates began in the 1990s and pit a marriage movement of traditionalists against feminist and liberal activists. Feminist critics have argued that the family as an institution is based on gender inequity as well as discrimination against same-sex couples and, historically, interracial couples (the Supreme Court struck down antimiscegenation laws only in 1967 with the case of *Loving v. Virginia,* but antimiscegenation laws remained on the books in some states until the 1980s). As such, some feminists have argued that society should abandon that social institution and instead focus on units such as the household, which might have a better chance of dividing up labor equitably and allowing for the vast diversity of kinship relations and families of choice that exist demographically in America but that are often marginalized and erased by dominant definitions of family.

Concerning the gender discrimination that has occurred in the patriarchal institution of marriage and the family, feminists point to the breadwinner-homemaker family model (the 1950s modern nuclear family unit) as an example of inequitable relations in which women are structurally made to be economically dependent on men. Because they are not paid for their household labor (witness Gloria Steinem's call for paying for homemaker's domestic labor in the 1970s), the female homemaker in this model is also exploited by a capitalist system that can profit from paying a lower family wage to the husband (since he does not have to pay for the domestic labor his wife performs for no wage) and can benefit from how the woman socially reproduces the husband and children and provides the man the emotional support necessary to continuing laboring in the workplace.[40] If the modern nuclear family arose precisely because it served the labor needs of that era of capitalism, a feminist addendum to that argument would be that it served the interests of patriarchy. Even with more women working outside of the home beginning in the 1970s, because of the wage gap between men and women (women currently earn 80 cents to the man's dollar for the same job, and median weekly earnings of women full-time workers were 80 percent of men's earnings as of 2004) patriarchal capitalism still benefits from gender inequity because employers can hire women more cheaply, gender work divisions lessen workers organizing to protect their rights, and unpaid housework lets families subsist on smaller wages for men too.[41]

Similar debates have occurred concerning the definition and status of marriage. Sociologist Judith Stacey has argued, for example, that rather than trying to get under a "bigger tent" of what counts as marriage, family diversity would be better served by recognizing and granting rights to a range of kinship relation arrangements, including domestic partnerships and marriage. Likewise, during the gay marriage debates, which heated up in the 2000s, some gay activists argued that rather than struggling to be granted the rights of marriage as an institution, they would do better to critique the institution because it is structurally discriminatory.

Since family opens such a space of performed social identity, often articulated through narrative, it is not surprising that television has always been one of the key battlegrounds for familial ideas. In her study of how 1970s television responded to the perceived cultural crises of the time, Taylor argues that TV families of the 1950s and 1960s were largely portrayed as harmonious, the building blocks of society and a consensus culture (*Ozzie and Harriet, Leave It to Beaver*), while 1970s families appeared under siege and in crisis due to significant changes like a spike in divorce rates during that decade (*All in the Family, One Day at a Time*). For Taylor, the 1980s TV witnessed a variety of family forms but was dominated by a retreat to nostalgic intact nuclear families (*The Cosby Show, Family Ties*).[42] As other critics have since noted, the 1990s TV families both continued in the 1980s vein (*Home Improvement, Seventh Heaven*) but also satirized family ideals through dysfunctional family sitcoms (*The Simpsons, Married With*

Children). Meanwhile, popular fictional shows in the early 2000s seem more explicitly to debate the variety of family forms emerging with recent demographic trends. Witness ABC's hugely popular nighttime soap, *Desperate Housewives* (2004–2012), which garnered a high of over 20 million viewers and top ratings depicting women struggling with their roles in a range of settings, including intact nuclear families, postdivorce families, single-parent households, and childless families.[43] In terms of audience reception of these TV images over time, a series of pioneering family television studies since the 1970s have shown how families use television in diverse ways to help shape selfhood.[44]

Reality TV itself has always been a remarkably familial genre, though the earlier examples of unscripted programming that display a similar obsession with the family do so in a different sociohistorical context. As Jeffrey Ruoff notes, *An American Family* is still the most widely circulated direct cinema documentary in U.S. history.[45] It aired just as large-scale social movements like women's liberation, civil rights, and gay rights were generating upheavals, and it put social changes like the soaring divorce rates into focus by charting an individual family's response to its time period. Earlier formal precursors also include the long-running madcap Chuck Barris game shows such as *The Newlywed Game* (first aired in 1966) and *The Dating Game* (premiered in 1965), which turned aspects of marriage and dating into farce.[46]

The large number of family reality shows include several recognizable subgenres: family switching shows (*Trading Spouses, Wife Swap, Celebrity Wife Swap, Black.White, Meet Mister Mom*); observations of family life (*The Real Housewives of Orange County; Little People, Big World*); celebrity family series (*The Osbournes, Run's House, Meet the Barkers, Being Bobby Brown, Breaking Bonaduce, Hogan Knows Best, Gene Simmons Family Jewels*); home and family makeover programs (*Extreme Makeover: Home Edition, Renovate My Family*); family workplace series (*Dog the Bounty Hunter, Family Plots, Family Business*); family gamedocs (*Things I Hate About You, Race to the Altar, Married by America, The Will, The Family*); parenting series (*Nanny 911, Supernanny, America's Supernanny, Showbiz Moms and Dads*); and historical reenactment programs with family settings (*Colonial House, Frontier House*).

Not surprisingly, recent public arguments about family and marriage often turn reality TV into prime fodder. Conservative groups frequently protest reality fare. Most spectacularly, complaints made by conservative activists from the Parents Television Council prompted the FCC to threaten

Fox with a fine of $1.2 million, the largest to date, for *Married by America* when it was on the air. The show had audiences pick mates for couples who could have gotten married on air (though none did and all the arranged couples stopped dating after the show). The protestors found it a vulgar trivialization of the institution of marriage and objected to randy bachelor and bachelorette parties.[47]

On the other side of the debate, progressive thinkers have used reality TV to make public arguments advocating a greater diversity of marriage and household arrangements. Cultural theorist Lisa Duggan, in a *Nation* article, explores public policy about state-sanctioned marriage in the context of the debates over gay marriage, critiquing, for example, "marriage promotion" by both the Clinton and the Bush administrations as a way to privatize social welfare. Duggan calls for a diversification of democratically accessible forms of state recognition for households and partnerships, a "flexible menu of choices" that would dethrone the privileged civic status of sanctified marriage and "threaten the normative status of the nuclear family, undermining state endorsement of heterosexual privilege, the male 'headed' household and 'family values' moralism as social welfare policy."[48] She uses reality TV as an example of current dissatisfaction with gendered traditional marriage and a marker of its decline, noting "the competitive gold-digging sucker punch on TV's *Joe Millionaire*" (which tricked eager women into believing they were competing to marry a millionaire) as an entertainment culture indicator of the statistical flux in marriage and kinship arrangements. She argues that the franchise confirms social anxiety that "marriage is less stable and central to the organization of American life than ever."[49]

Ultimately, regardless of the different ways the genre enters into existing political discussions, what is striking is that it continually becomes a site for family values debates. A case in point is how a couple competing on the sixth season of CBS's global scavenger hunt gamedoc, *The Amazing Race*, made headlines because critics accused the husband of exhibiting abusive behavior toward the wife in the series footage. The couple, entrepreneurs Jonathan Baker and Victoria Fuller, made the rounds of talk shows to protest that characterization but the main dynamic of press coverage has been to turn them into a teaching moment. Both went on the entertainment TV newsmagazine *The Insider* and were asked to watch footage of them fighting and respond to the charge that it looks abusive; Baker responds: "I'm a better person than that. I have to say I had a temper tantrum, you know, I pushed her, I never should have, and you know, I regret every moment of it and you know what, hopefully that experience will make me a better person. That's our story line, you know, that's who we were on television. That's not who we are in real life."[50]

Such a framing of that reality TV footage is emblematic: the show is perceived as somewhat mediated and constructed but still real enough to warrant a press debate. Through a bit of internal network marketing, Dr. Phil made them the topic of one of his CBS prime-time specials on relationships. Noting that the reality show sparked reams of hate mail and even death threats toward the couple, Dr. Phil explicitly argues that America was watching the couple and wanted to debate them in TV's public sphere. At the outset of the interview, he invokes and calls into being an imagined national public, saying "America was outraged and appalled by what they've seen," and after he exhorts the husband to correct his behavior, he concludes by saying, "So America doesn't need to worry about you?"[51]

Dr. Phil does not completely accept Baker's argument that he was only acting aggressively for the camera or that the editing heightened his behavior, and he admonishes the man for exhibiting bad behavior in any context, mediated or not. Dr. Phil is well aware of the construction of images that he himself perpetuates, and even draws attention to how Baker tries to manipulate this on-camera interview by coaching his wife, yet he insists on a substantial component of actuality in all of these depictions. In the press and popular response, the gamedoc couple (who later divorced) becomes a paradigmatic reality TV family example that can be used to analyze the state of the American family more generally.

Ultimately, reality programs add a new wrinkle to television's family ideas. The genre illuminates how the current definition of the family is up for grabs, and reality TV enters the debate arena in force. Instead of having nostalgia for the Cleavers as a model of the modern American family, viewers might one day have nostalgia for the Osbournes as a model of the postmodern American family. The amplified truth claims of reality TV comment on the social role of television itself as an electronic medium offering "public scripts" that, as the medium evolves, viewers increasingly want to interact with on the screen and participate in themselves. My next chapter will consider more fully the cultural politics of programs that link rhetorics of the family to neoliberalism.

Notes

1. U. Beck and E. Beck-Gernsheim, *Individualization: Institutionalized Individualism and Its Social and Political Consequences* (London: Sage Publications, 2002).

2. "Parsons/Bramhall," *Wife Swap*, ABC, January 12, 2005.

3. Andrew J. Cherlin, *Public and Private Families* (New York: McGraw-Hill, 2008), 461.

4. Historians now question how far back to date the nuclear family. Many assert the need to nuance the long-held theory of a total family revolution from premodern to modern families between the 1780s and 1840s due to industrialization. Coontz argues the conventional idea that industrialization ushered out the extended family does not hold true when one considers that the highest numbers of extended families occurred in the mid-nineteenth century. What most scholars do agree on, however, is that the white middle-class nuclear family model became idealized and codified in the Victorian period, even when the reality of people's lives differed drastically, and that it has been used to regulate ideas of family and behavior since then. Stephanie Coontz, *The Way We Never Were: American Families and the Nostalgia Trap* (New York: Basic Books, 1992), 12.

5. Andrew J. Cherlin, *The Marriage-Go-Round: The State of Marriage and the Family in America Today* (New York: Knopf, 2009), 7.

6. Ron Becker, "'Help Is On the Way!': *Supernanny, Nanny 911*, and the Neoliberal Politics of the Family," *The Great American Makeover: Television: History, Nation*, ed. Dana Heller (New York: Palgrave Macmillan, 2006), 175–192.

7. Lynn Spigel, *Make Room for TV: Television and the Family Ideal in Postwar America* (Chicago: University of Chicago Press, 1992).

8. Coontz and other historians have demonstrated that the 1950s fantasy family was not only the product of a statistical anomaly (unusually high rates of marriage and childbearing after World War II), but it was also rooted in damning contradictions and inequities; its new all-encompassing domestic ideals that, for example, asked women to return to the home after wartime labor and wholly subordinate their needs to their husband and children sparked the original desperate housewives and high rates of alcoholism. Coontz, *The Way We Never Were*, 37. See also Elaine Tyler May, *Homeward Bound: American Families in the Cold War Era* (New York: Basic Books, 1988), 11.

9. Ella Taylor, *Prime-time Families: Television Culture in Postwar America* (Berkeley: University of California Press, 1989), 2–3.

10. Herman Gray, *Watching Race: Television and the Struggle for "Blackness"* (Minneapolis: University of Minnesota Press, 1995).

11. For earlier arguments about "emotional realism" in popular music, see Stuart Hall and Paddy Whannel, *The Popular Arts* (London: Hutchinson, 1964), 269–283. Ien Ang, *Watching Dallas: Television and the Melodramatic Imagination* (London: Routledge, 1985), 47. Raymond Williams, *The Long Revolution* (Harmondsworth: Penguin, 1965), 64.

12. See Deborah Chambers, *Representing the Family* (London: Sage Publications, 2001).

13. Census data trends indicate that 50 percent of first marriages and 60 percent of second ones are likely to end in divorce within forty years. Coontz, *The Way We Never Were*, 3.

14. Susan J. Douglas and Meredith W. Michaels, *The Mommy Myth: The Idealization of Motherhood and How It Has Undermined All Women* (New York: Free Press, 2004).

15. Cherlin, *Public*, 22.

16. May, *Homeward Bound*.

17. Stacey, *In the Name of the Family*. Chambers, *Representing the Family*, 1–32. Jo Van Every, "From Modern Nuclear Family Households to Postmodern Diversity? The Sociological Construction of Families," *Changing Family Values*, eds. Gill Jagger and Caroline Wright (London: Routledge, 1999), 166–179.

18. "Bowers/Pilek," *Trading Spouses: Meet Your New Mommy*, episodes 103 and 104, Fox, August 3, 2004, August 10, 2004.

19. The March 3, 2002, debut had a 2.8 household rating and the show's ratings eventually exceeded five million viewers in the first season, though parts of the subsequent seasons had lower ratings. Adrian Deevoy, "Ozzy's Summer of Love," *Blender*, June–July 2002: 90–96.

20. Erik Hedegaard, "The Osbournes: America's First Family," *Rolling Stone*, May 9, 2002: 33, 33–36.

21. "A House Divided," *The Osbournes*, MTV, March 5, 2002.

22. Nancy Miller, "American Goth: How the Osbournes, a Simple, Headbanging British Family, Became Our Nation's Latest Reality-TV Addiction," *Entertainment Weekly*, April 19, 2002: 25.

23. Miller, *Entertainment Weekly*, 25.

24. Stewart M. Hoover, Lynn Schofield Clark, and Diane F. Alters, *Media, Home, and Family* (New York: Routledge, 2004). Anthony Giddens, *Modernity and Self-Identity: Self and Society in the Late Modern Age* (Stanford, CA: Stanford University Press, 1991).

25. Rebecca L. Stephens, "Socially Soothing Stories? Gender, Race and Class in TLC's *A Wedding Story* and *A Baby Story*," *Understanding Reality Television*, eds. Su Holmes and Deborah Jermyn (London: Routledge, 2004), 191–210.

26. Annette Hill, *Factual Entertainment and Television Audiences* (London: Routledge, 2005).

27. Becker, *Supernanny*, 175–192.

28. Josef Adalian, "Can Reality Feel Good?: As Nasty Shows Founder, Nice Gets Nice and Retro Since TV Economics Still Favor Unscripted Fare," *Variety* January 17–23, 2005: 19.

29. John Fiske, *Media Matters: Everyday Culture and Political Change* (Minneapolis: University of Minnesota Press, 1994).

30. Coontz, *The Way We Never Were*, 97.

31. Jason Fields and Lynne M. Casper, "The U.S. Census Reveals Change and Continuity in Family Life, 2000," *Major Problems in the History of American Families and Children,* ed. Anya Jabour (Boston: Houghton Mifflin, 2005), 492–500.

32. Stacey, *In the Name of the Family,* 7.

33. Dana Heller, *Family Plots: The De-Oedipalization of Popular Culture* (Philadelphia: University of Pennsylvania Press, 1995), x, xii.

34. Adam Nagourney and David D. Kirkpatrick, "Urged by Right, Bush Takes On Gay Marriages," *New York Times on the Web,* July 12, 2004, http://www.ny times.com/2004/07/12/politics/campaign/12REPU.html?ex=1090648734&ei=1& en=733bfb4a9e95ccd3.

35. "Senate Defeats Gay Marriage Ban," Associated Press, July 14, 2004, http://www.latimes.com/news/nationworld/nation/la-071404gaymarriage_wr, 1,7090909.story?coll=la-home-headlines.

36. Nagourney and Kirkpatrick, "Urged by Right."

37. Coontz, *The Way We Never Were,* 94.

38. Laura Kipnis, *Against Love: A Polemic* (New York: Pantheon, 2003), 23–24.

39. Cherlin, *The Marriage-Go-Round,* 10.

40. Cherlin, *Public,* 23.

41. Cherlin, *Public,* 98–99.

42. Ella Taylor, *Prime-time Families: Television Culture in Postwar America* (Berkeley: University of California Press, 1989), 2–3.

43. The show ranked second and averaged 13.9 million viewers. "Top 20 Network Primetime Series by Households: Season-To-Date 09/20/04–11/28/04," *Zap2It,* December 4, 2004, http://tv.zap2it.com/tveditorial/tve_main/1,1002,272| season||,00.html.

44. See David Morley, *Family Television: Cultural Power and Domestic Leisure* (London: Comedia, 1986); Morley, *Home Territories: Media, Mobility and* Identity (London: Routledge, 2000), 86–104.

45. Jeffrey Ruoff, *An American Family: A Televised Life* (Minneapolis: University of Minnesota Press, 2002).

46. *The Newlywed Game* aired from 1966 to 1974, 1977 to 1980, and as *The New Newlywed Game,* from 1984 to 1989. *The Dating Game* ran from 1965 to 1986 and as *The All-New Dating Game,* from 1986 to 1989, 1996 to 1999.

47. Frank Rich, "The Great Indecency Hoax," *New York Times on the Web,* November 28, 2004, http://www.nytimes.com/2004/11/28/arts/28rich.html?ex=1 102397227&ei=1&en=9736fb1bcb36aee1.

48. Lisa Duggan, "Holy Matrimony!" *The Nation,* March 15, 2004, April 7, 2004, http://www.thenation.com/doc.mhtml?i=20040315&s=duggan.

49. Duggan, "Holy Matrimony!" 1.

50. *The Insider,* CBS, January 19, 2005.

51. *Dr. Phil Primetime Special: Romance Rescue,* CBS, February 15, 2005.

Chapter 4

Family Values Debates: The Politics of the Family

If reality TV presents family as a spectacle, what are the attendant cultural politics and ideologies being circulated? What are the moral lessons and pedagogical messages on such programs? In this chapter, I further explore how reality TV is staging its own family values debate by analyzing programs about families in crisis. By assessing the cultural politics of several prominent reality shows that use a family crisis storyline, I demonstrate how they offer their own arguments about how best to approach family. I examine two related subgenres: the home makeover shows and the nanny intervention series. In one corner, we have a man with a bullhorn, ready to build a house. In the other, a Mary Poppins knock-off, ready to put children on what she calls the "naughty chair." The two share some especially aggressive political rhetoric.

These home makeover and parenting assistance shows circulate a problematic neoliberal rhetoric, of the kind critics have found on much of reality TV.[1] The home makeover shows (most notably ABC's *Extreme Makeover: Home Edition,* with host Ty Pennington, who whips out his bullhorn, slams on his hardhat, and tears down old homes to build up mansions) take their premise straight from nineteenth-century domestic science, which insisted that strong homes make strong families and thus a strong nation. Here, the notion is that by renovating dilapidated, outdated, or too-small homes, a reality program's intervention will effectively renovate struggling families. Meanwhile, the nanny shows provide experts, most often Mary Poppins–style British nannies, who swoop in to rescue parents who are supposedly in crisis and in need of better disciplinary techniques, more structure, and, it seems, a stiff upper lip.

In both cases of neoliberal rhetoric, the programs present families as private units that must be helped not by public aid but by corporate charity and private outsourcing. They suggest that the future strength of America as a nation depends on functioning private family units who can fend for themselves (and not require public resources). These series also privilege an older norm of a modern nuclear family unit over a newer postmodern diversity. They imply that the postmodern family forms need help to become workable, and that they should approximate the modern nuclear norm, or they could spark a crisis in society. By so obsessively trying to mold unruly families into an older modern nuclear family model, these shows, on one level, merely serve to underscore the tenuousness of that older norm.

Neoliberal Makeovers

Many forms of reality programming quite problematically norm the idea of neoliberal privatization as desirable and as a model of good, participatory citizenship. On the home makeover and nanny series, families look to corporations or charity for help rather than to the government, which becomes an attempt to justify a movement away from a welfare state in the United States. Often this neoliberalism comes in the form of a message of self-improvement, individual responsibility, and choice. If reality TV helps discipline subjects and citizens because it encourages people along paths of self-improvement, it does so by mobilizing some specific genre features. The genre adroitly generates cheaper content by getting viewers to put themselves on TV, such that audiences provide their own entertainment. As reality series prompt castmembers and viewers toward greater self-disclosure as a means of self-improvement (put yourself on TV, have your life judged, and become a better person), critics have convincingly argued that this message attempts to naturalize greater commercial and state surveillance of people (if people start to accept that cameras are always watching them and not see that as a problem, then they are being conditioned to accept greater surveillance of them by companies and by the government).[2] The self-improvement discourse also depends on promoting the idea that audiences can find opportunities for social learning and moments of emotional realism in the genre (again, dynamics Annette Hill has found in her audience study to be prevalent among viewers).[3]

In discussing this trend in which shows norm neoliberal citizenship, I am interested in analyzing how a message of self improvement becomes linked to ideas about other sites of social reproduction, like the family itself. Even though family reality series encourage a neoliberal self-regulation and a "project of the self" in terms of self-improvement, they do still retain a deep investment in larger social structures like the family as places where people are socialized. In my view, discourses of the family are a key space where rhetorics of the self and the state often come together in the reality genre. Helen Wood and Beverly Skeggs have argued that the genre's focus on self-making as self-regulation does not actually move subjects beyond traditional structures of social reproduction like the state or the patriarchal family.[4] Family reality series provide a test case for interrogating this issue.

On many reality shows that focus on the family, we can see how the state intervenes in legislating family forms (such as regulating access to the rights and economic privileges the state grants through marriage). But we can also see, simultaneously, elements that encourage the private monitoring of families. Relevant examples would include corporate philanthropy mixed with individual volunteerism, or so-called expert judgment of families as models for the moral judgments audiences are implicitly encouraged to engage in themselves. These dynamics are particularly evident in the home and family makeover subgenre, specifically the *Extreme Makeover: Home Edition* franchise and its short-lived imitator, *Renovate My Family.* These programs picture teams of experts who evaluate family life, lecturing participants and home viewers alike in family values as they worriedly assess new household forms. Most notably, it is families that depart from the older modern nuclear norm that need assistance (whether single-parent, blended, impoverished, or orphaned households). In an update of nineteenth-century domestic science rhetoric, their ideological tie between a rationalized home and a healthy family reveals further blurring of the traditional public–private sphere split.

On home renovation programs, for example, we meet families who are unable to afford their mortgages or who have seriously ill children with medical bills that the family cannot pay. Often, due to the debt caused by health care or employment problems (which are larger structural, institutional social problems), the family cannot afford to renovate a house that is on the verge of collapsing. In a response that bespeaks a diminishing public sphere, rather than advocating government aid in the form of low-income housing or social welfare safety nets, these series enact and laud neoliberal privatization and outsourcing. They renovate or rebuild homes into palatial estates and flood the families with new consumer goods. It is the prominently advertised corporate sponsors who contribute the materials and goods, while the network-financed design team encourages volunteers and local building companies to donate their labor. The implication is that a new home, specifically a materialistic paradise, will solve any problem the family is facing.

The most obvious, stunning example of neoliberalism appears on a 2005 episode of *Extreme Makeover Home Edition* in which former First Lady Laura Bush guest starred, traveling to Biloxi, Mississippi, to comfort Hurricane Katrina survivors. She came to praise the design team and ABC for their efforts to rebuild homes in hurricane-ravaged Gulf Coast areas. Her praise for a television program that has helped a small number of homes is in shocking contrast to the kind of wholesale government assistance that is needed to rebuild the region and that has clearly not been fully provided even today. The *New York Times* reported that producers instructed residents to "act surprised" when Bush walked into a community center to help distribute items donated by show sponsor Sears.[5] Meanwhile, Bush was quoted as saying that "It's going to take all of these (volunteers) working together to help people rebuild their lives" and that she was encouraged by the way governments, private organizations, faith-based groups, and individuals were working together to help ease suffering in the region.[6] Her comments about promoting faith-based organizations and private outsourcing match with the Bush administration's policies, as does her remark that she wished the show would rebuild a school or a community center to help more people. Here, the commercial, mass culture reality TV show, the product of ABC and Disney, would be taking on the role that the state (in the form of federal, state, or local government funding and programs) would have been expected to play.

Renovate My Family offers an added twist in which young host Jay McGraw counsels the families as well. The marketing of him as a counselor depends on him being the son of Dr. Phil McGraw, the Oprah-affiliated life coach of the *Dr. Phil* talk show, since Jay McGraw does not have professional credentials himself, other than the self-help books he has coauthored with his father or authored himself. Invoking pop psychology and his father's concepts of tough love and self-responsibility, the young McGraw advises families on alcoholism, impending divorce, and alienated teens. This series fits into the self-improvement rubric of this reality subgenre, and it exemplifies the way contemporary television uses a language of therapy as a main mode of address.[7]

In this reality format, the moment of revealing the new home is supposed to spark emotional realism in the family. Those highly valued weeping moments of purported authenticity allow viewers to trace what is presented as a real as opposed to a performed self (i.e., when the person is overcome and cries, it must be their so-called real self as opposed to the self they perform for the camera). These moments reflect contemporary anxieties about the status of identity in a media-saturated culture (such as questions about how you can tell if the person is being true-to-life on the screen, especially since screens are now all around us). What these programs reveal through their narratives more generally, however, is the movement toward neoliberalism in relation to the family specifically, and the norming of that ideology on such television shows.

In this chapter, I analyze reality shows that focus on expert advice about the home, parenting, or the running of domestic space. Such programs, through this expert advice, proffer the idea that aspirational self-improvement should be the end goal of the participant and viewer interaction with reality TV. Not only does the expert advice suggest that viewers should accept bourgeois values as the norm, it also models a version of neoliberalism. Specifically, these shows suggest that issues formerly associated with the state should more properly be outsourced to private experts who will solve problems; that is, fix broken families, whether through home makeovers sponsored by corporate advertising or through expert judgment of parenting skills and attempts to socialize parents into bourgeois parenting ideals, as on *Supernanny* and *Nanny 911* or on *Meet Mister Mom*.[8]

Programs like the nanny shows also display neoliberalism that attempts more broadly to legitimate the shift to postwelfare state governance in contemporary America. As Laurie Ouellette and James Hay and others have shown, this neoliberal rhetoric depends on how the shows laud private intervention and self-improvement, which promote broader discourses like welfare privatization and a neoliberal ideology of personal responsibility.[9] Ron Becker argues persuasively that the nanny reality shows reflect what he calls the "neoliberal makeover of the American family," that is, an effort to privatize the family unit and claim it as naturally primary and able to address all the necessary concerns of citizens. Thus the continued dismantling of the welfare state can be justified, as can the continued state effort to limit marriage rights (as when Bush's Healthy Marriage Initiative proposed spending federal funds to promote marriage at the same time the Bush administration was advocating a constitutional amendment preventing gay marriage by limiting marriage to "a man and a woman").[10]

I concur with this general line of argumentation about the neoliberal, private self-improvement framework on these shows. However, I also see a more explicit admission in these narratives that the older modern nuclear family norm is unstable and that it has internal inconsistencies, which underscores a clear internal contradiction in the accompanying neolib-eral rhetoric too. That tenuousness and weakness (an attack from inside the fraught and incoherent modern nuclear family unit ideal, as it were), emerges in how the storylines stage a contest between an older modern nuclear family unit norm and a newer demographic reality of postmodern family diversity. Another area in which these programs display narrative contradictions or "blind spots" that speak to the breakdown of ideologies is in their gender discourse. Many of the mothers depicted seem to suffer the effects of what Susan Douglas and Meredith Michaels term "new mo-mism," in which contemporary expectations now insist that mothers pro-vide complete, primary devotion to their children, define themselves first and foremost as mothers and only secondarily as career women (if they work outside the home), and that they put their children's needs first in order to be a successful mother.[11] While these programs frequently attempt to uphold that gender stereotype, they often fail to do so and instead focus on the mothers' dissatisfaction with that ideal in practice, or they implicitly register the incoherence and problematic contradictions of that ideal.

In addition to the aspirational self-improvement messages, these shows also speak to issues about television's status as a domestic medium. When programs bring cameras and experts into the home to level judgment and dole out advice, they mimic a long-standing dynamic on television, in which television brings the public world into the private, domestic sphere—or in this case, makes the private concerns of ordinary citizens a matter of mass public concern or entertainment. TV becomes a member of the family because it reaches audiences inside the home. That framework remains of central importance in viewers' (and producers') imagined rela-tions to programming even though television is increasingly being watched on handheld devices and in public spaces outside of the home.

Indeed, domestic space is a major issue reality TV engages, and, as I will discuss in this chapter, this issue is particularly evident in family reality series that bring experts into the home to evaluate their family life, whether that involves the quality of their home design or the effective-ness of their interactions with their children. The more general theoreti-cal issue about television being a domestic medium involves that fact that television brings the outside world inside via the screen. Television scholar Lynn Spigel has demonstrated how early TV marketed itself by claim-ing it could bring the larger world into the private household space, what theorist Raymond Williams called electronic communications' promise of "mobile privatization."[12] It pledged to allow the audience to experience a wider view of the social world, to see places they might never actually go, to control their interaction with society through this fantasy buffer zone of electronic media. Since reality TV gives viewers real people in unscripted situations, the genre somewhat collapses the difference between fantasy and reality in the images brought into the home through the television box. The castmembers living in domestic situations on the screen mirror some of the viewer's own domestic scenes. One reality subgenre explores such issues by temporarily switching people into each other's domestic spaces, whether to remodel their homes (*Trading Spaces*) or to reframe their family experience (like the wife swapping programs or *Switched*—a show about teenagers swapping lives for a few days). One dating series tests the compatibility of potential mates by actually moving a blind date, chosen by the contestant's family and friends, into the person's home for a week (*Perfect Match: New York*).

These kinds of programs intervene in the values cast and viewers attach to domestic space and familial roles. Furthermore, they tie those themes to the public sphere, debunking the idea that family is only a private sphere issue. The genre blurs the very distinction between a private and public sphere in its family portraits. TV's immediate electronic delivery of the social world into the domestic sphere, along with its often explicit attempts to address a national audience or some version of the public, brings the two spheres ideology of private and public into constant play.[13] From televised state funerals like Ronald Reagan's to big trials like O.J. Simpson's, television invokes a national public through an imagined community of viewers. Because reality TV adds another layer of truth claims to television's scenarios, it throws concepts of public versus private into greater complication, and it vociferously meditates on the issue. The genre reflects a fragmented public sphere by insisting on multiple ideal viewers, multiple family ideals, and multiple ways the domestic and public are imbricated. Call-in voting shows mine cultural anxieties about the fragmentation of a national audience (particularly in the post-big three network era) and about the status of participatory democracy (in vote-based gamedocs such as *Survivor: All-Stars, American Idol, The Voice, Dancing With the Stars, The X Factor, Big Brother*'s first season, *Married by America, Cupid,* and *Last Comic Standing*). While some programs picture regret or nostalgia about this national fragmentation through mass media, others celebrate its demise or imagine new ways for mass media to cohere multiple publics. Rupert Murdoch's *Showtime* reality series *American Candidate,* for example, selected the best political candidate from a pool of contestants that included the daughter of a former presidential candidate, Congressman Dick Gephardt. The program turned on the idea that politicians must now master the medium of television in order to be successful—or, in this case, to appeal to Showtime's marketing demographic. The series implied that one can best judge that ability through a reality program.

Meditating on these domestic space and private–public sphere issues, the subgenre of expert advice programs that are meant to groom homes and parents exist to buttress the family unit. However, in these series, that family unit most often is upheld as a private unit that validates a neoliberal agenda. And it is a unit that upholds white bourgeois values that Others are required to aspire to, even if they are barred from fully replicating them.

British Nanny Invasion

The two most prominent parenting shows, Fox's *Nanny 911* and ABC's *Supernanny* portray a severe tension between modern nuclear ideals and postmodern variations. In another iteration of the *Wife Swap-Trading Spouses* production dynamic, ABC purchased the British format of the show and Fox pirated the format and rushed its own version on air, with Fox premiering its version in the United States in November 2004, while ABC's appeared in January 2005. Both programs suggest that internal and external threats to the American family are so destabilizing that it must be saved by the colonial parent, who dispatches Mary Poppins–style nannies armed with common-sense childrearing philosophies. They implicitly recur to nineteenth-century domestic science ideals as well as mid-twentieth-century sociological theories such as Talcott Parsons's schema of functionalism and dysfunctionalism.

As a case study, these shows also depend on the idea that anxiety about expertise and professionalism contributes to consumer behavior. Worried parents buy self-help books, such as those proffered by the series as tie-ins. Likewise, they hire nannies to troubleshoot and solve their problems, much like management consultants for the family unit. The nanny format also relates to other programs, such as The Learning Channel's suite of shows about parenting and childbirth (most notably *A Baby Story*), all of which resort to expert advice and affirm the conventional modern nuclear family stereotype.[14] The nanny programs also demonstrate how reality programming can be framed as a pedagogical space where experts teach participants their preferred model of parenting, thereby also socializing them into certain values and beliefs.[15]

It is important to note that this neoliberal message is not the only one to be found on parenting shows across the reality TV genre. As an example of how the genre as a whole is engaging in a debate with multiple viewpoints (even though the neoliberal view might dominate in some areas), some of Bravo's parenting shows ironically lampoon neoliberalism. On their suite of shows, *Showbiz Moms and Dads, Sportskids Moms and Dads,* and *Showdog Moms and Dads,* the familial kinship behaviors that neoliberal rhetoric attempts to privatize or to make seem individualized and natural are instead satirized. The parents on *Showbiz Moms and Dads* are trapped by their desire to live vicariously through their children, and their efforts to replicate modern nuclear family unit ideals are no match for their own dreams of stardom. The parents on this reality documentary series continually abandon or displace nuclear family units. For example, mothers leave husbands and move with their children to Hollywood to promote their childrens' acting career, or they break up the nuclear family by sending young children out in touring theater companies on their own to pursue a larger career dream. The *Sportskids* parents are willing to make similar familial sacrifices in order to pursue vicariously dreams of sports glory. Meanwhile, the *Showdog* parents explicitly challenge traditional definitions of family as they poignantly attempt to define their families as their dogs, treating them like children and pampering them. In these reality series, good parenting is all relative. Thus, they underscore different parenting approaches and suggest that parenting is not a so-called natural category but rather a socially constructed one. Their ironic treatment of families (which can mean a house full of dogs or a station wagon full of child actors) directly fits Bravo's brand of marketing of satire and irony to its viewers.

Meanwhile, on *Supernanny,* the program's strong neoliberal rhetoric actually comes into conflict with elements that highlight the fragility and problematic nature of a modern nuclear family unit. The series suggests that these nuclear families should be private and autonomous (like neoliberalism tells them they should be), but they of course never truly are, because they often seek help from a larger extended family or from public or state programs, or they benefit from support by the state in all its myriad forms (from public schools to social security). The show, for example, sometimes praises extended family models. By way of registering problems with the nuclear family, it also highlights the idea of dissatisfaction with gender roles as a severe internal problem in nuclear family norms. Instead of supporting a "new momism" type of reliance on supermoms who sacrifice all for their children, even when they work outside the home, the program advocates a slight shift in the patriarchal family unit. It advocates a greater contribution to domestic labor by the fathers as the solution to a gender and labor problem.

Becker reads in the nanny shows an attempt to correct white heternormative nuclear family units who are seen as exceptions in their need for parenting help (i.e., they are dysfunctional, thus they do not threaten the idea of a functional nuclear family unit). As he notes, when nanny programs insist on natural, strong, autonomous families who can deal with individual, private problems within the family, they reinforce a neoliberal resistance to state and public programs, not just programs that would limit the supposedly "natural" work of the market but those that provide social safety nets—public programs that critics would say are necessary to the survival of citizens. He observes that "strong" families are far from being autonomous. On the contrary, they are supported by the state, as in those public schools but also in features like Medicare, the actual subsidization of suburban home ownership in the 1950s, and numerous other forms of assistance.[16]

I agree with his assessment, but again, I also see an added dynamic on these programs, a sharper fear that the modern nuclear family unit upheld as a norm is actually incoherent and untenable, and that perhaps these families in need of help are not the exceptions. Thus, the anxiety is not simply that the modern nuclear family unit has to compete with a variety of postmodern family forms. The fear is that the nuclear family unit is not actually functional, and that the struggling families are the rule. Star Jo Frost's brief socializing visit makes superficial changes. But, the program implies, the family would need constant policing by Frost for them to internalize those neoliberal norms, and the norms are often relaxed when Frost leaves. Also, the fact that a nanny is needed to rescue these families suggests that the system is failing to replicate itself "naturally"—the parents cannot rely on any "natural instincts," instead they must resort to the neoliberal practice of outsourcing as they hire a private expert to solve their parenting dilemma. The struggling families could seem the result of personal failures. Nevertheless, anxieties about the larger social system remain, given the fact that there are so many families the show presents as in desperate need of outside help.

This underlying fear about the tenuousness of the modern nuclear family unit is evident on the series in the repeated complaints of the parents: they feel isolated, overwhelmed, unable to discipline their children, and confused by evolving gender roles. The way in which the show stirs up a family crisis rhetoric is significant—it fans those fears and then does not fully resolve them by episode's finish, leaving them open-ended. One of the implicit anxieties the parenting shows express is about whether white middle-class ideals will still dominate, seizing the top of a hierarchy in a liberal pluralist framework. The series continually tries to socialize families into white middle-class ideals, which underscores a recurring theme involving a fear of cultural difference. Witness episodes where *Supernanny* Frost, for example, patronizingly tries to make African American families conform to white bourgeois ideals.

Epitomizing the self-help parenting reality format, *Supernanny* provides a collation of pop psychology childrearing techniques.[17] In a companion book authored by Frost, she describes the content as "common sense solutions" to frequent parenting issues (like kids with separation anxiety or who refuse to go to bed). Frost cites the origins of her theories in a vague amalgamation of popular knowledge: "I didn't invent the techniques. I suspect no one single person could put their hand on their heart and claim to have invented them out of the blue. By and large I've simply followed my instincts and observed parents and kids to see what worked and what didn't work."[18] Her most famous technique is called the "naughty step technique," in which she gives the children a structured time-out using ideas of consequence and respect. The technique is presented superficially, almost like a branding message. Parents bend down to explain in an authoritative tone why the offending behavior was wrong, the children remain on the naughty step for a designated time period and until they are ready to apologize, after which the parent hugs them. As a marker of that technique as a branding message, when the original version of the show premiered in the UK on Channel 4 in the summer of 2004 and became a hit, "Naughty step!" and "Your behavior is very naughty!" became popular catchphrases.

In establishing her authority as a so-called expert, Frost at once displaces a naturalized idea of family but also reinforces the idea of a mothering instinct. She insists that her fifteen years of nanny experience gave her pragmatic knowledge of "what works," even though she is not a mother herself and has no formal training. Frost writes: "I'm not a pediatrician, either, or a child psychologist. I've had no formal training to do what I do. Which puts me in much the same position as most parents, without the intense emotional attachment (although we nannies have feelings too!)." She goes on to insist on her expertise: "The big difference is that I've had many years of experience looking after all sorts of children at all stages and I'm not meeting these challenges for the first time. I've seen children through weaning and toilet training, teething, tantrums and the first day at school. Along the way I've observed behavior, listened to other people talking about child care issues and, most importantly, I've listened to my own gut instincts."[19] Frost asserts here that her expertise is based on experience parents would not have had, and also insists on naturalized parenting gut instincts that guide her and make her a sage to be consulted. Thus, she somewhat displaces a naturalized family unit model, because she exhibits this parenting instinct more strongly than the parents themselves do, and she does not have children herself. Yet her comment also implies that a natural mothering instinct resides in all women.

Here again, the show's neoliberal premise is that a dysfunctional nuclear family can be made functional by paying a private expert for help (and airing the process as a mass culture entertainment commodity). Some of Frost's parenting content does not actually reinforce the norm of the modern nuclear family unit, although much of it recurs to a Parson's model of functional and dysfunctional family behaviors. As she describes nannies as "the bridge between the child and parent" who must help families who have "become troubled," Frost identifies the root of parenting problems not in so-called bad children but in bad patterns of behavior that she can note and correct for people.[20] In a variation on functionalism, her book elaborates on her formula of her top 10 rules and applies them to the different stages of childhood development, with her rules involving a consequences and rewards sequence: "praise and rewards, consistency, routine, boundaries, discipline, warnings, explanations, restraint, responsibility, relaxation."[21] She emphasizes the need for boundaries and discipline and even points to the loosening of extended family ties as one factor in the "stress and isolation" of contemporary parenting, a notion that moves away from the modern nuclear family unit norm.[22]

Linking family and nation, the program characterizes the family crisis as a national crisis, sometimes explicitly. The voice-over narration in each episode's opening sequence hyperbolically exclaims, "It's a parenting emergency!" and "Can the Supernanny save these parents from absolute disaster?" Likewise, as I have previously noted elsewhere in my own review of the series, Frost tends to be melodramatic in her advice to the parents she is assisting.[23] She tells one frustrated couple that if they do not change their discipline strategies, they will create a juvenile delinquent. To another sleepless mother and father, she says, "I know you love your children, but the way you run this household is just not acceptable." In an episode entitled "Ririe Family," involving an overwhelmed mother of four, an under-involved father, and children who are beginning to grow physically aggressive with each other, Frost tells the couple: "As an Englishwoman, I can sit here and say you are the American Dream. However, I can see this going down the road to a nightmare if you're not careful." After the parents absorb their lesson, the mother says, "Jo gave us our life back. And that's our American Dream. . . . She gave us our family back."[24]

The show's narrative focuses on repeated elements and the assurance of success. It also involves a surveillance feature (when Frost evaluates video footage of the family), which follows reality TV's trend of picturing surveillance as desirable to viewers. Each episode follows a strict narrative formula, in which Frost arrives to spend a week with a troubled family, during which time she observes them, identifies problems, implements solutions, leaves to allow them to practice her techniques on their own for a couple of days (during which time she observes them using the television cameras), then returns to reinforce her teachings (in part by showing them video footage of their own behaviors as evidence). Each episode includes an ending update segment in which the show revisits the family to find out how they have been progressing several weeks after the Supernanny visit. Unfailingly, the participants insist that in spite of any initial skepticism they might have had, the visiting nanny has solved their parenting problems and improved their lives, as if to lend proof to the cliché that parents wish their children came with instructions.

The visual narrative in each episode works to establish audience identification with Frost and also underscores her gender message. For Frost, it is expected that the mothers will not be able to meet the superwoman ideal (of, say, the new momism). She urges them to adjust their expectations and she requires that fathers help more with domestic labor. Each episode aggressively repeats a similar story line: it begins with images of homes that are filled with ear-splitting tantrums, featuring shots of crying kids and playground meltdowns. When Frost observes their current parenting routine, we see her gazing directly at the camera in disbelief or exasperation, encouraging viewer identification with her point of view as judge of this family's behavior. She implicitly invites viewers to be the judge too, as the presence of the implied viewer here is established by these camera techniques. When she has a meeting with the parents to institute new rules and schedules, the mother usually breaks down in tears because she has failed to replicate a supermom ideal, while the reluctant father is asked to provide more parenting efforts. Their tentative attempts to implement the techniques at first meet with resistance from their brood, then success, with Frost's help. When Frost leaves, the parents usually falter slightly, necessitating her return and further instruction. In the concluding update segment, we witness a family happy with a new-found sense of order and purpose, replete with direct address interviews from children who like the new sense of structure and parents who no longer feel like failures. The show is repetitive, at every commercial break previewing scenes to come and summarizing previous ones. As with soap operas, the program uses that sort of repetition and summary to target an audience of distracted moms who are busy multitasking and will need to catch up with the show each time their attention is interrupted by childcare duties.

Gender role expectations serve as a primary point of conflict, which again, Frost often resolves by coaxing fathers into sharing more in parenting. Yet a strict gender role binary remains because the mother is supposed to remain the locus of nurturing and caregiving, even if she works outside the home (as some of the participant mothers do, but not all of them). The program captures the gendered "mommy wars" Douglas describes in the sense that there is bitter tension between mothers who work outside the home and mothers who stay home, and the working mothers feel a deep sense of guilt, based on cultural messages they are receiving. However, Frost actually dispels the new momism somewhat, because she insists that the father must play a greater role and that the mother should be allowed an accompanying reduction in her sense of responsibility. In an episode entitled "Jeans Family," a middle-aged couple with three young girls witness desired results when the traveling-salesman father gets "more involved." One man admits Frost castigated him for sitting in his recliner all day. In a continual reiteration of the new momism dilemma, the mothers repeatedly say they feel like failures when they cannot take on the roles of primary caregiver (with sparse help) and full-time career woman successfully. In "Ririe Family," Frost rescues the wife who fears she is "failing as a mother." Here again, instead of reinforcing the supermom ideal, part of Frost's solution is to engage the couch potato father with their four young kids.

The moments of emotional realism or emotional reveal occur during the parent meeting with Frost, and they often center on the women expressing frustration with their multiple roles and their inability to meet all of the demands placed upon them. Many are emotionally tied to their purportedly failing parenting measures and to their patterns of performed behavior in the household. They often burst into tears upon hearing Frost's critiques, yet quickly move onto the prescribed path of self-improvement through following the expert advice. The Ririe mother, for example, says of Frost's assessment: "It's kind of a slap in the face, but it's one that [we] needed."

In some episodes, the series attempts to discipline families who do not meet the modern nuclear family white bourgeois ideal. This dynamic implicitly articulates fears about more and more groupings appearing under the American family umbrella. The program's solution, implicitly, is to encourage these families to approximate an ideal they can never, by design and by the maintenance of those social hierarchies, fully reach.

In "Walker Family," Frost aids an African American extended family (a teenage nephew is living with them). She castigates the mother for what she calls "bad habits" such as spanking her children, babying her infant too long, allowing chaos in her house and aggression from the teenage boys living there.[25] The episode suggests that unless the parents change their behavior, the boys will become "big violent men." In so doing, it circulates and reinforces a stereotype linking young black men to violence. It also stereotypes the mother as having "bad habits" and running her family like a dysfunctional matriarch (in the vein of Moynihan Report stereotypes). Ironically, the mother actually runs her own home day care facility, while the father is a counselor at a juvenile detention facility. They have precisely the kinds of professional credentials Jo Frost does not have. And yet the series suggests that Frost must save them from sending their own violent juveniles onto the street. The family consists of mother Alice Walker (her name an irony given the way the episode reinforces the kinds of racial stereotypes contemporary author Alice Walker speaks out against), husband Anthony Walker, and the children who live with them: Anthony Jr., 12, Leila, 6, nephew Marcus, 17, and baby Alyssa, 14 months.

Frost's critiques of the Walker family are patronizing and reinscribe racial stereotypes. She also refuses to recognize some of mother Alice Walker's parenting approaches as coherent techniques that some childcare research supports (like attachment parenting, for example). She instead presents them as nonsensical and failures on Walker's part. Noting that she disagrees with spanking the children, Frost states, "it shouldn't take physical punishment for your kids to respect you and listen to what you're saying," and she goes on to denigrate the mother: "Alice's parenting skills are not effective but she's doing nothing to change them." She critiques Alice for being too attached to her baby, who, along with the six-year-old girl, still sleeps with the parents. She chastises the mother: "You've got her attached to you like a koala bear" and "she's become your pacifier." Along with the odd koala bear comment, which hints at bestializing racial stereo-types, Frost invokes racial stereotypes and exclaims: "now you've got me listening to rap music." She tells the parents to nip Anthony Jr.'s behavior in the bud because "he's not a big man yet," and in order to "teach him some respect," she sends the boy to meet a professional basketball player, Dwayne Wade of the Miami Heat, who is African American, in order, she says, to "give him a role model" he will actually heed. This kind of chan-neling of young black men into a fixation on professional sports repeats a problematic dynamic in which they are overly physicalized. In no episode about white teen boys who are acting out does Frost warn that they are not "big men" yet, implying that they could be a violent presence once they age—or that they will be characterized by being large physical presences. Thus, this episode enacts a neoliberal pedagogy with its private, corporate solution to familial problems, and it does so in a way that policies racial hierarchies.

Nanny 911 echoes the same structure and, while the content of the nanny advice differs at times from *Supernanny,* is largely similar to the ABC series as the original format.[26] It opens with a sequence set at "Nanny Central," an English thatched cottage where an elderly British nanny describes the problem family, then assigns one of her three junior nannies the task of coming to America to assist them. Gleefully banking on stereotypes and mimicking of British tropes such as Mary Poppins and British high tea, the series is obvious about the degree to which it is copy-catting another for-mat and is more intent on sensationalism about the families being in crisis than in depicting coherent parenting tips.

Rather than being aberrations that will correct themselves and thus prove the norm of the American family, the large number of frustrated families pictured and the repetition of their complaints make them seem part of a larger trend rather than exceptions. Nannies swoop in to bolster that family unit through rationalized and naturalized common sense. Their solutions make the family a private, individualized matter in which problems should be outsourced to paid experts, as in a neoliberal model. Yet the programs also, in moments, express a sense of deep anxiety about what the state of the nuclear family unit means for the state of the nation. However, again, the solutions are all private, outsourced ones.

Daddy Derby

By way of comparison, another parenting series echoes the family crisis rhetoric, a neoliberal outsourcing of solutions, as well as a sense of new gender roles that nevertheless entail a conventional gender binary and gender role dimorphism, with moms and dads still being expected to perform different roles based on an idea of inherent gender difference. NBC's extremely short-lived *Meet Mister Mom* removes mothers from two households for a week to watch the dads becoming increasingly frazzled and overwhelmed while trying to manage the kids and domestic duties. As I have previously noted elsewhere in my own review of the series, the program frames the narrative through the gender difference (women are the best caregivers, although men must learn to help out more).[27] Each episode opens with a voice-over intoning that even in the midst of "progress . . . some things never seem to change." We see a montage of Cleaver-style TV families positioned in a meta scene: they are in black and white in their living rooms watching families on TV. The competing reality TV families take their places in this montage and turn into color images, suggesting that we are going to see a real-life update of the 1950s TV family ideals. The series is thus self-conscious about the fact that society gets many of its gender myths from TV, since TV reflects and helps reinforce or even shape popular gender ideologies. NBC's press release describes this gendered parenting theme as a spectacle offered up for comedic amusement: "Each episode showcases the comedy that ensues when two very busy families realize just how irreplaceable mom is in their daily lives. Humorously told from the children's perspectives, every episode will also include valuable information for families on how to better manage their lives together."[28]

The series hones in on gender roles in families, specifically couch potato dads who let moms do all the work. This premise suggests the show will force passive dads to change for the better, as they find new respect for their better halves and will, after this reality TV experiment served up for viewer entertainment, pitch in more. However, while the fathers might learn to do a bit more housework, kid supervision, or group organizing, they are still simply helping mom with her naturalized roles of nurturer, caregiver, cook, maid, other-focused angel in the house. That notion references the broader discourse of perfect, self-sacrificing mother found in the new momism rhetoric. In fact, in large part what the dads learn is that household labor is exhausting, they would prefer not to do it themselves, thus they must better appreciate their wives (the group of women pictured comprised of both stay-at-home mothers and those who work outside the home).

The premiere, a representative episode, establishes the vanishing mother premise as well as the reality gamedoc format.[29] While the mothers go to a spa for the week, competing dads will be graded by experts on four key areas: nutrition, housekeeping, time management, and parenting. After a series of assigned family projects, in addition to the daily routine, the two families reunite and meet in an elementary school classroom (with its implication of an educational mission) to discover the winner, who receives a $25,000 college education savings account from State Farm, the show's sponsor. The competing families in this episode are the Smiths and the Potters, both of Austin, Texas. Dan Smith is the director of human resources in a hospital, wife Leslie a full-time psychologist who also maintains their home almost single-handedly. As the youngest of their three sons, four-year-old Mitchell, explains helpfully of the father, "he does nothing" at home. The Smiths feature roughhousing boys, while the Potters have three daughters. Father Tom is a salesman often on the road, while Linda is a "classic stay-at-home soccer mom," as our voice-over intones, carting the girls around to games.

The mothers seem anxious at being away from their children, a sign that they are feeling the pressures of the idealized new momism, in which their raison d'être is their nurturing devotion to their children. They have difficulty relaxing at the spa. However, rather than reinforcing this stereotype, this episode's storyline of boy family versus girl family tension suggests approvingly that the children might be more radical than the parents. During one head-to-head competition, in which the dads have to build cars to race each other in a soapbox derby, one Potter girl observes, "Just cause they're boys doesn't mean they're any better than us." The show delights in this girl power message, showcasing an interview with the youngest Potter daughter, a scrappy soccer tyke, who says, "I think girls are stronger because they're tougher and they actually have more muscles than the boys." This idea that girls can be more assertive in sports goes only in one direction, however; girls can do boy-associated activities, but boys rarely do girl-associated activities on the show.

Thus, the episode's potentially feminist structural critique of gender role stereotypes is reduced to a postfeminist rhetoric of personal choice and personal preference, rather than a broader societal-level criticism. The prize for the winner of the soapbox derby brings this point home in the most egregious way possible. A huge crate is hauled in and opened to reveal the reward: two maids. Two white women with cleaning equipment and matching uniforms step out of the huge crate, as if they had been shipped there, in order to clean the house of the winning father. The implication is that since the wife is not there to do the housecleaning, the husband can outsource it to other women. None of the participants seem disconcerted by this development, only happy to have the chores done. That sequence provides a neoliberal solution, private outsourcing, to gender role tensions involving domestic labor.

The program's standards for evaluating effective and noneffective parenting are vague, which has the effect of making what they call good parenting seem arbitrary. As the increasingly disheveled dads muddle through the week, the family projects they are required to do seem to be based on no clear criteria for selection (hosting a sleepover party for their kids, house-sitting odd pets like a llama), as does the judging of their performances. Fathers get high marks for efficiency, caring, and patience, and strict monitoring of what the kids eat. Cleanliness also garners lofty praise, again, a category that reinforces nineteenth-century domestic science in suggesting that a clean home leads to a healthy family. One dad wins points for bonding with the llama. The other suffers demerits for how many fudge pops his son, little Mitchell, devoured during the week (many). Unseen judges leave cards with grades (in primary colors and letters in a childhood-style scrawl) and statements to be read by the returned mothers.

The program's neoliberalism becomes more evident in the dynamics of the judgment and reward sequence, which culminates when the State Farm representative arrives to dole out a check to the winning family. Meeting at a public school to instruct people on parenting techniques implies that family is a public issue. However, the idea of family being a matter for public concern is immediately undercut, because that concern has been outsourced to private corporations. The fact that the prize will be used to help pay for exorbitant college costs is yet another instance of neoliberalism, since it moves a structural social issue of class disparity and lack of educational access into the realm of private businesses (and reality shows), who get to adjudicate who is worthy of funding.

The show debunks the myth that a mother's work is easy, speaking to the statistics about complacent husbands "letting" working women do the majority of the household labor. Yet while urging the fathers to "help out" more, the series nevertheless suggests that home and childcare are still the woman's job. The show does not, for example, feature any stay-at-home fathers. The program is more of a throwback than it purports to be. While some of these families have working moms, distinguishing them from the 1950s TV family, the conventional gender role dimorphism still reigns supreme. Each episode ends by encapsulating the purported educational mission of the show, summarizing what the families have learned. As the families leave, happily reunited, they offer their final thoughts. Leslie says she hopes Dan learns that "it's not just one single person that runs the family, it's everybody pitching in." Dan expresses his newfound desire not to take his working wife for granted, in an unintentionally hilarious speech: "The last thing that Dan Smith needs to do is to allow Leslie to do everything so that she is finally convinced: What do I need him for? What does Leslie Smith need me for?" Dan worries that since he is not the only wage earner in the family, he will no longer have a clear role defined by his gender, and that he will become obsolete. Tom expresses his greater appreciation for homemaker Linda by saying, "My God, what a valuable person she is . . . the glue that held everything together" in their team. He has reinforced his idea of a rationalized division of labor for men and women, and he has recurred to a new momism kind of naturalization of the mother figure. As the show frames his comments approvingly, it also upholds these ideas.

Extreme Home Makeover, Neoliberal Edition

Like the domestic science rhetoric of good parenting on nanny shows, home makeover shows establish an ideological tie between a rationalized home and a healthy family. In so doing, they reveal further blurring of the traditional public–private split. Developing out of the earlier *Extreme Makeover* plastic surgery reality series, ABC's *Extreme Makeover Home Edition* program is the flagship program and epitomizes neoliberal rhetoric.

The series offered a fantasy resolution to the problem of affordable, adequate housing, but it did not offer a substantive solution. Strikingly, the show that billed itself as a feel good fix to housing crises has now itself suffered the effects of the housing crisis stemming from the 2008 recession, because it has been canceled (ending after the 200th episode on January 13, 2012, although ABC will continue to run some *Extreme Makeover* specials). Even the magical corporate philanthropy and private volunteer solution to housing crises that *Extreme Makeover* production company Endemol offered could not magically solve systemic housing problems. In addition to ratings declines, the show was having increasing trouble finding enough donated supplies and volunteer builders to complete its rapid renovation projects. In housing funding problems the program itself caused, some families who had homes made over by the series infamously went into foreclosure when they could not pay the mortgages or taxes. The company tried to donate funds for mortgages and even began a practice of leasing the property for the 14-day renovation, making the improvements done during that time tax exempt. Similarly, Fox's *Renovate My Family* producer Rocket Science Laboratories gave families a lump-sum to cover taxes on the renovations (including an extra amount to cover taxes on the payment itself). But the focus on such programs was never on the actual economic and class issues but rather on the products and consumption.

In each episode of *Extreme Makeover,* the narrative format has a design team, led by carpenter Ty Pennington, spend a week redoing the home of a what they dub "a deserving family." The lucky family is sent on vacation for the week, often to Disney World (ABC thus engages in cross-marketing corporate synergy and product integration for parent company Disney). Families apply for this philanthropy by submitting pleading videos explaining their plight, and the opening sequence of each episode includes clips from the submission video. Part of each episode's dramatic tension comes from a procedural drama issue: can the design team renovate a home in one week, a prohibitively short amount of time for an effort that should take four months or more, not seven days. The team is joined by contractors and workers or volunteers, often numbering in the hundreds. Drawing on a home and garden improvement or do-it-yourself format, the program also discusses how to undertake such renovations, especially in added featurettes on construction included in the DVD releases of each season or on freestanding televised behind-the-scenes specials that served to expand ABC's content.[30] Dramatic tension is also culled from the seemingly staged banter of the design team, as when designer Preston Sharp is presented as the opposite of carpenter Paul DiMeo, a binary narrative opposition the series tried hard to mine for humor, with Sharp the metaphysical poet butting heads with DiMeo the feet-of-clay pragmatist.

The show aggressively promotes consumerism with its elaborate product integration, and it implies to the families that material goods will solve all of their problems.[31] Creator Tom Forman insists the show is not about materialism, saying his pitch to ABC was "good homes for good people," and that they carefully screen for people who really need assistance.[32] The situations of the families they choose to help range from a crew of foster kids trying to stay together to single parents struggling with financial problems. In the program's first season, one episode depicts a home makeover for eight siblings trying to stay together after both their parents died within days of each other ("The Cadigan-Scott Family"), another helps a widow with nine kids ("The Walswick Family"), and another aids a family whose father is in Iraq serving in the National Guard ("The Woslum Family").[33]

Yet the visual and rhetorical emphasis is on the home renovation products and the gorgeous mansions the team creates.

The feeling of sympathy with the suffering families is relentlessly emphasized in the narrative. In the episode with the eight orphans, for example, Pennington explains that this family of seven sisters and one brother, all aged 23 or younger, has suffered because the two eldest siblings had to move home and become the legal guardians of the younger kids, otherwise some would have been sent to foster care. Their tiny house is bursting at the seams and falling into disrepair. Pennington asserts a home makeover is a chance to keep the family together and to help them "move on" from the tragic deaths of both their parents from heart attacks. The eldest daughter, who has sacrificed mightily to stay at home and keep her family together, gets her own suite and support from the crew for her efforts. The sentimentalism is particularly heightened in the application videos, where each family must prove they are needier than the next by pitching their misery, and they often dissolve into tears. Each episode sentimentalizes the design team as well, with close-ups of, for example, shopping guru Tracy Hutson tearing up or of Pennington trying (unconvincingly) to exude empathy.

The show conscripts both community members and viewers to join in a process in which structural social problems felt most acutely on the level of housing are being framed as problems that can best be solved by private efforts involving corporate philanthropy. The producers' rhetoric also emphasizes this neoliberal community message. Forman argues: "It's not about ratings or awards. This is all about community. It's about making a difference in the life of a good family that's down on its luck and just needs a helping hand. We all need a little help sometime."[34] Senior producer Conrad Ricketts says he sees the building process, in which neighbors in these communities pitch in, as "kind of like the barn-raisings of the 1900s." He also insists that because they get so much local press coverage while building, "what you see is really the truth," they cannot fake anything or cut corners or run late.[35] The series is thus participatory in a distinctive way and banks on citizen desires to "make a difference" or "lend a hand and help a neighbor." When the show arrived in a community, they asked the neighbors to pitch in, and people turned out by the thousands. Some helped to build, some raised money, some helped decorate (which meant anything from making scrapbooks to arranging plants). Like a recruiting video for Habitat for Humanity (Disney makes donations to that organization when consumers purchase the DVDs) this reality series encourages viewers to want to be a part of this humanitarian effort because it showed so many people participating. The flocks of fans lining the street holding welcome home signs and chanting "move that bus" for the big reveal of the new house indicate how eager people are to feel like they can join in (a reveal moment meant to spark weeping and emotional realism). The implication is that each viewer would get their chance when the show arrived in their area. The massive ratings for the show for most of its run, as when it routinely finished in the top 10 in weekly ratings in its first several years on the air, indicate viewer eagerness to feel like they can join in, perhaps making the program a bellwether of how unhappy people are with the decline in a sense of community (pace much-debated arguments about a popular sense of the decline of communities).[36]

The families who need help are often families headed by single women or that feature some kind of alternative family structure that is represented as unstable or in need of bolstering and assistance. For example, when the series focuses on foster families, it takes a problem of social services and foster care (children broken up into different homes that suffer from a lack of financial support and resources) and turns it into a problem that can symbolically be solved by corporate America through one high-profile act of philanthropy. Again, after building the new home, the production team sometimes lobbies for private donations to help the families pay for increased taxes and mortgages. In "The Mendoza Family" episode, the producers choose a family headed by a single Latina mother who is a social worker raising a daughter and two foster sons, and who also reaches out to the six siblings of the boys, all of whom also live in foster care in other households. She gathers together the entire brood of siblings living in foster care for weekend visits with each other. The ABC program remodels her home in order to increase dramatically the space the mother has at her disposal, making it easier for her to take in foster children and providing a space for their far-flung siblings to gather. While this individual family has been helped by corporate charity, this act makes no structural change in the foster care system or its resources, and yet the program encourages viewers and participants to see these private acts of giving as the solution to a widespread social problem. In "The Harris Family," the series similarly rewards another single mother whose home has flooded, "Sweet" Alice Harris, an African American woman who has been serving her Watts neighborhood in South Central Los Angeles for 35 years. In an act echoing the Mendoza episode, the program builds her a larger home where she can take care of herself and also better serve the community.

The most extreme example of this dynamic in which the need for state-funded social services is framed as a matter of private concern is the episode about the eight siblings who are orphaned. The producers imply that by building the children a new home, the home itself will solve all of their problems. Similarly, another episode about a single mother involves a white working-class family of nine left bereft by the father's death from cancer. In "The Walswick Family," the design team remodels their home and makes it larger, turning the need for a social safety net into a private concern.

Other episodes are representative in the sense that they touch on major categories of need that the show deems to be legitimate when the families apply for their help by sending in the video tape auditions. Some families have been stricken by the illness of a family member and the inability to pay medical bills, a dynamic which obviously speaks to the need for greater health care coverage. The series instead implies that private solutions will solve the problem. "The Zitek Family" receives a remodeled home to help in the care of their paralyzed son, while "The Powell Family's" new home is designed to help them cope with their son's rare cell disorder and debilitating asthma and allergies. Several families are found worthy of aid because the father has made sacrifices to be a minister of some kind ("The Powers Family," "The Cox Family"), while others are aided because the father is a soldier and does not make enough money to support the family's housing needs ("The Woslum Family").

Instead of questioning the class system and distribution of wealth that make some families fall into poverty, the series insists everyone can pull themselves up by their bootstraps, with some assistance from corporate America. The prevailing ideology is, again, similar to nineteenth-century domestic science: good homes make good families, and good families are the building blocks of a strong nation. Many episodes pair these recurring messages with patriotic gestures of flag-waving as well as expressions of religious faith. These families, the programs suggests, must be saved through charity, or at best faith-based initiatives, not government reform. The episode involving the National Guardsman is particularly manipulative because ABC manages to prevail upon the Guard to send him home for leave for the week. They want him to reunite with his family on camera. Apparently, the intervention of network TV can get a soldier sent home on leave and can reunite a family. Similarly, critic Jennifer Gillan points to how the series deployed neoliberal messages alongside frontier mythology in the season two finale focusing on veterans, when it helped build a new home and a community center for the family of rescued prisoner of war (POW)

Jessica Lynch's fallen Navajo comrade, soldier Lori Piestewa, which became a way of assuaging guilt over more Native "vanishing Americans."[37]

As the television program provides families with assistance, instead of the assistance of social welfare programs, it also proffers a troubling idea, the suggestion that simply by watching the show, viewers can feel they have contributed to helping solve serious social problems, merely by consuming the program. Televised entertainment here becomes a substitute for social justice. On one hand, Forman admits the show's limitations but also makes serious humanitarian claims for it. "It's still a network television show and I don't want to pretend we're doing the work that Habitat for Humanity has been doing, but for that one family maybe we are." He goes on to say: "I think it's become something more than a television show." While Habitat has families work on their home sites too, to feel human dignity in their own situation, *Home Makeover* emphasizes an implausible, almost magical makeover of a home while the family in question vacations in Disney World.

The ideological fairy dust here obscures the economics and cultural politics involved in the show's neoliberal message. As in the parenting series, the sense of family crisis is solved by recourse to private efforts, which will maintain the family as autonomous. These programs are promoting neoliberal rhetoric most strongly when they imply that the strengthened family justifies further dismantling of the welfare state and undercutting of the kinds of social safety nets these networks are providing with their so-called expert help, paid for by corporate advertisers who are purchasing the attention of the viewers. Those viewers are encouraged to tune into this entertainment with a pseudosociological claim in order to feel a vicarious sense of helping their community or of furthering their own, individualistic self-improvement and family improvement.

As a footnote to the series, when current First Lady Michelle Obama also appeared on the program in 2011, her episode was different in its cultural politics, instead linking volunteerism and mass culture. But what is striking about this example is that instead of being a more recognizable volunteer effort, the volunteer work here is done in the context of a reality TV show that is, of course, a mass-circulated commodity packaged as entertainment that profits ABC and Disney. On that episode, Pennington and crew build a community center for homeless veterans in Fayetteville, North Carolina. On the broadcast, Obama promoted her Joining Forces national initiative promoting volunteer efforts to assist veterans and their families, cofounded with Dr. Jill Biden, wife of Vice President Joe Biden.

Obama cited the show's building renovation as an example of the kind of volunteer effort she urges.[38] However, the episode does not depict an on-going volunteer effort but rather a moment of high-profile corporate philanthropy, one that does not even appear as particularly philanthropic when one considers that it is filmed to be made into a mass media commodity that profits a media conglomerate. In my next chapter, I turn more fully to a different aspect of the family media spectacle, the gender wars.

Notes

1. Laurie Ouellette and James Hay, *Better Living through Reality TV: Television and Post-welfare Citizenship* (Malden, MA: Blackwell Publishing, 2008).

2. Mark Andrejevic, *Reality TV: The Work of Being Watched* (Lanham, MD: Rowman & Littlefield, 2004).

3. Annette Hill, *Reality TV: Factual Entertainment and Television Audiences* (London: Routledge, 2005).

4. They see this process as part of the biographical project of the reflexive self that social theorists such as Ulrich Beck and Anthony Giddens have identified. Helen Wood and Beverly Skeggs, "Notes on Ethical Scenarios of Self on British Reality TV," *Feminist Media Studies* 4, no. 2 (2004): 205–208. Ulrich Beck, *Risk Society: Towards a New Modernity* (London: Sage Publications, 1992). Anthony Giddens, *Modernity and Self-Identity: Self and Society in the Late Modern Age* (Stanford, CA: Stanford University Press, 1991).

5. Anne E. Kornblut, "Laura Bush Joins Hit Makeover Show as It Focuses on Storm Victims," *The New York Times*, September 28, 2005, http://www.nytimes.com/2005/09/28/national/nationalspecial/28makeover.html.

6. Stephen M. Silverman, "Laura Bush Guest Stars on *Extreme Makeover*," People.com, September 25, 2005, http://www.people.com/people/article/0,,1110624,00.html.

7. Mimi White, "Television, Therapy, and the Social Subject; or, The TV Therapy Machine," *Reality Squared: Televisual Discourse on the Real*, ed. James Friedman (New Brunswick, NJ: Rutgers University Press, 2002), 313–322. See also White, *Tele-Advising: Therapeutic Discourse in American Television* (Chapel Hill: University of North Carolina Press, 1992).

8. See Gareth Palmer for how so-called experts on lifestyle television function as mouthpieces for socializing consumers into bourgeois values. Gareth Palmer, " 'The New You': Class and Transformation in Lifestyle Television," *Understanding Reality Television*, eds. Su Homes and Deborah Jermyn (London: Routledge, 2004), 173–190, 173.

9. Ouellette and Hay, *Better Living*; Palmer, *Understanding Reality Television*.

10. Ron Becker, "'Help Is On the Way!': *Supernanny, Nanny 911,* and the Neo-liberal Politics of the Family," *The Great American Makeover: Television: History, Nation,* ed. Dana Heller (New York: Palgrave Macmillan, 2006), 175–192.

11. Susan J. Douglas and Meredith W. Michaels, *The Mommy Myth: The Idealization of Motherhood and How It Has Undermined Women* (New York: Free Press, 2004).

12. Lynn Spigel, *Make Room for TV: Television and the Family Ideal in Postwar America* (Chicago: University of Chicago Press, 1992), 9.

13. Relevant to my discussion here is how critics have complicated Habermas's idea of a bourgeois public sphere of civic engagement, showing how the public and private intertwine, how multiple publics exist, and how mass media helps enact those multiple publics (departing from Habermas's Frankfurt School view of the media as a debasing influence on audiences). Jürgen Habermas, *The Structural Transformation of the Public Sphere: An Inquiry into a Category of Bourgeois Society,* trans. Thomas Burger and Frederick Lawrence (1962; Cambridge, MA: MIT Press, 1992). Nancy Fraser, *Unruly Practices: Power, Discourse and Gender in Contemporary Social Theory* (Minneapolis: University of Minnesota Press, 1989), 113–143.

14. See Rebecca L. Stephens's explication of The Learning Channel shows and their cultural work of upholding a status quo. Stephens, "Socially Soothing Stories? Gender, Race, and Class in TLC's A Wedding Story and A Baby Story," *Understanding Reality Television,* eds. Su Holmes and Deborah Jermyn (London: Routledge, 2004), 191–210.

15. Annette Hill, *Factual Entertainment and Television Audiences* (London: Routledge, 2005).

16. Becker, *Supernanny,* 180.

17. See http://abc.go.com/primetime/supernanny/index.html.

18. Jo Frost, *Supernanny: How to Get the Best from Your Children* (New York: Hyperion, 2005), 10.

19. Frost, *Supernanny,* 11.

20. Frost, *Supernanny,* 11.

21. Frost, *Supernanny,* 14–15.

22. Frost, *Supernanny,* 13.

23. Leigh H. Edwards, "British Nanny Invasion: Review of *Supernanny,*" *PopMatters,* March 28, 2005, http://www.popmatters.com/pm/review/supernanny-2005/. In the following four paragraphs, I am adapting and updating material from my published review of the series.

24. "Ririe Family," *Supernanny,* ABC, season 1, episode 8, March 21, 2005.

25. "Walker Family," *Supernanny,* ABC, March 12, 2007.

26. A newer nanny show, *America's Supernanny* (2011–), on Lifetime, imports the format into an American context, with an African American nanny.

27. Leigh H. Edwards, "Good One: Review of *Meet Mr. Mom*," *PopMatters*, August 2, 2005, http://www.popmatters.com/pm/review/meet-mr-mom-050802. In my analysis of the series in the following paragraphs, I am adapting and updating material from my published review of the series.

28. See http://www.nbc.com/Meet_Mister_Mom/.

29. *Meet Mister Mom*, NBC, August 2, 2005.

30. See http://www.amazon.com/gp/product/B000AJJNJU/104-7369028-3956764?v=glance&n=130&n=507846&s=dvd&v=glance.

31. Critic June Deery has demonstrated that the program offers an aggressive pedagogy of consumerism, in which the self can be remade precisely through conspicuous consumption. Deery, "Interior Design: Commodifying the Self and Place in *Extreme Makeover, Extreme Makeover: Home Edition*, and *The Swan*," *The Great American Makeover: Television, History, Nation*, ed. Dana Heller (New York: Palgrave Macmillan, 2006), 159–174.

32. *Extreme Makeover Home Edition: The Most Inspiring and Unforgettable Makeovers from Season 1*, DVD, Buena Vista, 2005.

33. "The Cadigan-Scott Family," *Extreme Makeover: Home Edition*, ABC, season 1, episode 12, May 23, 2004. "The Walswick Family," season 1, episode 10, May 9, 2004. "The Woslum Family," season 1, episode 2, February 22, 2004.

34. *Extreme Makeover Home Edition: The Official Companion Book* (New York: Hyperion, 2005), 5.

35. *Extreme Makeover*.

36. See debates sparked by the national best seller, Robert D. Putnam's *Bowling Alone: The Collapse and Revival of American Community* (New York: Simon & Schuster, 2001).

37. Gillan further demonstrates how the series models neoliberal citizenship for viewers when it invokes American frontier mythology and an idea of neighborliness. Gillan, *"Extreme Makeover Homeland Security Edition," The Great American Makeover: Television: History, Nation*, ed. Dana Heller (New York: Palgrave Macmillan, 2006), 193–210.

38. "Marshall Family," *Extreme Makeover: Home Edition*, ABC, September 25, 2011. Colleen Curtis, "Joining Forces with Extreme Makeover: Home Edition," September 23, 2011, http://www.whitehouse.gov/blog/2011/09/23/joining-forces-extreme-makeover-home-edition.

Chapter 5

Wife Swap: Gender Wars

Continuing to explore the narrative trends in reality programs about the family, I now turn to a programming format that asks participants to judge each other's parenting, homemaking, and partnering skills by swapping homes and lives. These programs provide us with a particularly apt case study for further examining gender role dynamics on reality TV, because the idea of a battle of the sexes, as in some gamedoc shows, is a central narrative conceit. Not only do these programs norm gender role dimorphism (the husband-provider and the mother-caregiver, even if she works outside the home), they also map race and class hierarchies onto this central narrative of gender, partially questioning some norms and stereotypes while reinforcing others.

Mostly focused on having women trade places for several days to two weeks, series such as *Wife Swap* and *Trading Spouses: Meet Your New Mommy* highlight a rhetoric of crisis in the family unit—a rhetoric scholars have shown to be commonplace in public discourse about the family.[1] In each instance of cultural expression in which the idea of family crisis is articulated, it is important to detail the kinds of social fears such a rhetoric is responding to in specific sociohistorical contexts.

In this instance, I have been arguing that reality TV responds directly to tensions and anxieties about the changing shape of households and definitions of family in the United States. The larger social tension between family models, specifically the movement from the modern nuclear family to a postmodern diversity of family forms, becomes evident in this subgenre of family switching shows most intensely through the debates the participants have with each other. After learning the protocols and norms each woman utilizes in her own home, the visiting mother is asked to institute rules changes, in which she instructs her host family in new behaviors meant to improve their family dynamic or the running of their household. In making these changes in another family's life patterns, all the participants are forced to express and defend their standards and ideologies about family life.

The crisis rhetoric often appears in the voice-over narration in these programs, in which judgments are expressed, from the program's narrative point of view, about the problems each family exhibits (judgments reinforced by the selective narrative and visual editing of each episode). Each family is presented as having some flaw or shortcoming that could throw it into peril, and it is up to the visitor to correct the problem. Alternatively, the original mother of each home is herself implicitly encouraged to correct the issue based on her experience of seeing her behavior refracted back to her through this media representation and through the judgments of a peer, specifically a stranger chosen precisely for having views that oppose her own. The program narration and editing upholds certain norms and depends on taking binary oppositions and bringing them into a liberal pluralist consensus by the end of each episode. In so doing, the programs fit into what scholars have identified as the dominant ideological mode of address of current television—liberal pluralism. Nevertheless, through picturing a process of judgment and debate between the participants, the series introduce a degree of uncertainty about proper norms or imply that there are a number of different norms possible or behaviors worthy of value. Thus, the current state of "the American family" appears as a matter of debate.

In addition to framing the family in terms of crisis and debate, these programs also draw conflict from identity categories such as gender, race, class, and sexuality. While the staging of family debates might slightly decenter or denaturalize some older norms about kinship relations, the way the programs address identity categories is largely regressive, in the sense that, again, they tend to question some stereotypes but aggressively reinforce others. Locating the performance of these identity categories in the context of the family, the series reinforce traditional social hierarchies, specifically by privileging white patriarchal family models. Regarding gender on reality TV, in their special issue of *Feminist Media Studies* focused on this topic (which included an article of mine about gender stereotypes on reality TV), Sujata Moorti and Karen Ross note the importance of examining the status of gender difference and gender binaries on reality TV and how these narratives are used to produce models of gendered selfhood.[2] On the troubled history of depictions of race on television, Herman Gray has pointed out that TV traditionally has tended to keep race "at arms' length."[3] Sasha Torres has noted the need for more scholarship analyzing race on TV, arguing strongly that TV depends on racial difference to organize images, narratives, and discursive flows—and in order to signify.[4] In my view, these family switching reality shows epitomize that dynamic.

As the framing narratives set up structuring binary oppositions, gender often takes center stage. As in the nanny shows, one underlying message proffered by the programs is that men should accept a more expanded set of domestic duties as their emerging social role. Because the women leave the home during the experiment period, the men and children, the program implies, must necessarily learn to appreciate her and her labor for them more. Her contribution to the household, previously invisible, is made visible. The sometimes implicit directive that emerges by episode's end is that the men should help their busy wives with childcare, cooking, cleaning, and laundry. However, this imperative to "help out more," a constant refrain in the comments of the participants, does not disturb a binary of gender difference in which the household is organized around the mother's role as a nurturer-caregiver. Even if she works outside of the home, she is still expected to perform this role in which she engages in the social reproduction of her husband and children.

The use of comedic elements in these reality sitcoms and docusoaps plays a key role in assuaging anxiety about changing gender roles in society. TV scholars Patricia Mellencamp, Mary Beth Haralovich, Susan Douglas, and Jennifer Gillan have all demonstrated how certain television genres, such as the 1950s star-sitcom or its update, the celebrity reality domestic sitcom, use comedy to express indirectly gender tensions germane to their own sociohistorical moment.[5] As their arguments suggest, for example, in 1950s episodes of *I Love Lucy*, Lucy Ricardo keeps trying to enter show business and move beyond her role as wife and mother, but each time she fails and she and her husband Ricky laugh off her attempts. However, this laughter does not resolve the gender tensions, instead leaving them evident and unresolved. Domestic sitcoms of the 1950s thus comment on gender tensions of the epoch, as the wives both reasserted and subverted gender norms. Joanne Morreale argues that by the late 1950s and into the 1960s, traditional family sitcoms did the cultural work of trying to restabilize the traditional modern nuclear family that U.S. culture was attempting to norm after the war. Gillan reads in modern celebrity reality sitcoms like *The Osbournes* a combination of these strategies, merging both the humorous rebel of the 1950s and the happy homebody of the 1960s and *Leave It to Beaver*, and she insists that the resulting open-ended story lines on *The Osbournes* speak to viewers because they are more accurate for a current, postmodern existence, as opposed to earlier sitcoms focused on narrative closure and certainty.[6] Indeed the tensions on reality programs about the family, not just celebrity families, also speak to a negotiation among different models of the self as performed and changing gender role norms constantly in tension and under debate. Again, I would identify the relevant sociohistorical context here as the shift to the postmodern family or a diversity of forms with no narrative closure.

When addressing difference directly, through race or sexuality, the series eagerly promote a kind of corporate multiculturalism, turning superficial diversity into another commodity and eschewing substantive cultural differences. The edited narratives continually recur to a model in which an updated modern nuclear family (with a working wife) rooted in white bourgeois values is normed. Meanwhile, all other signs of "difference," whether gay couples or African American extended families, are tolerated but are presented as marginal, not normed. In that sense, this programming continues a conservative trend Herman Gray noted in the 1980s, in which black families represented on television in programs such as *The Cosby Show* were positioned in relation to a white bourgeois norm and were accepted in the precise degree to which they approximated that modern nuclear family norm.[7]

In switches involving intact white nuclear families and single mothers, for example, while the single mother is shown as valiant in her efforts, the nuclear family is presented as the rational, functional model. In terms of class depictions, while wealthy families who flaunt their conspicuous consumption are criticized, impoverished working-class families are shown to be noble in their struggles but not enviable or part of the norm. In all of the alternative households pictured, for example, whether marginalized based on race, sexuality, income, or alternative worldviews (such as atheists, astrologers, Buddhists, Wiccans, or rock star parents who do not wish to replicate middle-class, middle-age norms), the children continually express a sense of frustration or irritation at their marginalization and some degree of longing for so-called normal family models. While the program narratives critique as excessive any intense nostalgia for an older version of the modern nuclear family, satirizing the idea of women as obedient homemakers, they nevertheless limit the range of new norms.

Production and Marketing Contexts

ABC's *Wife Swap* and Fox's *Trading Spouses: Meet Your New Mommy* are both based on a British format, and they initially sparked controversy because the ABC show hired the British executive producers from the 2003 original series, while the Fox show was the copycat production that beat *Wife Swap* to air, both premiering in 2004 within months of each other. *Trading Spouses* debuted on July 20, 2004, while *Wife Swap* first aired on September 20, 2004.[8]

The series also exhibited distinct marketing strategies. ABC promoted *Wife Swap* as a much more so-called high culture or high brow version (with all the class distinctions and hierarchies implied by a claim of high versus low culture) of reality TV. In promotional materials, ABC lauded the series as one which drew more strongly on documentary traditions, made sociological claims to record the current state of families faithfully, and featured some degree of public service being performed; that is, instructing viewers on proper behavior and giving participants the chance to better themselves and their marriages as a result of their experiences on the program. In press interviews surrounding the U.S. premiere, for example, *Wife Swap* executive producers Stephen Lambert and Jenny Crowther drew attention to their background as documentary filmmakers as well as their work in television news. Lambert argued that they did not offer a cash reward on their series, in contrast to *Trading Spouses,* because "The reward is the hope that your relationship will be stronger as a result of taking part in the show. Our experience in the UK and already with the episodes we've been doing in the States [is that] marriages have been strengthened as a result of this."[9]

Fox's show, meanwhile, was promoted as part of Fox's suite of reality shows focusing on conflict and sensationalism, and their marketing for the show continues to emphasize those elements. In one particularly high-profile 2005 marketing campaign, for instance, Fox ran frequent televised ads with clips of one of their most sensationalistic episodes. The advertisements featured the "God warrior" woman, a fundamentalist Christian from Louisiana who, during her episodes, became enraged with a Massachusetts family and their beliefs in astrology. The promotional clip, run during Fox programs and on the network website, features a screaming, wild-eyed woman almost foaming at the mouth and yelling: "They're tampering with the dark side. This is tainted. I am a God warrior, and I don't want anyone tainted doing anything with my family." While screeching these words, the woman rips apart the sealed envelope, left for her by the guest mother, describing how the $50,000 the family earned by being on the program was to be spent.

As this marketing encapsulates, instead of portraying a substantive difference of opinion concerning religion, the Fox series is intent on offering up the "God warrior" as a spectacle, an extreme instance of religious fervor meant to be an object of ridicule and controversy. The woman, Marguerite Perrin, from Ponchatoula, Louisiana, runs a dance studio and lives with her husband, daughter, and granddaughter. Perrin switched homes with Jeanne D'Amico Flisher, a hypnotherapist who lives with her husband Chris Flisher, an astrologer, and their four children. The husband and wife team also hosted a local radio show entitled "Love Talk USA." During one sequence while guest hosting that radio show, Perrin was asked to talk with a self-declared Christian astrologer and instead walked out of the studio during the middle of the radio show. Her host family was shocked to learn of her reaction, since she did not have any aggressive interactions with them during the making of the two-part episode arc (2005).[10] Fox made the moment of eruption the centerpiece of their marketing. It is precisely that kind of focus on conflict and sensationalism that characterizes their framing of their show.[11] They returned to milk this dynamic further when they later brought Perrin back, an unprecedented move, for another two-part episode (2007).[12]

The reception of the two series in the popular press mimics this distinction between them. Many reviewers followed the lead of this kind of promotional rhetoric and lauded the later ABC show over its earlier Fox rival, specifically by pointing to its high culture aspirations, and to taste markers, which are inevitably linked to class status and a norming of bourgeois values, as sociologist Pierre Bourdieu so influentially demonstrated. Noting the high culture sheen, what Bourdieu would term the "cultural capital," of this show, one reviewer, while dubbing *Trading Spouses* "Fox's sleazy knockoff," described *Wife Swap* as "a rare reality show that is classy and says some things about family values and dynamics while still being entertaining. It may have elements of a reality show as we know it—the artificial setup, for one—but it's closer in tone to a documentary series."[13] Another reviewer makes similar distinctions between the two programs: "ABC's *Wife Swap* is a much more intricately plotted, well-cast and videotaped entry that actually examines family values and cultural differences in an informative, entertaining, almost documentarian, way. *Trading Spouses* is a rush-job rip-off of that idea." The reviewer goes on to note the criticism Fox has taken for purportedly pirating formats.[14] Another media critic finds that "ABC's show, although still constructed by crafty reality-show editing, has more of a sociological class study flavor to it."[15] Even when some reviewers are critical of both, they still note the format's "sociological potential."[16]

Such marketing speaks to the specific claims to documentary fidelity, public service, and self-improvement that characterize many formats in reality TV as a hybrid genre. It also underscores the degree to which the family as a topic generates popular interest precisely because it has been a battleground in the media over issues of moral values, identities, and social hierarchies. In addition, the degree to which the two series are marketed in contrasting ways reflects the two networks' different marketing imperatives and product identities, and the strategies they use to capture target audiences. As part of suites of reality programming on their networks, these programs share some marketing and target demographics with other reality series on their networks.

Narrative Structures

The two programs differ in the frameworks for their narratives. While *Wife Swap* is structured in one-hour free-standing episodes, *Trading Spouses* uses a two-episode arc for each family narrative. Since *Trading Spouses* is also a gamedoc, the narrative depends more on conflict and competition. While each family is assured of winning $50,000, they do not know how the money will be spent until the visiting mother makes that judgment. The moment in which the visitor takes up the decision-making power is a surprise twist, in which everyone learns that the visiting mother has the right to decide how the host family will spend their winnings.

However, both series are similar in their strong dependence on binary oppositions to organize their narratives. Each family swap is set up to emphasize some key tension point between the two households, one designed to spark conflict, sensationalism, and ratings, even if the participants themselves are unaware of the framing tension. The relentless narrative and visual emphasis on the opposition suffuses each episode. TV narratives in general most often depend on binary oppositions; a particular emphasis on contrasting ideas, such as masculine versus feminine codes and their connotations, helps structure the discourse or narration process, which shapes and directs story events, on television programs.[17] For both series, the voice-over narration joins with the story editing and narrative discourse to communicate the show's narrative point of view, or the agency behind the story-telling. Sarah Kozloff, discussing the complexity of authorship and the author function on television, calls this dynamic the "implied author," or the "textual construct" that is "the viewer's sense of the organizing force behind the world of the show."[18] I would add that there is also an implied viewer in these shows, as the program addresses an imagined viewer as part of the text itself.

For both series, the implied author levels harsh judgments of the women and their parenting and household management skills, and it organizes each episode around a reductive binary opposition between the two families, based on categories such as gender roles, class, racism, taste, religious beliefs, regional differences, standards of household cleanliness, and parenting standards. In the opening sequence for *Wife Swap,* we hear dramatic music and see images a city, suburbs, and rural homes as the voice-over intones: "Each week from across America, two families are chosen," followed by the graphic: "It will change their lives." We then see images of first one family, then the other standing in front of their homes in an almost American Gothic-style portrait while the voice-over narration establishes opposing stereotypes for them. Smiling winningly at the camera, the participants clearly have no idea how the voice-over narration is framing them. As we see intercut scenes flashing ahead to the conflicts that unfold when the women swap homes, the voice-over then tells us: "Each wife is about to get a new husband, new children, and a new life" while a graphic reads: "They swap lives for 2 weeks." After more clips of scenes prefiguring the conflicts to come, the voice-over offers this marketing summation: "Real homes. Real lives. Real drama."

In an episode involving a switch between a rural ranch family in Delaware and a suburban self-declared "luxury hairstylist" in Ohio, the voice-over narration encapsulates class differences in the opening description of them. Accompanying an image of the parents and two children and their horses, standing in front of a barn, we hear: "This week, the Ridgely family from Delaware. Wife Jen is a tough as nails cowgirl who works the ranch 24–7. Husband Randy is a professional bull fighter who treats his wife more like a ranch hand than a spouse. Their two daughters aged 7 and 3 have tons of chores and aren't permitted to whine or cry." The scene of the family standing in front of their house shifts and the camera provides a humorous close-up of the tiny three-year-old perched precariously on her horse's saddle, looking scared and ready to cry. In a related technique involving thematic and visual juxtaposition, the series often uses a humorous juxtaposition in which a visual image contradicts what a speaker has just asserted to be true. In this particular episode, shifting to an image of a woman in a fur coat standing with her husband and two kids in front of an opulent brownstone, their son playing a video game, the voice-over continues: "And from Ohio, the Corrao family. Kim is a glamorous high maintenance mom whose husband allows her to live a pampered, party girl lifestyle. Their two spoiled children are prone to frequent tantrums."[19]

In this short point–counterpoint sequence, we quickly learn implicit norms—that is, that hard work is to be valued, but a woman should not work so hard that she is no longer feminine, nor should the children be worked too hard for their age. Meanwhile, materialistic women need to learn to rein in their consumerism to some degree to pay more attention to their children. Additionally, submissive husbands must become more assertive.

Such oppositions based on gender, race, or class differences are framed as core oppositions that are foundational (as, for examples, tensions between dominant and marginal versions of masculinity and femininity), while other sets of oppositions, such as tidiness, are framed as personality differences. One *Wife Swap* episode sets up, in the opening voice-over narration, a gender binary between a Wiccan high-priestess "whose husband worships the ground she walks on" versus a "traditional stay-at-home wife and mother of two kids, whose husband expects her to do everything for him."[20] By the end of the episode, both women have been trained in a new gender role that is framed as more "normal." The Wiccan mother has been chastised for being too independent, her husband trained to be more assertive, and their children given the chance to have alternative influences beyond Wicca. The homemaker mother has benefited from her husband offering to help her around the house more. The show's pedagogy is to frame each woman as being on opposite extremes of a spectrum of gender role behaviors and to pull them toward some imagined norm in the center, in which the women must be nurturer-caregivers and the men must provide them with some degree of assistance.

In contrast, sometimes the binary oppositions seem aggressively contrived, as in one *Wife Swap* episode that describes one woman as "disorganized, with 25 pets" and the other as "an obsessively tidy woman who hates animals."[21] Both learn a less extreme model of cleaning their homes and the animal hater learns to tolerate animals and even gets her own pet after her experience of swapping homes. Yet the disagreement over the proper cleanliness of a home or the status of pets seems to be attributed to personality quirks rather than substantive differences.

The binary oppositions often involve class, which then becomes tied to parenting values. The show rejects materialistic moms but also ridicules rural working-class moms. In the second two-part episode of *Trading*

Spouses, for example, wealthy blonde Californian Samantha Pilek trades her beach house for the mobile home of Lisa Bowers, the mother of a working-class family living in a rural area in Massachusetts. Bowers is denigrated by the program's narrative both because she is described as having "poor taste," but also because she is shown to be too bossy and has alienated her husband and children. The two sets of behaviors are connected throughout the narrative. When Bowers arrives to live with the Pilek family, Samantha's husband, a yacht captain, begins avoiding her due to her gruff behavior, and she alienates their neighbors and finally ends up drinking and crying in her guest room. Pilek, meanwhile, has a more positive experience with the Bowers family. She is framed as having good grace and good manners, implicitly due to her class status, and she promptly encourages the daughter of the house, Katy, to approximate more closely normed gender roles by turning away from being a tomboy into being "a girly girl" who likes fancier clothes and has her hair styled at a salon. As a consequence of these narrative dynamics, in this instance at least, higher class status is framed as equating with better parenting. In other episodes, lower class status, described as a common folk or salt of the earth status, is sometimes favored for better parenting.[22]

On another episode of *Wife Swap,* Jodi Spolansky, a Manhattan millionaire heiress who has "never worked a day in her life" and has four nannies to care for her three children, changes places with Lynn Bradley, a working-class rural New Jersey bus driver and wood chopper with two kids and a husband who does not help her with the chores.[23] Lynn's husband Brad challenges Jodi's snobbery while Jodi's husband Steven ridicules Lynn as a country bumpkin. After several shouting matches, for example, Brad and Jodi start to communicate, share different viewpoints, and see beyond their material goods, the trappings of social status, and other props of identity. They make friends with each other. Brad listens to Jodi and decides he should help around the house more and try to be a more sensitive husband. As a result of living Lynn's life, Jodi resolves to spend more time with her kids. However, Lynn is so alienated by Steven's ridicule and unwillingness to listen to her that she leaves the opulent Spolansky apartment a day early, and Steven seems merely bemused by the whole experiment when the two couples meet to discuss what they learned. The show likes to have it both ways: the edited narrative focuses on people critiquing their own preconceptions, but it also makes fun of the cast and sometimes pigeonholes them itself.[24] While framing Brad as a boor for his upper-class pretensions and dismissiveness toward Lynn, the episode also plays a parody of *Deliverance*-style bluegrass music as a leitmotif in Lynn's scenes and sensationalizes things she does not know about the city.

These episodes try to fit their material back into a liberal pluralist framework of consensus by the end. However, some episodes have to work harder than others to do so, especially when they have moments in which the prevailing ideology fails to account for a moment of conflict and the text simply moves on, failing to explain away the conflict. Both programs end each episode with a meeting between the swapped mothers in which each attempts to instruct her counterpart on her failings and areas on which she needs to improve. Most encounters involve some tension and defensiveness followed by a sense of appreciation at learning something from the experience.

This kind of moment can sometimes stem from class conflicts that erupt into physical confrontations and Jerry Springer–style fights. On the "Ridgely/Corrao" episode of *Wife Swap* mentioned above, for example, the ranch family from Delaware comes into conflict with the materialistic family from Ohio. While *Trading Spouses* has only the wives meet in person at the end of the taping, *Wife Swap* has both couples meet across a table. In this episode, after the ranch mother calls the Ohio mother "a slut" and her submissive husband "a sap," the two women begin yelling at each other and the rural husband, a professional rodeo cowboy, flips over the table, then confronts the suburban husband, a grocery wholesaler, and punches him.

This episode thus pictures gender role tensions, because an earlier model of hard-bodied masculinity (prowess through physical labor) competes with a more recent, information-age model of masculinity in the form of the businessman. The episode amplifies this gender conflict. As the cowboy throws the punch, the color image is frozen into a black and white freeze-frame image. The Ohio man yells at the cowboy: "I'm suing your ass" and then bellows: "Security, call the police." The image then jump cuts into a later direct address interview with the cowboy couple as the voice-over intones: "The couples declined to return to the table but agreed to talk about what went down." The cowboy husband explains his viewpoint: "Definitely both wives were arguing across the table, I jumped up and flipped the table over, and her husband got some cowboy education." We cut to the visibly shaken Ohio man, his wife by his side, who says: "I guess that's how they do it on the farm. They just, you know, it's hit first and ask questions later, and I feel bad in the fact that if they're raising their kids and all about their kids and how great structure is, maybe they can tell their kids that their dad punched a guy in the face on national TV."[25]

Given no resolution to that conflict, the program leaves it open-ended and instead shifts to the next standard stage of the narrative, in which parents are reunited with their children. In this episode, that stage launches with the odd, truncated voice-over narration: "After a round of interviews with the local sheriff, the couples are about to be reunited with their children." The rushed transition, which obviously fails to address fully the preceding conflict, highlights how unresolved the narrative is. These reunion scenes are followed by the standard closing sequence, in which we are given a family update to see the changes that have happened in each family since the switch, and each discuss what they have learned from the process. Both claim to have learned "how lucky" they are, and both incorporate some elements from the visiting mothers, which is the standard liberal pluralist resolution that in this instance does not paper over the conflict that occurred in earlier scenes.

Narrative and Identity

The series also force the female participants to explain their own sense of identity. They must leave household manuals for the visiting mother, in which they describe their beliefs about childrearing, gender roles in marriage, their daily routines, rules for their children, and the relationship between work and family life. These manuals, also available on the network websites, force the women to provide a profile of themselves. The visiting mother must attempt to live that story for a period of time, effectively performing the woman's character as described, before she can change the rules and institute her own code of conduct and operations for the home. In these series, that story process gains another layer of complexity, since the women write answers to questions in order to detail what I term their own "character narrative" that the visiting woman will try to play.

One result of this dynamic is that these series imply that social identity is an arbitrary performance—one can switch places with someone else and inhabit their social identity or choose to change their social identity. By the end of the episode, these women often report deciding to change something about their own identity based on their performance of someone else's, or they notice that they have automatically altered some aspect of their personality as a result of playing someone else. The selfhood being articulated here is thus more a postmodern, decentered, performed self, not an older model of a rationalized, humanist self with an essential, unchanging core. The role of narrative in shaping identity on these programs is crucial, and it is often through the narrative tropes that we find this fraught sense of identity emerging. This use of narrative opens up a set of larger questions about how reality TV creates "character narratives" for participants.

Again, what many of these programs share is the suggestion that one can learn to find one's true self through media narratives, an idea the genre repeatedly links to family stories. Cultural theorists have long argued that the family itself is a space of identity formation through narrative.[26] Many of these reality TV narratives create identity through mass-mediated versions of the family. We know that domestic behavior itself is a theatrical performance. Spigel has argued convincingly that early sitcoms of the late 1940s through the 1950s treated families as theater troupes as opposed to approximations of real families, consequently framing family life as a theater of roles for the middle class.[27] In contrast, reality TV is exactly concerned with conveying "real" families in the 1990s and 2000s, but here the actual families become theatrical in part because the genre's edited narratives filter them through the history of the TV family sitcom as a dominant cultural narrative.

Race and Gender Conflict

In the family swapping format, the narratives of binary oppositions organized around class, gender, and race reveal prevailing attitudes and norms concerning these identity categories and social hierarchies. The issue of how reality TV is both reflecting and shaping gender and racial norms and stereotypes has been a matter of particular concern to television studies scholars. The family swapping series provide a particularly helpful case study for opening up larger questions about the depiction of race and gender on reality TV. In this section, I will provide a fuller textual analysis of one exemplary episode of *Wife Swap* that strikingly encapsulates race and gender issues, and I will use that discussion to raise larger issues about the reality genre more generally.

In their attention to functional and dysfunctional models, both programs often cover for class, race, or gender-based conflict. While participants argue over the importance of cleaning or organization or appropriate levels of emotional closeness or the right way to approach consumer culture for their children, they are often more centrally responding to these broader tensions. In one particularly heated episode of *Wife Swap,* for example, Maryland mother Shelley Elliot criticized Sue Burkhalter of Mississippi for having lax house rules, while Burkhalter castigated Elliot for running her house as too strict a disciplinarian. But the core of their conflict was cultural, i.e., stemming from different cultural practices associated with different racial groups, and with conflict over racist ideas. White mother Burkhalter kept a "mammy" cookie jar in their kitchen, and African American mother Elliot was forced to explain to the white family why the jar was offensive. Meanwhile, Elliot's husband and children took Burkhalter to a black church for the first time. The white family emerges lauding the idea that their horizons have been broadened, while the African American family was relieved to have the experience ended. Accounts of the controversial episode in the popular press congratulated the white family for learning to be "more open-minded."[28] The role the Elliot family implicitly plays in this episode is to educate a Southern white family out of racist views and stereotypes. The nurturing of the white family remains the focus, while the alternative views of the African American family provide a new sense of corporate multiculturalism to the white household.

Another racially charged episode on *Wife Swap,* "Flummerfelt/Bray," pushes stereotypes to an extreme but ends with a liberal pluralist resolution. ABC bills the episode as picturing how "two integrated families swap lives and push racial stereotypes to the limit." In both families, the wives believe that gender roles as defined by their husbands are based on their husband's race. A black wife with a white husband begins by arguing that "all black men are male chauvinist pigs," while the white wife with a black husband argues that "black men in my experience typically know who they are as men" as she embraces her role as a submissive wife to "a real man" who leaves all the child and homecare to her because "that's what women do."[29] Over the course of tense encounters between the families the black wife decides to be more maternal and to question her stereotypes about black men, while the white wife with a black husband becomes less submissive, asks her husband for more help around the home, and begins to suggest to her five home-schooled children that they might be allowed to move beyond traditional gender roles if they so choose. The program tries to script both families into perceived norms involving race and gender.

Fascinating Womanhood

A fuller example of the intersection of race and gender issues can be found in another *Wife Swap* episode, one that provides a level of complexity that begs more extensive discussion. This particularly telling episode places race and gender roles in American families on the table and offers it up for debate. The episode, "Fuentes/Lawson," turns the participants into types, fitting them into familiar television narratives.[30] In creating their character narratives, the series generative quick narrative arcs of development, encouraging audiences to sympathize with or identify with these people—though sometimes framing some of them as villains to be judged negatively. Viewers fit a larger reality TV schema in which they are asked to be, in John Corner's formulation, both voyeurs and judges of each person's performance of self.[31]

The ABC network website describes the central narrative for this episode, just as the voice-over narration at the beginning of the episode sets the stage: "A female police detective, who believes a woman can do anything a man can do, swaps places with an obedient, stay-at-home mother who believes her role is to fulfill her husband's demands." By framing each woman as a type and providing a central narrative of conflict, this storyline shapes the episode in terms of reducing people to stereotypical characteristics and proffering competing value systems as a source of central conflict and dramatic strife. Each episode uses soap-opera conventions to feature a great deal of summarizing and previewing after and before commercial breaks, which targets an audience demographic of busy mothers looking in intermittently from household labor. After setting up the central premise and offering previews of conflict between these opposing women and their value systems, the episode spends several minutes fleshing out the before the swap situation in each household. Each episode mixes sequences of the families interacting with each other intercut with footage from direct address interviews to the camera, some filmed while the participant is engaged in a task and is commenting on it, others in the now-standard reality TV style of confessional, to a stationary camera while they are alone. These confessional moments work to establish a sense of intimacy or identification with the viewer.

The narrative frame moves insistently toward a liberal pluralist resolution, in which both women will learn something from the other. They are both encouraged to make some positive changes in their household based on their experience of living someone else's life (and of having their own household and own experiences offered up on national TV for the judgment of the home viewers). Most participants, when prompted about what they hope to gain from being on the show (a question the voice-over poses), will reply that they hope to teach others some of their helpful values and learn new strategies and about things they can improve. The focus is on personal growth and self-knowledge through inhabiting someone else's life and through media scrutiny of their own. The narrative encourages both parties to compromise about their competing ideals, thus pressing for some kind of consensus middle ground.

As it pushes for this pluralism, the voice-over narration and the editing elucidate the kinds of values the program is norming in the way they frame and treat participants. Some of these recurring norms include the idea that men should help more with domestic duties, women should be able to work outside the home, but they must not place work over family to the degree that they do not spend enough time with their children and husband. There is a recurring emphasis on family time at the dinner table, clean homes (although not obsessively clean), open communication among parents and children (although not overly lax boundaries), and individualism and self-expression for all members of the household (although the episodes seem worried about too much individualism and atomization of household members). Recurring objects of derision include "pampering" oneself too much, a prohibition established by recurring shots of women getting facials and pedicures at spas, or indulging oneself with too much shopping, with stock shots of the women with overflowing shopping bags. Tell-tale tropes the series uses to signify families in trouble include household members going off to eat dinner alone, going off to watch TV alone in their own rooms, or spending a lot of time on the telephone to friends rather than interacting with family members. Through gazing at a series of examples that are tested against each other, the series offers a trial and error pedagogy in which this implicit value system is reinforced by the narration each time, cumulatively.

The episode critiques women for being either too independent or too submissive. In quick contrasts between the two households, the opening sequence cuts back and forth between them. For the "tough, independent-minded" workaholic California mom, the voice-over tells us, "Lillian Fuentes is a cop who works 18 hour days" and leaves her "fiancé and his mom to pick up the slack." For the stay-at-home mom who yearns to be a "domestic goddess," the voice-over intones, "Dawn Lawson thinks a woman's place is in the home," and under her husband's "dictatorship," she tries to fulfill his every need, and she "even clips his nails." While Dawn follows the rules of a book from a housewifery book from the 1960s that she wants to emulate, Lillian, as we see in quick preview shots of her living in the Lawson household, finds her submissiveness to her husband ridiculous, saying in a direct address interview to the camera: "If that's what marriage is all about, they can have it." As the voice-over proposes the standard question: "What do they hope to gain from the swap?", we see Lillian telling the camera she hopes to have a "reality check" about how her life is going, while Dawn wants to share her household strategies and "allow the husband to experience being the king of his house."

The set-up identifies this core opposition as the problem each woman must learn from in this experience. The premise sets up both women as extremes, the overly independent career woman versus the overly submissive housewife (which speaks to larger contemporary "mommy wars" tensions between working moms and housewives), and equates their lifestyles as equally off-kilter or outside of an implicit norm. Ominously noting the problems Lillian's independence has caused in her family, over a picture of Lillian and husband Bill rushing around in their solo daily business, the voice-over intones: "Financier Bill hasn't always wanted such a tough, independent-minded woman," noting that the two once broke up over this issue because Bill "wanted a stay-at-home wife and mother." The set-up also establishes the idea that even when she does spend time with her two young sons, Lillian is primarily focused on work, because she spends that time quizzing them and running them through drills about proper fire and personal safety. The episode also critiques Lillian for spending some of her sparse spare time pampering herself rather than bonding with her kids, as we see images of her getting facials at a spa.

Dawn, meanwhile, comes in for harsher critique for subscribing to outmoded ideals. Thus, while both women are criticized for being outside of some implicit norm, Dawn is the worst offender in this example—the workaholic mother fits a new system of norms better than the 1960s throwback mother. Introducing the opening segment about her, the episode uses breezy music appropriate to a *Leave It to Beaver*–style sitcom. As it returns to that leitmotif each time it pictures her household, we know she is being ridiculed. Tellingly, we see a preview of Dawn, at the table meeting between the two couples that ends each episode, saying that she has always had this feeling inside of her that she wants to "be June Cleaver." She follows the teaching of Helen Andelin's 1963 book, *Fascinating Womanhood,* which purports to teach women how to be a "domestic goddess," by being a diligent wife and mother, cooking, cleaning, doing interior decorating, and always catering to her husband's needs.

Again, we know the book is being ridiculed because when the segment about her opens, we see a graphic of a large book opening to show her cheerful home. Dawn, explaining how she follows the book's guidelines, says she tries to "look nice when he comes home"; she puts on makeup, meets him at the door and takes his coat and shoes, and lets him know that "he is on a pedestal." For his part, her husband Demetrius equally subscribes to his vision of traditional gender roles and divisions of labor, saying, "I wear the pants." Dawn seems conscious that her values might seem out of step in the twenty-first century, saying, "I believe it's important to honor and submit to your husband, things a lot of women might find degrading." While she celebrates her "pleasure in doing drudgery," and the episode features shots of her weekly book group meeting to discuss the teachings of *Fascinating Womanhood,* the voice-over undercuts her by describing her as "shackled to her house" because the family only has one car; thus, she usually stays home and has to ask Demetrius permission to go anywhere. As Demetrius's teenage son Calvin and the couple's two young sons flash by on screen during family montages, Calvin, in direct address interviews to the camera, expresses his displeasure at his strict father who will not "listen to him." By equating the son's easily recognizable sense of being oppressed with Dawn's situation, the voice-over again denigrates her expressed values, as the narration describes "no independence for Dawn and no independence for Demetrius's kids either."

As she discusses her reliance on 1950s sitcom ideals or the book she treasures, Dawn often insists that her desires preceded these media texts, asserting that the texts simply offer her expression and justification for what she already feels. But since the episode explicitly describes her as "passive" and undermines her portrayal of herself as a happy "domestic goddess," it also implies that rather than expressing some "nature" of her own, these texts actually exert too much control over her, becoming fantasies she subscribes to and follows. At the ending table meeting, when Lillian criticizes her passivity and submissiveness, saying it does not make sense to her, nor does the book, she makes fun of Dawn as being a "time capsule." Dawn begins crying and says the book "gave me validation for what I felt inside of me already." The episode implicitly presents itself as a much more rational and logical pedagogical media model that will meld nicely with the common sense of its imagined community of viewers.

Other staple components of the episode similarly emphasize the core opposition posed, specifically the degree to which both women depart from the series' implicit favored norms, and the degree to which Dawn is further beyond the pale. As Dawn reads about Lillian's approach to parenting in her household manual, it causes her to posit and question the very purpose and nature of marriage. She wonders if Lillian does everything for herself, "what do you need a husband for, then?"

Strikingly, the episode does not address race at all. This omission is particularly telling: Dawn and Demetrius are an interracial couple, she is white and he is black. While she tries to return to the time and mindset of her 1960s wife manual, the irony here is that in some parts of the country, it would still have been illegal for her to be married to Demetrius in the 1960s (since the federal antimiscegenation statute was not struck down until 1963 with the Lovings of Virginia; antimiscegenation laws in some states remained on the books through the 1980s). She idealizes what she calls "good old days" she wishes to return to, but during that time period she would have been banned from marrying her husband.

Gender and Race on Reality TV

The liberal pluralism and corporate multiculturalism evident in the portrayal of race on family-swapping shows matches up with the dominant trends in portrayals of race in the reality genre more generally. In a notable example, on *Black.White.*, producers use makeup to swap the identities of a white and black family for several weeks. While the white patriarch began the show by dismissing racism, he eventually realizes the reality of racial discrimination based on his own experiences, but the series relentlessly sensationalizes the spectacle of people in whiteface and blackface as well as the conflicts between the families as they live in close quarters with each other. That kind of portrayal is in keeping with the assimilationist rhetoric that scholar Herman Gray has detailed as stemming from 1980s television and the rise of popular black family sitcoms such as *The Cosby Show* (with the focus on the family itself as "universal" framing black families in terms of cultural norms).[32] Gray notes that networks are always eager to package as a sellable commodity programming that address hot social topics of the day, from single motherhood to teen pregnancy to multiculturalism, and as part of TV's goal to "generate profits by identifying and packaging our dominant social and cultural moods."[33]

More generally, representations of race on reality TV present a struggle over meaning, especially on reality family programming, where the idea of race becomes a way to talk about anxieties concerning the breakdown of the white nuclear family unit. Similarly, regarding the larger issue of gender role depictions on reality TV more generally, as I have noted elsewhere in my earlier work, I would argue that reality programming as a genre uses the repetition of gender role stereotypes as stock tropes.[34] In my view, gender emerges in reality programming as a set of generic conventions in which individual shows frequently transgress and then reassert traditional gender role expectations. Many reality series depict a man or woman as departing from these gender codes, crossing the barriers of older notions of acceptable masculine or feminine behavior. Yet the programs also ultimately reinforce patriarchal gender categories, often by showing the transgressive behavior to be an exception that proves the rule.

Wife-swapping shows join the battle of the sexes by reinforcing a gender role binary. They partially question but ultimately a reestablish some version of traditional gender role norms. They use ideologies of the family to naturalize gender difference.

The gender ideas the programs uphold correspond closely to conventional patriarchal models, what Michael Kimmel, citing sociologist R. W. Connell, would call the versions of "hegemonic masculinity" and "emphasized femininity" articulated as norms or favored ideals for any given society and time period. In twentieth-century America, hegemonic masculinity involves an idealized fantasy of masculinity, what Erving Goffman characterizes as " 'a young, married, white, urban, northern, heterosexual, Protestant, father, of college education, fully employed, of good complexion, weight, and height, and a recent record in sports.' "[35] Emphasized femininity describes an exaggerated ideal in which women comply with male desires, privilege social over technical skills, accept gender inequality, and comply with the hegemony of a patriarchal social sphere and labor organization. As reality TV shows transgress these older socially constructed ideas of gender, they critique those models as outdated and no longer dominant, but they simultaneously return to them as norms. Thus we see how the genre questions a conceptual boundary between two social identity categories, like masculine and feminine, but in the way that it moves across those boundaries, it reasserts the original categories.

Reality programming banks off of evolving ideas of gender by turning this sense of gender change and transgression into a repetitive trope; it is the continual process of transgressing and simultaneously reasserting patriarchal gender role models that is meant to generate viewer pleasure through the repetition of this trope. I read the shows' gender representations not as a reflection of reality but rather, as in all reality TV, imagined possible versions of reality—these programs are making narrative arguments about sociocultural ideas. Again, critics have also proven how the reality elements are nothing new to television, and how primetime fictional programming has always itself critiqued the "real" by incorporating documentary forms and theorizing the fiction/nonfiction mix.[36] On a larger level, I would argue that the "cultural work" reality programming does is to explore the volatility of changing ideologies of human behavior while reasserting or partially returning to more traditional social norms and models.

All of these gendered dynamics work to norm stereotypical ideals of masculinity and femininity. I see this dynamic, where shows question social changes and then try to recur to traditional social role behaviors, as part of a larger process in reality TV. As I have been arguing, the genre becomes an important site for imagining changes in patterns involving not just gender and race but also larger social units like the family—social changes such as women impacting the labor force in greater numbers, the state of the postmodern fragmented family unit, and the advent of same-sex marriage. As I noted earlier, critics Lynn Spigel and Cecelia Tichi have shown how television has always projected a fantasy of the heterosexual white middle-class suburban nuclear family unit as its ideal target audience. Reality TV explores alterations to such ideas of gender and race and related social structures even as it keeps returning to traditional norms. My next section traces these norms, all framed in the discourse of family, in historical reality programming.

Swapping Eras

Historical switching shows that place families in a different time period (and ask them to follow the culture of that era) offer another example of testing family values through comparison. PBS's *Frontier House* makes some family values arguments that are in keeping with how other reality shows question and reassert traditional family norms. It makes structural critiques of nineteenth-century discrimination and the gendered inequity of the institution of marriage and property ownership. However, it nonetheless reinforces frontier mythology, ignoring how Manifest Destiny resulted in dispossession and displacement of Native Americans, and it also upholds the American dream ideology while ignoring the structural class inequity that makes that ideal unattainable for many.[37]

Some reality programs perform the cultural work of historicizing the evolution of the American family. In the popular BBC/PBS historical House series, the shows do the cultural work of both questioning naturalizing modern norms of family as participants project those norms onto their experience of the past. *Frontier House* provides a particularly useful case study of these dynamics, as it links the American family to American history and frontier mythology.

Depicting three families of modern-day time travelers who immerse themselves in the rough and tumble culture of 1883 Montana, PBS's *Frontier House* series provides a critical, self-reflexive interrogation of romanticized visions of the U.S. nineteenth-century life on the frontier. Not simply a melodramatic retelling of history as escapist fantasy, the series reflects on trends within public history to attempt to represent history with multiple viewpoints.[38] As it portrays how modern participants experience discomfort with the gender, race, and familial norms of the Montana territory as they try to reenact, the series explicitly debunks the romance of Wild West Hollywood films or TV shows like *Little House on the Prairie*. Producer Simon Shaw notes these romantic media visions prompted him to launch the series and motivated some participants, and that the harsh living conditions forced everyone to abandon these fantasies.[39]

Yet at the same time, even while it tries to offer less idealized versions of history based on the cast's lived experiences of material conditions, the show nonetheless ends up reinforcing frontier mythology, specifically an on-going investment in the idea that the American West establishes American exceptionalism by fostering freedom, individualism, and opportunity (just as Frederick Jackson Turner theorized it in the 1890s).[40] The series' narrative continually returns to a vision of liberal pluralism, one that privileges an Anglo-American cultural legacy even as it critiques the excesses of Manifest Destiny or the history of racism. The show thus offers an updated version of frontier mythology in the context of television's current dominant ideological mode of address, liberal pluralism, and in the context of recent popular culture versions of corporate multiculturalism.

The status of the American family is one of the main thematic cruxes where this process of demythologizing and simultaneously making new, updated mythologies is evident. Utilizing the techniques of literary analysis, specifically attention to text and context, or historicized textual analysis, this section examines these issues in the program's narrative, themes, and character development. The series' form and content both contribute to these ideological themes.

Myths Debunked

The show's production history and context illuminate the series' recurring narrative focus on debunking myths. The opening tag line of each episode promises to show viewers "the real frontier" behind "the romanticized mythologies." The concept for this most American version of an historical reality series followed upon the success of the British House series on the BBC, a suite of programs including *The 1900 House* (1999), *The 1940s House* (2001), *The Edwardian Country House* (2002, called *Manor House* when it aired stateside on PBS), and *Regency House Party* (2004). While those series were joint productions by Channel 4 and Wall to Wall Television, Wall to Wall came to the United States and partnered with the PBS station, Thirteen/WNET in New York to produce *Frontier House* and later *Colonial House* (2004). Other production companies have used this format, including a CBC series called *Pioneer Quest: A Year in the Real West* (2000) in Canada and a German series called *Black Forest House,* both about the nineteenth century.

Going into production in 2001 and airing in 2002, the series followed three families for six months as they tried to survive and provide for themselves on their assigned homesteads in the Montana wilderness, securing food and shelter, caring for farm animals and growing crops, and making ready for the winter. The historical focus involves the Homestead Act of 1862, a bill Abraham Lincoln signed into law stating that public land belonged to the people and could be given free to citizens; homesteaders could claim up to 160 acres by filing a claim, living there at least half the year for five years, improving the land ("prove up"), and then getting the deed at the end of that period. The series notes that the filer has to be the head of the family, at least 21 years of age, and a citizen (or about to become one). It cites other restrictions that reflected the social hierarchies of the times, such as the fact that single women could apply but married women could not, because they lost most of their legal rights when they married (through the idea of coverture, where the wife falls under the husband's legal rights). Though the experiment was designed to end before the start of winter, the families were judged by historical experts on how well they could have survived based on their preparations.

Discussing his inspiration for *Frontier House,* British series producer Simon Shaw emphasizes his childhood dreams of the Wild West. In the companion book to the series, Shaw writes:

> Beyond childhood romps playing cowboys and Indians I was spellbound by the lure of a life where men and women pitched themselves against a world full of rugged challenges. For years, every movie, television show, comic, and book detailing heroic adventures in cow towns and across prairies was a favorite escape from my real life, growing up in a small village in the middle of England.[41]

When he had the chance to recreate 1880s frontier life in Montana, Shaw says he felt "my dream was about to become a reality." What is notable about his explanation for his motivations in making this series is that he has his own American dream, shaped by U.S. mass media. He wants to be transported to a fantasy world of adventures and pioneers, the Wild West. He acknowledges that his idea of the West has been shaped by "the treasured kitsch" of Hollywood films, especially John Wayne movies, and by shows like *Little House on the Prairie.*

The applicants and eventual castmembers also cite their idealistic notions of the frontier as motivation for participating in this series. The production company put out a call for participants and over 5,500 families applied, responding to the advertising query: "It's time to make American history. . . . Could you live as a pioneer out in the American West?"[42] Shaw overviews the timbre of the applications, noting that most had a dream of "returning to a simpler time," finding the roots of the American dream, and making lives for their families on the Western land. He concludes that "it became clear that the dream of carving a new life out in the untamed land of the West was still a potent force in modern America."[43]

The three families chosen similarly specify these romanticized visions. All reflect on the idea of a simpler time bringing families closer through an agricultural lifestyle—the kind of nostalgia for a rural life that is a typical response to the urbanization and industrialization of modernity. Gordon Clune, a 40-year-old Los Angeles business man and president of his own company, brought his homemaker wife Adrienne (39), an Irish immigrant, teenage daughter Aine (14) and two young sons Conor (8) and Justin (12), along with their teen cousin Tracey (15). On his application, he explains he is nostalgic for the farm life he grew up with in Canada: "I admit I have a romanticized notion of a simpler life, a life that existed for me that I would like to share with my family" (Shaw 23). Student Nate Brooks (27) and social worker Kristen McLeod (27), an engaged couple from Boston who got married on the series, cite the opportunity to revisit Nate's experiences growing up on a self-sufficient farm and "the chance to reconnect to the land and to human history through a challenging experiential endeavor" (Shaw 21). Nate's father Rudy (68), a retired corrections officer, spends the first two months on the homestead with Nate until Kristen arrives for their wedding and move-in; he cites the chance to live this agricultural life again with his son.[44] Likewise, Karen Glenn (35), a nurse from Nashville, cites nostalgia for her parents' rural upbringing as a reason to apply for her blended family, consisting of second husband Mark (44), a college instructor, and her children Erinn (12) and Logan Patton (8).

Once the cast and crew make it by wagon train to the Montana plains where they are living and shooting the series, however, the idealized notions quickly give way to harsher realities. The participants repeatedly note their sense of frustration over the hard work, loneliness, and isolation, and the palpable sense that they might not have been able to survive the brutal labor conditions required to keep a homestead farm going. Whereas the first episode, "The American Dream," shows applicants eager to leave the modern rat race and live a frontier life, by the second episode, "Promised Land," the families are tired and focused on survival.[45] Noting the common media fantasy of *The Little House on the Prairie* television series, Erinn Patton says she thought it would be like becoming Laura Ingalls Wilder, but now she realizes there is so much work to be done every day, even for the children, that no one would have time to sit around and braid their hair like the Wilders. In an episode focusing on their hardships, "Survival," Gordon Clune notes that "God's country is like a two-edged sword. It's beautiful, but it can also be a hell." An exhausted Mark Glenn sighs, "you want to explain to me exactly what's fun about your hands cracking and bleeding" every day.

The series focuses on their frustrations with nineteenth-century norms involving gender roles, race, and older patriarchal family forms. As the three families struggle to survive under 1880s conditions, the women often express their frustrations with onerous domestic duties like laborious cooking and cleaning and yearn for male roles that provide for more freedom. While the men eventually find agency in their roles outside laboring, the women are left to do cooking and laundry all day, chained to their homes. In the final episode, "The Reckoning," Adrienne Clune notes that while the rest of her family eventually adjusted to the hardships and experienced personal growth, it felt like a six-month labor camp for her. The teen girls in her household explicitly rebel against their gender role expectations and start working in the fields and eschewing the heavy dresses of the time.

In addition to critiquing nineteenth-century gender norms that gave women less freedom and agency, the series also critiques nineteenth-century racial prejudices by exploring what it would have been like for Nate, who is African American, and Kristen, who is Anglo-American, as an interracial couple on the frontier. While they would have had more freedom in the West than in the East, where many states had antimiscegenation laws, they still would have faced discrimination, such as the fact that their eventual interracial children would not have been allowed to go to school with the white children. Their fellow castmembers quickly eschew the racist nineteenth-century practices, all voting that they would have allowed Nate and Kristen's children to attend the school if they had had any (or if they were to eventually). Here, the program historicizes racism in the nineteenth century but misses the opportunity to examine it in the twenty-first century. By allowing the castmembers to imply that overt racism no longer exists, the series reinforces a simply liberal pluralism while failing to emphasize the degree to which systemic structural discrimination and prejudice still exist. In a direct address interview, Nate and Kristen note their interest in examining how nineteenth-century societies treated race, but Kristen herself quickly papers over racism in her own time, saying that she knows Nate has "faced racism" but that she has yet to experience it.

The series critiques efforts to naturalize the family unit in the sense that, as it places three 2001 families into an 1883 historical context, it draws attention to gender role tensions, estrangement between parents and children, and a feeling of isolation caused by such intense focus on a nuclear family unit. At the program's end, Nate and Kristen are judged most able to survive the winter by the experts, in large part because they are a young, childless couple. The Clunes try to offset the burden of many children who would not survive the harsh winter by saying they would send half the children to live in a nearby town, but the historians reject that plan as historically inaccurate. During much of their time adjusting to frontier life hardships, the families, far from coming together as units, begin to focus on themselves as individuals, feeling isolated from each other as they spend all their time on daily chores, struggling to keep themselves and their farm animals housed and fed.

In addition, as the families note the restrictiveness of the nineteenth century and learn to value their greater degrees of freedom in the twenty-first, they also see on-going tensions concerning the family that link the two time periods. As all the women emphasize how tedious the nineteenth-century women's work of cooking and laundry is in the family unit, they also ponder the choices they make in the twenty-first century about working outside the home or being stay-at-home mothers, just as they assess the modern conveniences that influence their choices. Similar tensions about how to define gendered roles emerge for these families in the historical context just as it does for them in their modern lives, with many of the women bucking parts of their historical role and noting that their choice to do so will likely make them more assertive in their modern lives too.

Anxieties over how families will manage these tensions, and whether it will break them apart or threaten their survival, take on new importance in the frontier context but likewise filter over into their modern lives, as the Glenn blended family endures great tension between the husband and wife, who wind up separating after the series ends. The program implicitly contemplates anxieties about changing familial norms in the twenty-first century United States. The tensions in the Glenn blended family in particular speak to the struggle between the older modern family norm and emergent postmodern family variety.

This kind of demographic family change in the twenty-first century is thrown into greater relief by sending modern families back into a nineteenth-century context in which they are asked to focus on nuclear families on the frontier as labor units. As a frontier social arrangement, the families find the laboring nuclear unit to be problematic and isolating. Mark Glenn, in particular, continually notes that he has had trouble "finding a role" for himself, because his wife runs the family and the children "aren't his," and he does not enjoy being a stepparent. He does not feel he has a clear role in the homestead labor unit, because he has no regular duties but rather does what is needed around the farm, while his wife and stepchildren all have a daily routine of tasks. When asked to build a fence to keep cattle out when a neighboring rancher drives them through the area, Glenn argues that he has finally found "a role for the man." Karen, meanwhile, speaks frequently in direct address interviews about how she wishes Mark would "quit his whining," that he would learn to accept "not always being in charge," and that he would come to understand that she will always "be a package deal" with her children, not separate from them. Their blended family tensions are in marked contrast to what nineteenth-century roles would have asked of them (with a male head of household making the decisions). The juxtaposition of the two time frames underlines the couple's personal tensions (many sparked by gender role tensions of today).

Revising Frontier Mythology through Reality TV

This process of debunking myths for a different, more critical vision based on experiential history emphasizes an education mission for the show along with the reality genre entertainment tropes. This combination of education and entertainment fits, of course, with public television's purported public service mission, and many television scholars have detailed how this dynamic shifts more toward entertainment with reality TV.[46]

Yet the series does make its own critical historical discourse. It uses the techniques of reality programming to merge twenty-first century castmembers with nineteenth-century storylines. The program is part docusoap in the sense that it uses some documentary techniques, like diary confessionals, direct address chats with the camera, unobtrusive observational documentary styles mixed with voice-over narration and interviews with the interlocutor edited out. It also features elements of the gamedoc, because it focuses narrative energy and conflict on which family will be judged better able to survive by the end of the experiment. Some participants played up this competition dynamic. Karen Glenn and others accused Gordon Clune of breaking the ground rule of historical accuracy by "finding" a boxspring mattress to use, by "trading" with modern neighbors for food at one point, and by bringing his own whiskey still as his luxury item to trade alcohol for goods. While other castmembers chose to focus on the experience rather than the game element, the show's edited narrative does keep returning to the idea that only 30 percent of families survived the five years needed to make land claim stick, thus encouraging the survival of the fittest rhetoric. The program interweaves historical narratives and details about the postbellum era with the personal stories of the reality show participants, and the producers talk frequently about learning more about the twenty-first century through this encounter. Notably, when the teen girls get bored in the Clune household, they turn to the video diary cameras for entertainment, making home movies to keep themselves entertained, focusing on twenty-first century mass media interactions.

   Critic Jonathan Bignell has argued for the critical reflexivity of the House series overall, asserting that as they explore the constructedness of historical conditions and ideologies, that same lens can be turned on the present, and the series give viewers the raw materials for that questioning process. As Bignell writes: "The recreated reality of the past may be highly constructed and mediated by practices of narration and editing, but it opens up viewing positions that reflect on the differences of ideology between then and now, both positively and negatively, and on how the constraints of a television format can expose the ideological constraints of a social world glimpsed in microcosm."[47] The programs do take on specific inflections in terms of their cultural politics in the British series versus the American ones. For example, Bignell argues that *The Edwardian Country House* (*Manor House*) ultimately focuses on the community of the house, which, while class-stratified, hierarchical, and enforced, reveals the interdependence of the groups of people living there and emphasizes the communal over the individual.

   In contrast, *Frontier House* is emphatically about the triumph of the individual and the failure of community. While some participants explicitly set out to find the community of a supposedly simpler time on the prairie, all are reduced to the limits of nuclear family by the end, having given up on their neighbors to a large extent, because of heated contentiousness and competition between some of them. While the series' edited narrative tries to salvage some sense of camaraderie by having the children learn to get along by going to frontier school together (a one-room schoolhouse with a teacher reenacting educational techniques from the time), the recurring emphasis is nevertheless on my property, my family, and, consequently, my isolation. Gordon Clune insists that the show proves his family can survive as a family, and that even when they consistently broke the rules of historical accuracy, it showed the pioneer spirit of opportunism and entrepreneurialism, and the willingness to do anything to feed their children and to survive. Somewhat melodramatically, in the finale, he insists that settlers risked their lives to come homestead, just as his family has done by being on this program. Through their editing, the episodes likewise critique Gordon's attitude, implying that his questionable ethical decisions are not in keeping with a purer frontier spirit of the kind the series implicitly lauds. When Gordon tries to justify "trading" with modern neighbors for food, he claims he is suffering from malnourishment and almost from starvation, as he quickly loses weight during his long days of hard labor. As producers carefully bring a doctor to verify that Gordon is not losing more weight than he would be expected to, the voice-over narration frequently notes that Gordon's claims are groundless. The historical experts who judge the families in the final episode likewise note how Gordon's behavior threatens the accuracy of the historical experiment and all the hard work the other families put in in order to achieve "authenticity."

Yet even as the program offers this kind of self-reflexive, critical historical discourse that debunks mythologies, it nevertheless reinforces ideas of American exceptionalism. In the final episode, which returns the cast to their modern lives, Mark Glenn critiques Gordon Clune's avaricious behavior and reflects on what the frontier experience was like for him. Noting, like many castmembers, how hard it was to return to the twenty-first century, Glenn argues that people brought their competitive, commodity-driven behavior from the twenty-first century but that the nineteenth century was purer. He calls the twenty-first century an "unnatural space" in which "principles are all for sale," and argues that people need a 12-step program to recover from it and return to the truer frontier life. In spite of all his complaints during the series, Glenn argues that he now misses his homestead, family, and neighbors and that they "could have made one hell of a good community." All of the children, likewise, bemoan the consumer culture they have returned to, which now bores them from so many choices yet so little to do; Logan argues, "you have so much stuff that you're just bored with all of it." The teen girls both feel out of place, insisting, in a somewhat surprising about-face, that the homestead gave them confidence and a sense of accomplishment, but they are now bored with their modern life.

The clearest example of how the series reinforces a revised version of frontier mythology, in which the frontier is critiqued for its hierarchy and false myths but then romanticized anew for being a building ground of the American spirit, also comes in the final episode. While still at the homesteads, the cast learns of the 9/11 attacks. Adrienne Clune sews an American flag of the period, and the series focuses dramatic weight on her as she talks about being an immigrant and finding in this frontier experience "the spirit and vitality and energy and go and get it attitude" of America, saying "a lot of it comes from this homesteading experience" of this earlier generation. She and Gordon both expound on how the experience has brought their family closer together and given them the ability to survive anything. In spite of how the series debunks gender and familial norms in many ways, the program ultimately emphasizes how much this has been a family experience, underlining the idea of family as a building block for the nation.

Another aspect of the series that reinforces frontier mythology is the fact that it underplays the fact that Native American land dispossession is what made the "free land" homesteading movement possible. While an early episode features a Native American hunter who brings food to the hungry families (since they cannot hunt during that time of the year because of modern-day game restrictions but the Native American neighbor can because of his hunting rights), and the series uses this as an occasion to note that his peoples were pushed off their land by the settlers, it is only addressed in passing. The narrative focus is more on the bravery and hardships of the settlers in a way that romanticizes them. In addition, while the show emphasizes how the families have personal empathy for their visitor, it does not dwell on larger social critiques of U.S. government treatment of the Native Americans. Likewise, the series features a Chinese immigrant merchant at a recreated frontier store, but producers edited out a storyline in which he is run out of business because of racism (an event that happened frequently historically). It instead focuses on the families' pleasant trade transactions at the store, just as it focuses on Kristen Brooks's cheerful declaration that "it's all love" in terms of how others respond to her interracial marriage with Nate rather than elaborating more on nineteenth-century racist practices and their legacy today.

Ultimately, the series attempts to recapture the "structure of feeling" of 1880s Montana, the shared values or ideologies of this particular group or society, their collective cultural unconscious. It therefore focuses on delivering Ien Ang's "emotional realism" in television, a sense of accuracy in the treatment of psychological situations, even in the midst of hyberbolic dynamics. The primetime soap opera viewers she queried, for example, were aware that this emotional realism they found in *Dallas* emerges out of the artifice of fictional narrative genre patterns, yet they still valued that staged realism.[48] In the case of reality TV in general, critic Annette Hill has shown that viewers tend to look for moments of authenticity, particularly in moments of revelation or confession in direct address interviews. *Frontier House* certainly highlights those moments. We incessantly hear these families talk about how much they are learning about themselves as a result of this experience, and their emotional journeys of self-discovery become narrative focal points in the edited episodes. This focus on the self is also typical of the genre. Hill has shown that reality series often emphasize the idea that participants and viewers can learn something from the program, and Mark Andrejevic has detailed the prevalence with which participants see the reality show experience as a path toward self-growth and personal knowledge (a dynamic which he, again, critiques for playing into emerging marketing strategies).[49] Critics have established as central to the genre the cultural politics of this focus on the self.[50]

In keeping with the genre trends, the program focuses on character and individual personal growth. It gives each family a backstory, placing them into a nineteenth-century story and character arc, turning them into frontier settlers. In a bonus "Behind the Scenes" featurette on the DVD set of the series, Shaw and other production team members note their surprise at how each family began to think they really were homesteaders. The series' edited narrative focuses on characters and their narrative arcs. Part of their character narratives involve how they fear audiences will view them. Karen Glenn, in particular, argues in the finale that no matter how people respond to her and the break-up of her marriage on camera, she knows what she calls her church family will accept and love her for who she is.

In this case, the focus on the self serves to convey the series' reinforcement of an updated, more self-reflexive, yet nevertheless still individualistic American dream and still possessive frontier mythology. We see individual families and individuals as relatable characters through their own "character narratives" of development, the story arcs emphasized in the narrative structure of reality shows. We are encouraged, for example, to identify with the first-person direct address confessional documentary camera moments (in interviews or diaries) when the women express their frustrations with onerous domestic duties, or the interracial couple are prompted to think about what it would have meant to seek more freedom and mobility on the frontier (as opposed to the antimiscegenation laws back East). While the televised America we see is a more inclusive and multicultural one, it still depends on the idea of the frontier (here a postmodern media one) as a crucible for the formation of personal and national identity.

As with the other reality family programs I have discussed in this study, such historical shows both question and reinforce American family norms and stereotypes. More than that however, these programs capture the anxiety and ambivalence prevalent in the culture concerning changing demographic patterns of gender and the family. The history programs highlight that anxiety and those norms by taking people out of their historical context and asking them to live in another (where, of course, the participants do not so much come into contact with the ideologies of that other historical period as they, rather, engage with those of their own). Yet even these programs, much like celebreality family shows, parenting, home makeover, and spouse-swapping shows, still naturalize the modern nuclear family unit. Alongside their naturalization of family as a core component of nation, these shows also often slightly query but ultimately reinforce regressive ideologies of gender and race and political arguments such as neoliberalism. Taken as a whole, then, reality family programs question some norms but reaffirm others, all while appealing to viewers through their attempts to encapsulate social changes and larger cultural moods in reference to the always-in-flux American family. In my conclusion, I bring together this discussion of how reality TV markets a major theme of social conflict alongside how it uses trends in new media in order to assess where the genre is headed in the future.

Notes

1. Linda Gordon, *Heroes of Their Own Lives* (New York: Viking, 1988), 3.
2. Sujata Moorti and Karen Ross, "Reality Television: Fairy Tale or Feminist Nightmare," *Feminist Media Studies* 4, no. 2 (2004): 203–205.
3. Herman Gray, "The Endless Slide of Difference: Critical Television Studies, Television, and the Question of Race," *Critical Studies in Mass Communication* 10, no. 2 (1993): 193.
4. Sasha Torres, ed., *Living Color: Race and Television in the United States* (Durham, NC: Duke University Press, 1998), 2.
5. Patricia Mellencamp, "Situation Comedy, Feminism, and Freud: Discourses of Gracie and Lucy," *Critiquing the Sitcom: A Reader,* ed. Joanne Morreale (New York: Syracuse University Press, 2003), 48. Mary Beth Haralovich, "Sitcoms and Suburbs: Positioning the Fifties Homemaker," in *Where the Girls Are: Growing up Female with the Mass Media,* eds. Joanne Morreale and Susan Douglas (New York: Times Books, 1995).
6. Jennifer Gillan, "From Ozzie Nelson to Ozzy Osbourne: The Genesis and Development of the Reality (Star) Sitcom," in *Understanding Reality Television,* eds. Su Holmes and Deborah Jermyn (London: Routledge, 2004), 54–70.
7. Herman Gray, *Watching Race: Television and the Struggle for "Blackness"* (Minneapolis: University of Minnesota Press, 1995).
8. Noel Holston, "Tell Mom She's Traded: Will 'Wife Swap' Play Second Fiddle to Fox Knock-Off, 'Trading Spouses'?," *New York Newsday,* NYNewsday.com, 10/7/04, September 29, 2004, http://www.nynewsday.com/entertainment/tv/ny-ettel3987393sept29,0,7781865.
9. Holston, "Tell Mom She's Traded."

10. "Perrin/Flisher," *Trading Spouses,* Fox, November 2, 2005, November 9, 2005.

11. Eric J. Hudson, "Family Gets Real on National TV," *The Boston Globe,* boston.com, 12/1/05, October 30, 2005, http://www.boston.com/news/local/arti cles/2005/10/30/family_gets_real_on_national_TV

12. "Perrin/Malone-Brown," *Trading Spouses,* January 19, 2007, January 26, 2007.

13. Charlie McCollum, "Fox Clone Is No Match for Classy 'Wife Swap,'" September 27, 2004, 10/7/04, *Mercury News,* mercurynews.com, http://www.mer curynews.com/mld/mercurynews/entertainment/televisions/9766721.htm

14. Jonathan Storm, "Moms Away: Fox's Wife-Swap Entry Doesn't Add up to Much," *The Philadelphia Inquirer,* philly.com, July 27, 2004, 10/7/04, http://www. philly.com/mld/philly/entertainment/9249817.htm,.

15. Rob Owen, "TV Previews: 'Wife Swap' A Light Sociological Study," *Pittsburgh Post-Gazette,* post-gazette.com, September 25, 2004, 10/7/04, http://www. post-gazette.com/pg/pp/04269/384952.stm.

16. Matthew Gilbert, "ABC's 'Wife' Is Divorced from Real Life," *The Boston Globe,* boston.com, September 29, 2004, 10/7/04, http://www.boston.com/ae/tv/ articles/2004/09/29/abcs_wife_is_divorced_from_real_life?

17. Jonathan Bignell, *Media Semiotics: An Introduction* (Manchester: Manchester University Press, 2002).

18. Sarah Kozloff, "Narrative Theory and Television," *Channels of Discourse Reassembled: Television and Contemporary Criticism,* ed. R. Allen (London: Routledge, 1992), 67–100, 78.

19. "Ridgely/Corrao," *Wife Swap,* ABC, May 1, 2006.

20. "Thompson/Askam," *Wife Swap,* ABC, March 6, 2004.

21. "Pitts/Policchio," *Wife Swap,* ABC, September 26, 2004.

22. "Bowers/Pilek," *Trading Spouses: Meet Your New Mommy,* episodes 103 and 104, Fox, August 3, 2004, August 10, 2004.

23. Spolansky/Bradley, *Wife Swap,* ABC, September 29, 2004.

24. Leigh H. Edwards, "Identity Props: Review of *Wife Swap,*" *PopMatters,* October 11, 2004, http://www.popmatters.com/pm/review/wife-swap-2004. In the next several paragraphs, I am adapting and updating points from my published review of the series.

25. "Ridgely/Corrao," *Wife Swap,* ABC, May 1, 2006.

26. Heller, for example, refits Freud for the postmodern family on this question. She revises his idea of the family romance, a narrative search for origins stemming from the family experience, into what she calls a postfamily romance, or family plots that reflect the new configurations of gender, narrative, and private space from the 1960s onwards. Dana Heller, *Family Plots: The De-Oedipalization of Popular Culture* (Philadelphia: University of Pennsylvania Press, 1995), x, xii.

27. Lynn Spigel, *Make Room for TV: Television and the Family Ideal in Postwar America* (Chicago: University of Chicago Press, 1992), 10. Mary Beth Haralovich, "From Sitcoms to Suburbs: Positioning the 1950s Homemaker," *Quarterly Review of Film and Video* 11, no. 1 (1989): 61–83.

28. "A Happy Ending for the *Wife Swap* Couples," *Us Weekly,* January 3, 2005, 37.

29. "Flummerfelt/Bray," *Wife Swap,* ABC, February 23, 2005.

30. "Fuentes/Lawson," *Wife Swap,* ABC, December 12, 2005.

31. John Corner, "Performing the Real: Documentary Diversions," *Television and New Media* 3, no. 30 (2002): 255–269, 268.

32. Gray, *Watching Race*, 60.

33. Gray, *Watching Race*, 69.

34. Leigh H. Edwards, " 'What a Girl Wants': Gender Norming on Reality Game Shows." *Feminist Media Studies* 4, no. 2 (Summer 2004): 226–228. In the following paragraphs, I am adapting and updating part of my article on this issue.

35. Michael S. Kimmel, *The Gendered Society* (New York: Oxford University Press, 2000), 11.

36. John Caldwell, *Televisuality: Style, Crisis, and Authority in American Television* (New Brunswick, NJ: Rutgers University Press, 1995). James Friedman, ed., *Reality Squared: Televisual Discourse on the Real* (New Brunswick, NJ: Rutgers University Press, 2002).

37. Leigh H. Edwards. "The Endless End of Frontier Mythology: PBS's *Frontier House.*" *Film & History: An Interdisciplinary Journal of Film and Television Studies* 37, no. 1 (2007): 29–34. In this section, I am adapting and updating some points from my published article on the series.

38. See Marita Sturken, *Tangled Memories: The Vietnam War, the AIDS Epidemic, and the Politics of Remembering* (Berkeley: University of California Press, 1997); David Glassberg, "Public History and the Study of Memory," *The Public Historian* 18, no. 2 (Spring 1996): 7–23; Donna Graves, "Representing the Race: Detroit's *Monument to Joe Louis*" in *Critical Issues in Public Art: Content, Context, and Controversy,* eds. Harriet F. Senie and Sally Webster (New York: HarperCollins Publishers, 1992), 215–227.

39. Simon Shaw, with Linda Peavy and Ursula Smith, *Frontier House* (New York: Atria Books, 2002).

40. Frederick Jackson Turner, *History, Frontier, and Section: Three Essays* (Albuquerque: University of New Mexico Press, 1993).

41. Shaw, *Frontier House,* vi–vii.

42. Shaw, *Frontier House,* 1–2.

43. Shaw, *Frontier House,* 2.

44. The companion book explains that the arrangement is due to Kristen's severe allergy to horses, which were much used in the initial wagon train and home-building, though the series itself never gives that background.

45. All citations of particular episodes are drawn from the DVD set, *Frontier House,* PBS Home Video, 2002.

46. Susan Murray and Laurie Ouellette, eds., *Reality TV: Remaking Television Culture* (New York: New York University Press, 2004); Richard Kilborn, *Staging the Real: Factual TV Programming in the Age of Big Brother* (Manchester: Manchester University Press, 2003); Su Holmes and Deborah Jermyn, eds., *Understanding Reality Television* (London: Routledge, 2004).

47. Jonathan Bignell, *Big Brother: Reality TV in the Twenty-First Century* (London: Palgrave, 2005), 85–86.

48. Ien Ang, *Watching Dallas: Television and the Melodramatic Imagination* (London: Routledge, 1985), 47.

49. Annette Hill, "*Big Brother:* The Real Audience," *Television and New Media* 3, no. 3: 323–325. See also Hill, *Reality TV: Factual Entertainment and Television Audiences* (London: Routledge, 2005); Mark Andrejevic, *Reality TV: The Work of Being Watched* (Lanham, MD: Rowman & Littlefield, 2004).

50. See, for example, Laurie Ouellette, " 'Take Responsibility for Yourself': *Judge Judy* and the Neoliberal Citizen" in Murray and Ouellette, *Reality TV,* 231–250.

Conclusion: The Futures of Reality TV

The future of reality TV lies in transmedia stories that can make an emotional appeal to viewers, sparking them to want to follow these real people portrayed as characters on the screen as the content continues on other media platforms (from music albums to web pages to smart phone apps). Rather than mere sensationalism, the genre is making substantive arguments at the heart of contemporary social issues, whether that is how media shapes people's everyday lives or how the family unit is still central to American social life. As it uses its signature documentary–fiction hybrid mix, reality TV continues to depend for its success on active fans and their interactive participation in the programs they love, from *American Idol* to the *Kardashians*. To answer the question of where reality TV is going in the future, it is helpful to consult where it has been in the recent past.

"Television Ate My Family": Reality TV and the Return of *An American Family*

A good illustration of how reality TV has evolved over time is a reality forerunner, the PBS documentary series *An American Family* (1973), and the recent fictionalized HBO film *Cinema Verite* (2011) about the making of that series. In the change in how that show was perceived then versus now, one can see how reality TV both impacts and exhibits American family values. The PBS series was a reality TV pioneer because it took the observational documentary techniques popularized in the 1960s and looked at a so-called typical American family in a time of social upheaval and demographic change in the 1970s. Its mixture of observational documentary with fictional TV genre codes, what producer Craig Gilbert dubbed "a real-life soap opera," is precisely what characterizes today's reality TV genre.[1]

An American Family was controversial in 1973 because it let millions of viewers see private family conflict. Filmmakers Alan and Susan Raymond chronicled substantive family tensions and a marriage's disintegration. The Loud family was a white, upper-middle-class suburban Santa Barbara, California, nuclear family comprised of salesman father Bill, housewife Pat, and five children. Pat and the philandering Bill ended up divorcing (although they live together today). Their son Lance Loud was openly gay and became a gay icon after the show aired. In a later documentary, *Lance Loud! A Death in An American Family* (2003), the Raymonds showed how the pressures of fame affected him and chronicled his life as he was dying from HIV. He charged: "Television ate my family."[2]

An American Family presented the Louds as representative of the state of the American family in the early 1970s. The program emphasizes Pat's conflict with Bill over his extramarital affairs and contrasts his detached behavior with her bond with her children. It captures her push to have her concerns taken seriously, which illuminates the gender politics of the women's liberation movement era. The dramatic tension culminated in a producer-orchestrated moment in which Pat kicks Bill out of the house on camera. The Raymonds note that while their goal was simply to "hold a mirror up to society" using a cinéma vérité documentary style, the series created a huge controversy. Some critics called it an innovative snapshot of American life while others dubbed it sensationalism and suggested that the camera's intrusion is what tore the family apart. The Raymonds argued with Gilbert over his desire to highlight negative aspects of the family's life and about how much he tried to prompt action.[3]

The program's millions of viewers (averaging 10 million weekly, an extremely impressive number then) and extensive debate about it in the popular press made it a symbol of changing 1970s American cultural norms.[4] Also important is how the series influenced later programming. It inspired the British TV series, *The Family* (1974), itself a precursor to later reality genres like the 1990s British docusoap, and it was a central influence on *The Osbournes* (2002–2005), which has itself spawned many copycats.

At the time of its release, *An American Family* sparked a debate about the ethics and ramifications of its use of documentary. Most notably, anthropologist Margaret Mead, writing in *TV Guide,* lauded its potential ethnographic benefits: "It is, I believe, as new and significant as the invention of drama or the novel—a new way in which people can learn to look at life, by seeing the real life of others interpreted by the camera." She argued: "I do not think *An American Family* should be called a documentary. I think we need a new name for it, a name that would contrast it not only with fiction, but with what we have been exposed to up until now on TV."[5] In reply, Pat Loud sounded a clarion call warning about the potential for exploitation and the negative effects of mass media voyeurism and sensationalism: "Margaret Mead, bless her friendly voice, has written glowingly that the series constituted some sort of breakthrough, a demonstration of a new tool for use in sociology and anthropology. Having been the object of that tool, I think I am competent to say that it won't work."[6] Their debate demonstrates how the series became a site for larger ethical discussions.

The documentary reflected changing American values, especially new views of family as a social unit due to the 1970s marriage and family patterns, such as a major spike in divorce rates. It spoke to the shift from the modern nuclear family ideal to a new postmodern family diversity of forms. In televising changing mores in an actual family, the PBS series became a lightning rod.

Some critics feared the show would negatively influence American values, promoting materialism and triviality. The Louds were slammed for everything from perceived bad parenting to exhibitionism. The melodrama and the materialism came in for especially harsh critique. The *Village Voice* review argued: "If this were a sane civilization, it would be a ridiculous show." Meanwhile, one *New York Times* reviewer concluded that the series only offered "their approximation of the American Dream—an eight-room ranch house, a horse, three dogs, a pool, a Jaguar, a Volvo, a Toyota, and a Datsun pickup."[7]

Cinema Verite updates these concerns for our own cultural moment—a moment defined by the dominance of reality TV in our media landscape. If emerging documentary TV techniques were sparking early discussions of sensationalism in the 1970s, that debate is now a full-blown roar in the 2000s. Now, the debate is about the status of the "real" in American culture and in digital media culture more generally, as reality TV has become a global phenomenon. The film speaks to the theory that reality TV reflects an anxiety about truth claims that have become increasingly suspect in our digital era of easily manipulable images. It also takes note of ongoing family values debates that were emerging in the 1970s and have only amplified since. Lance Loud's idea that television can "eat your family" has become a truism, given that so many celebrity and noncelebrity families break up after being on reality TV. Today's reality show castmembers often attribute their family disintegration to the pressures of filming alongside harsh press and audience judgment (witness eight divorces on Bravo's *Real Housewives* franchise in its five years).[8]

Cinema Verite illustrates how television culture both builds and displays American values over time. No longer as much a story about family change, the HBO film is more a meditation on what reality TV indicates about society and what this genre has done to American culture. The film underscores how Pat Loud and her family later said they felt exploited by Gilbert and were misrepresented. The family went on a press tour after the 1973 series began airing, trying to tell their side of the story. Also frustrated with the original series, the Raymonds updated their take on the family with the documentary *An American Family Revisited: The Louds 10 Years Later* (1983). *Cinema Verite* focuses on the effects of producer Gilbert tampering with the Loud family and their lives. It ponders the ethics of his prompting events and crossing privacy lines Pat Loud tried to maintain, and it even references rumors of an affair between Gilbert and Pat Loud. Fittingly, it uses fictionalized film with elements of documentary in order to comment on reality TV.

No longer a discussion of whether a family depicted on television is accurate or enviable, *Cinema Verite* looks back at the Big Bang of reality TV and implicitly questions whether the genre is a good or a bad development. The film argues that the series was exploitative and that the reality TV aesthetic it spawned represents an ugly pandering to the camera by both producers and casts. Given how prevalent reality TV is now, partly because it is cheaper and quicker to make than scripted television, this ethical debate may not impact the survival of reality TV. However, it has much to say about shifting American mores and how the genre has influenced them. Current reality stars now embrace the very exploitation earlier observers warned audiences to fear, as we have seen with Kim Kardashian's assertion that most people now see the dystopian *The Truman Show* and its TV control of televised lives as a good thing.

Current reality TV shows pick up that very debate, insisting that their use of documentary is legitimate, even as those programs change what documentary means in different contexts. *An American Family* made arguments about family change and became a player in that debate, not just reflecting but also shaping American family values in the process. In some similar ways, a show like MTV's *Teen Mom* takes up stances in family values debates and itself becomes a heated topic of discussion, precisely for how it might influence social views with the themes it depicts. What is different now, however, is how self-conscious today's reality shows are about the way the cameras can influence the people's lives they depict, and how today's reality stars tend to accept that impact because they take part in a newfound desire for media fame.

New American Families of Reality TV

Updating a controversial reality family program to the present, MTV's *Teen Mom* franchise (which includes *16 and Pregnant, Teen Mom,* and *Teen Mom 2*) has become a flashpoint for debates about teen pregnancy. Even though teen pregnancy numbers are down overall, the show has sparked a controversy in the press about whether or not it glorifies teen moms by making them reality TV stars, and in so doing, does it, in effect, encourage teen pregnancy. The show focuses on the trials and tribulations of these young women, many struggling to stay in school or maintain a job, having no or little relationship with the baby's father, and many depending on their own family and parents to help them and their baby survive. Yet the "TV effect" of turning these women into household names and giving them reality celebrity precisely because they were 16 and pregnant is what critics question. The majority of the press coverage on the show tends to argue that it does not glorify teen pregnancy and that the teen pregnancy numbers are down. Meanwhile, some pundits who are critiquing the show are clearly using it as a chess piece in the family values debate—that is, turning it into a so-called bad values example in order to argue for their own ideologies and values.

I would argue that what the show primarily does is to suggest that the lives of teen mothers are important and are worthy of attention, and that they are largely filled with struggles that viewers would not want to have. The show emphasizes how many of these young women rise to the challenges they face, and how they show courage and a strength of will in order to do so. The program also makes a strong feminist critique of gender relations, because it sides narratively with the young women who are always pictured as doing the majority of the childcare. In the edited storylines, the show implicitly (and sometimes explicitly) critiques many of the young fathers, many of whom either do not see childcare as "a man's responsibility" or refuse to have any involvement or responsibility for the children. The franchise also implicitly criticizes some schools that refuse to let pregnant girls or teen moms attend because they would appear as bad role models to other students. MTV rejects that fear by putting these young women on TV, and it sides with the teen moms in sympathetically portraying their frustration and disappointment at not being able to attend school. Nevertheless, even given these strong social critiques, the reality fame dynamic is still present. As with other reality programs, some of the teen moms pictured try to parlay the TV appearances into fame and even an entertainment industry career. Thus the show does present contradictory messages.

Taken together, those two dynamics suggest that the effect of the show is to make arguments about the difficulties of teen pregnancy and also to convey how the media impacts family in today's media-saturated culture. The reality TV fame piece becomes a commentary on how the genre makes celebrities out of real people depicted as characters on television, which involves a new model of fame and stardom updated to our reality TV moment. The TV effect of the teen moms as TV stars also comments on how an interaction with media has become integral to people's identity constructions in today's culture. More specifically, it also comments on how media interaction shapes family behaviors and ideas of family.

Shows like *Teen Mom* are making their own arguments about what family is, what it means, and what it should or will look like in the future. I would submit that, like many other family reality shows, the *Teen Mom* franchise makes a particular kind of argument about the family: it privileges older stereotypes and norms of the modern nuclear family unit while also registering the fact that most families do not look like that norm (and never have). The franchise stages a debate between the older norm of the modern nuclear family unit and the newer norm of a postmodern diversity of family forms (postdivorce, single parent, blended, etc.). While it emphasizes the prevalence of the postmodern family, because it focuses quite sympathetically on teen moms in trouble who are struggling to shape families at all, the program nevertheless foregrounds the anxieties and risks of family instability and looks back nostalgically at an older modern nuclear family ideal.

The show's ideological message is one of liberal pluralism, in the sense that it accepts a diversity of family forms and cultural approaches to child-raising (such as extended family households). That message is in keeping with the MTV network's usual mode of address (promoting liberal pluralism version of tolerance and diversity, although a limited version). Yet the franchise does express yearning and desire for an older modern nuclear family unit norm. It pictures as more stable the young mothers who return to live with their parents and are taken care of as part of their modern nuclear family unit with their own parents, now making that unit an extended family unit. Perhaps most notably, the franchise focused narrative attention on the one couple who did marry and become a modern nuclear family unit spending large portions of the program excitedly covering their wedding. When that marriage broke up, the show presents it as tragic, even though the teen frames it as the best decision, lauds her ex-husband as a good co-parent, and expresses happiness with a boyfriend who cohabitates with her. Thus, while the program emphasizes the symbol of a modern nuclear family ideal, what it actually depicts is the reality of postmodern family diversity and the rise of households of various kinds as a new mode for social life in America.

Teen Mom is also indicative of the new media culture trends reality TV utilizes. Fans can interact with the teen mom cast via blogs, their tweets are included onscreen when episodes re-air, and audiences spark a volatile debate about the show. The cast themselves discusses how it is hard to be under the judgmental eye of so many viewers, because they get some positive feedback but also some harsh criticism, as the show clearly becomes a flash point in a heated family values debate. The show itself tells a transmedia story, with online content including webisodes. Throughout, the emphasis is on garnering sympathy for the cast (although the documentary–fiction hybrid genre mix clearly sparks the opposite reaction in some audiences, it nonetheless manages to foster strong emotions in either direction). The young women get to have their voices heard even more directly through their blogs and through follow-up interviews.

While *Teen Mom* is like *An American Family* was in the 1970s in terms of being highly controversial in its themes, one element that is different now is how much fans shape the franchise and how many more chances the castmembers themselves have to get their opinions aired. Because of the transmedia storytelling, the *Teen Mom* cast would never have to try and create their own press tour to get their version of their story heard.

In addition, these young moms do not think television could "eat their families." In today's culture, for some of these reality castmembers, to appear on camera seems to be a validating experience, as if being on camera offers proof that their lives matter or that media attention itself gives their lives meaning. Meanwhile, their audiences join them in participating in this media attention, becoming a bigger and bigger part of the program themselves. That interaction drives reality TV into its future as a booming multiplatform network of texts.

Notes

1. Jeffrey Ruoff, *An American Family: A Televised Life* (Minneapolis: University of Minnesota Press, 2002), 53.

2. *Lance Loud! A Death in An American Family* (2003), http://www.pbs.org/lanceloud/about/.

3. Alan Raymond and Susan Raymond interview, Archive of American Television, Academy of Television Arts & Sciences Foundation, 2010, http://www.emmytvlegends.org/interviews/people/alan-raymond-and-susan-raymond.

4. Ruoff, *An American Family*, xv.

5. Margaret Mead, "As Significant as the Invention of Drama or the Novel," *TV Guide*, January 6, 1973, A61, A63.

6. Pat Loud, "Some Second Thoughts from *An American Family*," *Los Angeles Times*, March 4, 1973, 7.

7. Quoted in Ruoff, *An American Family*, 102.

8. Joyce Eng, "Is Reality TV the Kiss of Death for Marriages?," *TV Guide*, May 26, 2009, http://www.tvguide.com/News/Reality-TV-Marriages-1006332.aspx. Virginia Heffernan, "Too Much Relationship Vérité," *The New York Times*, April 17, 2011, http://opinionator.blogs.nytimes.com/2011/04/17/too-much-relationship-verite/. Tracie Egan Morrissey, "22 Families Affected by the Reality TV Divorce Curse," *Jezebel*, May 2, 2011, http://m.jezebel.com/5796713/.

Selected Bibliography

Allen, Robert C., and Annette Hill. *The Television Studies Reader*. London: Routledge, 2004.

Andrejevic, Mark. *iSpy: Surveillance and Power in the Interactive Era*. Lawrence: University Press of Kansas, 2007.

Andrejevic, Mark. *Reality TV: The Work of Being Watched*. Lanham, MD: Rowman & Littlefield, 2004.

Ang, Ien. *Watching Dallas: Television and the Melodramatic Imagination*. London: Routledge, 1985.

Barnouw, Erik. *Documentary: A History of the Non-Fiction Film*. 2nd rev. ed. New York: Oxford University Press, 1993.

Becker, Ron. " 'Help Is On the Way!': *Supernanny, Nanny 911,* and the Neoliberal Politics of the Family." *The Great American Makeover: Television: History, Nation,* edited by Dana Heller, 175–192. New York: Palgrave Macmillan, 2006.

Bignell, Jonathan. *Big Brother Reality TV in the Twenty-First Century*. London: Palgrave Macmillan, 2006.

Caldwell, John. "Prime-Time Fiction Theorizes the Docu-Real." *Reality Squared: Televisual Discourse on the Real,* edited by James Friedman. New Brunswick, NJ: Rutgers University Press, 2002.

Caldwell, John. *Televisuality: Style, Crisis, and Authority in American Television*. New Brunswick, NJ: Rutgers University Press, 1995.

Chambers, Deborah. *Representing the Family*. London: Sage Publications, 2001.

Cherlin, Andrew J. *The Marriage-Go-Round: The State of Marriage and the Family in America Today*. New York: Knopf, 2009.

Connell, R. W. *Masculinities*. 2nd ed. Berkeley: University of California Press, 2005.

Coontz, Stephanie. *The Way We Never Were: American Families and the Nostalgia Trap*. New York: Basic Books, 1992.

Corner, John. "Afterword: Framing the New." *Understanding Reality Television,* edited by Su Holmes and Deborah Jermyn. London: Routledge, 2004.

Creeber, Glen, ed. *The Television Genre Book*. London: British Film Institute, 2001.

de Certeau, Michel. *The Practice of Everyday Life*. Berkeley: University of California Press, 1984.

deCordova, Richard. *Personalities: The Emergence of the Star System in America.* Urbana: University of Illinois Press, 1990.

Deery, June. *Consuming Reality: The Commercialization of Factual Entertainment.* New York: Palgrave Macmillan, 2012.

Douglas, Susan J., and Meredith W. Michaels. *The Mommy Myth: The Idealization of Motherhood and How It Has Undermined All Women.* New York: Free Press, 2004.

Dovey, Jon. *Freakshow: First Person Media and Factual Television.* London: Pluto, 2000.

Dyer, Richard. *Stars.* London: British Film Institute, 1998.

Edwards, Leigh H. *Johnny Cash and the Paradox of American Identity.* Bloomington: Indiana University Press, 2009.

Edwards, Leigh H. "Twitter: Democratizing the Media Versus Corporate Branding," *FlowTV* 9.14 (May 2009). http://flowtv.org/2009/05/twitter-democratizing-the-media-corporate-branding-leigh-h-edwards-florida-state-university/.

Ellis, John. *Visible Fictions: Cinema, Television, Video.* 2nd ed. London: Routledge, 1992.

Fetveit, A. "Reality TV in the Digital Era: A Paradox in Visual Culture?" *Media, Culture & Society* 21, no. 6 (November 1999): 787–804.

Feuer, Jane, Paul Kerr, and Tise Vahimagi. *MTM: "Quality Television."* London: British Film Institute, 1984.

Friedman, James. *Reality Squared: Televisual Discourse on the Real.* New Brunswick, NJ: Rutgers University Press, 2002.

Frith, Simon. *Sound Effects: Youth, Leisure and the Politics of Rock.* London: Constable, 1983.

Gillan, Jennifer. "*Extreme Makeover Homeland Security Edition.*" *The Great American Makeover: Television: History, Nation,* edited by Dana Heller, 193–210. New York: Palgrave Macmillan, 2006.

Gillan, Jennifer. "From Ozzie Nelson to Ozzy Osbourne: The Genesis and Development of the Reality (Star) Sitcom." *Understanding Reality Television,* edited by Su Holmes and Deborah Jermyn, 54–70. London: Routledge, 2004.

Gillan, Jennifer. *Television and New Media: Must-Click TV.* New York: Routledge, 2011.

Gordon, Linda. *Heroes of Their Own Lives.* New York: Viking, 1988.

Gray, Herman. *Watching Race: Television and the Struggle for "Blackness."* Minneapolis: University of Minnesota Press, 1995.

Hall, Stuart, and Paddy Whannel. *The Popular Arts.* London: Hutchinson, 1964.

Hay, James, and Laurie Ouellette. *Better Living Through Reality TV: Television and Post-welfare Citizenship.* Malden, MA: Blackwell, 2008.

Heller, Dana. *Family Plots: The De-Oedipalization of Popular Culture.* Philadelphia: University of Pennsylvania Press, 1995.

Heller, Dana, ed. *The Great American Makeover: Television, History, Nation.* New York: Palgrave Macmillan, 2006.

Hill, Annette. *Reality TV: Factual Entertainment and Television Audiences.* London: Routledge, 2005.

Hill, Annette. *Restyling Factual TV: Audiences and News, Documentary and Reality Genres.* London: Routledge, 2007.

Holmes, Su, and Deborah Jermyn, eds. *Understanding Reality Television.* London: Routledge, 2004.

Inness, Sherrie A. *Tough Girls.* Philadelphia: University of Pennsylvania Press, 1999.

Izod, John, and Richard Kilborn. *An Introduction to Television Documentary.* Manchester: Manchester University Press, 1997.

Jenkins, Henry. *Convergence Culture: Where Old and New Media Collide.* New York: New York University Press, 2006.

Jhally, Sut. "Image-Based Culture: Advertising and Popular Culture." *Gender, Race, and Class in Media: A Text-Reader,* edited by Gail Dines and Jean M. Humez, 2nd ed., 249–257. Thousand Oaks, CA: Sage Publications, 2003.

Kilborn, Richard. *Staging the Real: Factual TV Programming in the Age of Big Brother.* Manchester: Manchester University Press, 2003.

Kimmel, Michael S. *The Gendered Society.* New York: Oxford University Press, 2000.

Kompare, Derek. "Extraordinarily Ordinary: *The Osbournes* as 'An American Family.'" *Reality TV: Remaking Television Culture,* edited by Susan Murray and Laurie Ouellette, 97–116. New York: New York University Press, 2004.

Lewis, Justin. "The Meaning of Real Life." *Reality TV: Remaking Television Culture,* edited by Susan Murray and Laurie Ouellette, 288–302. New York: New York University Press, 2004.

Lipsitz, George. *Time Passages: Collective Memory and American Popular Culture.* Minneapolis: University of Minnesota Press, 1990.

May, Elaine Tyler. *Homeward Bound: American Families in the Cold War Era.* New York: Basic Books, 1988.

Mittel, Jason. *Genre and Television: From Cop Shows to Cartoons in American Culture.* New York: Routledge, 2004.

Modleski, Tania. *Feminism Without Women: Culture and Criticism in a "Postfeminist" Age.* New York: Routledge, 1991.

Moorti, Sujata, and Karen Ross. "Reality Television: Fairy Tale or Feminist Nightmare." *Feminist Media Studies* 4, no. 2 (2004): 203–205.

Morley, David. *Family Television: Cultural Power and Domestic Leisure.* London: Comedia, 1986.

Morley, David. *Home Territories: Media, Mobility and Identity.* London: Routledge, 2000.

Murray, Susan. "'I Think We Need a New Name for It': The Meeting of Documentary and Reality TV." *Reality TV: Remaking Television Culture,* edited by Susan Murray and Laurie Ouellette. New York: New York University Press, 2004.

Murray, Susan, and Laurie Ouellette, eds. *Reality TV: Remaking Television Culture.* New York: New York University Press, 2004.

Nichols, Bill. *Introduction to Documentary.* Bloomington: Indiana University Press, 2001.

Nichols, Bill. *Representing Reality: Issues and Concepts in Documentary.* Bloomington: Indiana University Press, 1991.

Palmer, Gareth. "'The New You': Class and Transformation in Lifestyle Television." *Understanding Reality Television,* edited by Su Homes and Deborah Jermyn, 173–190. London: Routledge, 2004.

Pozner, Jennifer. *Reality Bites Back: The Troubling Truth about Guilty Pleasure TV.* Berkeley, CA: Seal Press, 2010.

Raphael, Chad. "The Political Economic Origins of Reali-TV." *Reality TV: Remaking Television Culture,* edited by Susan Murray and Laurie Ouellette, 119–136. New York: New York University Press, 2004.

Ruoff, Jeffrey. *An American Family: A Televised Life.* Minneapolis: University of Minnesota Press, 2002.

Shorter, Edward. *The Making of the Modern Family.* New York: Basic Books, 1975.

Skeggs, Beverly, and Helen Wood. "Notes on Ethical Scenarios of Self on British Reality TV." *Feminist Media Studies* 4, no. 2 (2004): 205–208.

Spigel, Lynn. *Make Room for TV: Television and the Family Ideal in Postwar America.* Chicago: University of Chicago Press, 1992.

Spigel, Lynn. *Welcome to the Dreamhouse: Popular Media and Postwar Suburbs.* Durham, NC: Duke University Press, 2001.

Spigel, Lynn, and Jan Olsson, eds. *Television after TV: Essays on a Medium in Transition.* Durham, NC: Duke University Press, 2004.

Stacey, Judith. *Brave New Families: Stories of Domestic Upheaval in Late Twentieth Century America.* New York: Basic Books, 1990.

Stacey, Judith. *In The Name of the Family: Rethinking Family Values in the Postmodern Age.* Boston: Beacon Press, 1996.

Stephens, Rebecca L. "Socially Soothing Stories? Gender, Race and Class in TLC's *A Wedding Story* and *A Baby Story.*" *Understanding Reality Television,* edited by Su Holmes and Deborah Jermyn, 191–210. London: Routledge, 2004.

Storey, John. *Cultural Theory and Popular Culture: An Introduction,* 4th ed. Athens: University of Georgia Press, 2006.

Taylor, Ella. *Prime-time Families: Television Culture in Postwar America.* Berkeley: University of California Press, 1989.

Tichi, Cecelia. *Electronic Hearth: Creating an American Television Culture.* New York: Oxford University Press, 1991.

White, Mimi. *Tele-Advising: Therapeutic Discourse in American Television.* Chapel Hill: University of North Carolina Press, 1992.

White, Mimi. "Television, Therapy, and the Social Subject; or, The TV Therapy Machine." *Reality Squared: Televisual Discourse on the Real,* edited by James Friedman. New Brunswick, NJ: Rutgers University Press, 2002.

Williams, Raymond. *The Long Revolution.* Harmondsworth: Penguin, 1965.

Index